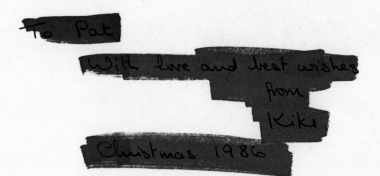

To Pat

With love and best wishes
from
Kike

Christmas 1986

SOLDIER INTO SPY

SOLDIER INTO SPY

The Memoirs of
ROLAND RIEUL

WILLIAM KIMBER · LONDON

First published in 1986 by
WILLIAM KIMBER & CO. LIMITED
100 Jermyn Street, London, SW1Y 6EE

© Roland Rieul, 1986
ISBN 0-7183-0613-9

Typeset by
Print Co-ordination, Macclesfield, Cheshire
and printed in Great Britain by
The Garden City Press
Letchworth, Hertfordshire SG6 1JS

To Trix
and in gratitude to all
my brave comrades

Contents

List of Illustrations

*Many of above photographs are reproduced
by courtesy of Monsieur Philippe Allemann*

Illustrations in the Text

Acknowledgements

I gratefully acknowledge the help and encouragement of my friend Keith Harrap in getting my manuscript into print. I would also like to thank Mrs M. Mills for assistance with the translation and to Mr A. Cheek for his valued recommendation.

R.R.

CHAPTER ONE

Home for Harvest

People who appreciate the delights of camping know the sweetness of the early morning in the woodlands, especially high woodlands, moist only with dew. They know the tangy scent of the undergrowth, the poignant bird song high above and the pleasant hum of the tractors in the distance. But in June 1940, sleeping out in this wood near Toul in north-eastern France, we soldiers of the 6th French Division were aware only of the pungent smell of powder, the whistling of shells and the discordant din of the oncoming tanks intent on ploughing through our last defences.

Before taking my place in what I thought was to be the final stand, I decided to go along to the cook-house for a mug of coffee, perhaps my last, and to get the latest news from the one really in the know, the company cook.

The customers were not in good spirits that morning and even the *patron* had lost his characteristic Provençal good humour. He stood there, with an anxious frown, pouring out the coffee, with cap rammed down, cigarette dangling and in no joking mood.

'Hullo, what news today?'

'We're up the creek. Can't ch'er see the look on their mugs? The Jerries are strutting down the Champs Elysées. I 'ears they've even crossed the Loire and you know what that means.'

I knew all right. I had realised it long ago, but with some others I had pinned a last hope on the belated appointment of General Weygand, at one time Chief of Staff to General Foch, our victorious leader of World War I. Now I had to face facts. We were already on our knees and surrounded on all sides. We could not, short of a miracle, expect to see the outcome of the battle. However, there is no truer word than 'While there's life, there's hope', and at all costs morale must be kept up. I, as sergeant, must set an example. Perhaps this should be easier for me; my father had been French and my mother, English. So far, only half of me was bearing the full weight of the onslaught. The other half was still in possession of all its considerable resources. The Jerry had still not set foot in England

and the Royal Navy was supreme. Our allies (so I told myself) would hold the fort till history repeated itself and America came to our assistance. Besides, are not the British past-masters at losing the first battle only to win the final one? Having convinced myself while sipping my coffee that this was what would happen again, I felt it was worth while to put these arguments to the men by way of encouragement.

'We're not up the creek yet!'

Plenty of contradiction was immediately forthcoming.

'This chap still believes in Santa Claus.'

'We shall never give in,' I retorted.

'So says our bloody-fool-General. He'd as soon see us slaughtered like a lot of ruddy sheep!'

Morale was very low and this heckler seemed to have overwhelming support, but I continued to press the point.

'"We" does not only mean France. I'm speaking of Great Britain and the British Empire.'

My assertion didn't seem to impress my listeners – rather the reverse.

'Some hopes. We've seen what *they* can do!'

'They'll clear off as usual!'

'Have *you* seen any of them anywhere except at Montmartre?'

But Ramus, our humorist, came to my aid with: 'Yes, and they burnt Joan of Arc.'

Yet the more I thought about it the more firmly convinced I was.

'Don't forget they've got the strongest fleet in the world, and there's the RAF.'

'Don't talk about the RAF to us,' said one.

'Did *you* see any British planes at Montmédy?' asked another.

'I admit we saw very few planes at all,' I argued, 'but the only ones we *did* see *were* British. Ours were all busy waiting for orders!'

'For orders! Fat lot of good *that* was. We've been sold out. Everybody knows *that*.'

It was the cook who brought this conversation to an end.

'In the meantime we've got it coming, mate. The General's given orders for rifles to be distributed to all orderlies and to everyone who hasn't got one, even to me! And he says we're to fight to the last man.'

I left them to their morbid speculations and went off to visit the lieutenant thinking that he would be more responsive. I found his expertly camouflaged car labelled 'Do not disturb'. He was asleep. In fact, since the situation had turned against us, he spent most of his time sleeping. He had been as keen as any before but now he had become a fatalist. He fully understood that disaster was upon us and had already thrown in the towel.

I wondered what I could do while awaiting developments and decided to write home to send reassuring news. This done, I had to face the problem of what to do with the letter. We were encircled and without communications. All I could do was put it into my pocket.

Suddenly, from the stone where I had been sitting writing, I spotted some activity among the men nearby, and called over to my friend the sergeant-major; 'Hey, Bouchet, what's going on?'

'It's all over, old man. The General's capitulated. He'll be meeting the Boche this afternoon to fix terms.'

Another, and until then, a highly valued friend repeated what Bouchet had just told me, but added jubilantly: 'We are saved!'

'What about France?' I asked him. 'She isn't saved.'

In a flash I realised the magnitude of our calamity and was overwhelmed with a feeling of despair. I looked scathingly at this soldier who felt no concern for his country so long as he could save his own skin. He realised this was no time for pleasantries and made himself scarce, throwing me a parting glance which obviously meant 'poor fool'.

In fact, I was on the horns of a dilemma. On the one hand, to fight to the last man, to die a hero under arms, sounded most impressive to me, a 'pupille de la nation' (I was so described because my father, an officer in the French Army, was killed in action in 1915). On the other hand, what about my recent argument, that the outcome was not necessarily determined by the result of the first battle? I decided that there was nothing for me to do but accept the situation and hope some day to avenge it.

The news of our surrender ran like lightning through the company. Everyone was talking about it. Some said we should all be made prisoners of war, others that we should be sent home as soon as hostilities were at an end. On the other hand, there were those who thought that captivity would be brief. One farmer from the Calvados was already congratulating himself that he would be home for harvest!!

And all this time, the battle was going on; for the surrender was not yet official. Wounded were being brought back from the edge of the wood where the front line was still repelling the onslaught of the *Feldgrau* (as the German Infantry, in their field grey uniforms were called). Sometimes there was a lull, and sometimes the intensity of the battle was redoubled, until all at once there was a cease fire.

Speculation was rife. It was all over evidently, because the Jerry planes were passing overhead but dropping no bombs. Progressively, during the day the true patriots felt the growing oppression of defeat. Not that it was any fault of theirs. Our corps had consisted of the 6th Infantry Division flanked by the divisions of the 6th North African and the 6th Colonial. It had fought tenaciously in the breach at Montmédy, and had only fallen back under orders.

Morale was perceptibly affected. But those who had at first taken the news of our surrender as a blessing, lost their confidence as time passed and nothing happened. One was so impatient that he blurted out:

'What the hell are they waiting for? Why don't they take us prisoners?'

'Oh shut up!' replied his neighbour.

We waited for over an hour without hearing a single shot. All was calm. Suddenly, the distant sound of a bugle could be heard and we recognised the call: Cease Fire.

This time it was official. A colonel gave orders to the Artillery alongside us.

'Spike your guns. Burn all military papers including your pay books.'

This was no sooner said than done. The Boche would not get anything from *me*, and what a blaze there was across where the adjutant had his tent. He was burning the company books and to fan the flames he had added a million francs in notes. A lovely one thousand franc note fell at my feet. I picked it up, held it to the flame and lit my cigarette.

A sudden shot, very close in the undergrowth, made me start. A young officer had blown his brains out. Was that an act of weakness or of strength? I was not sure and this was no time for deliberation. The Jerry might arrive at any moment. Explosion followed explosion; the Artillery were carrying out the order. Machine-gunners were destroying their weapons by jamming them in the spokes of field guns. All was in a ferment of preparation and geared for departure but where or how, no one could predict. We could only hope for the best.

We teamed up with our friends and waited about in little groups for hours, with ever increasing anxiety. It was already growing dusk when our ears caught a sound of movement.

'That's it. There they are.'

A German patrol of nine or ten men was approaching rapidly along the forest road, each man grasping a tommy-gun at the ready. A sergeant, bringing up the rear, shouted in very good French; 'Throw down your arms. Take your mess-tins and follow the path leading behind our lines.'

The ragged column fell in mechanically, proceeding slowly through the wood. Germans appeared on all sides, cutting off any possibility of escape through the undergrowth. NCOs shouted orders at the top of their voices and the other ranks echoed their commands with the words '*Los! Los!*'

At every '*Los*' our old friend the comic or 'Titi parisien' named Ramus, responded with the mocking 'wow-wow' of a lap-dog.

It was quite dark by the time the column wound slowly out of the wood, but every now and again we could make out corpses lying by the wayside, whether French or German we couldn't tell, but what did that matter? That was the fortune of war. They were now at peace whereas what about us? Where were we bound for that black night, with all these devils screeching words at us which we could not understand, but which we found in no way reassuring?

The column halted at the foot of the hill and a German voice warned us in bad French that any man leaving the path for any reason whatever, would be shot. We stayed there for several hours without moving forward a yard. Men stood and squatted or lay on the ground. I was cold and I wasn't the only one. We had all had enough of being prisoners already. We felt like sheep, but without any wool! Even Ramus had stopped his commentary.

At last the flock was on the move again and the Huns drove us eastward with dogs into the sunrise. At length we found ourselves on a tarred road, crowded with military traffic, and were able to see at first-hand the enemy equipment. From their comments it was clear that our men were greatly impressed by the colossal magnitude of the German war machine, and full of indignation against those responsible for sending us to fight with such inadequate equipment. What I heard said about our statesmen does not bear repetition. Ramus had the last word; 'The sods!'

Soon our guards were reinforced by motor-cyclists. We halted in a meadow and were told we could have one hour. It was lovely country and nothing was stirring on the hills round about. The guard seemed to have diminished and suddenly it struck my mind that this might be a moment to break away, but not alone. I did not feel courageous enough to tackle that. I wondered if I could find someone else to share the risk, but my suggestion was received with:

'Are you mad? What'd be the good of that, when they say we're off to Nancy to be demobbed?'

All at once, whistles blew and dogs started barking. We had to get going again in spite of the weariness which was beginning to make itself felt. Some found it more than ever difficult after the halt, weighed down as they were with too much tackle, but the Boche forced the column on by shooting down stragglers.

'This isn't the time to get belly-ache!' commented Ramus.

It was then about half past two in the afternoon and we had just come through a terrible storm. It had not lasted long but we were all drenched to the skin. In a garden on the right, we came upon the first civilians we had seen. A young woman in black stood, dazed, staring at the ruins of her home which had been razed to the ground. Near her, seated on a box, there was an old man in tears. These wretched people were so immersed in their own disaster, that they did not even notice the miserable column which was passing slowly along the road. But the prisoners, despite their own misfortune, could not help pitying these poor people.

We had now travelled for twenty-five kilometres and at last began to see the first houses on the outskirts of the great industrial town of Nancy. I shall never forget the welcome the inhabitants gave us. They did all they humanly could, in the face of brutal German opposition, to provide us with food and drink, and to give us comfort and encouragement for the ordeal ahead. On the way up the long hill on the other side of the town, a pretty girl (maybe the *putain de Nancy* of bugle-call fame) took hold of my arm and joined our ranks, chatting gaily the while. A brute of a Boche tore her away, but to our delight, she clenched her fist and gave him a resounding blow on the cheek. Taking advantage of his astonishment, she then made her escape by darting between the bystanders and disappearing in the crowd. I shall never forget you and the new heart you put into me, undaunted daughter of Nancy!

At long last we found ourselves in a barbed wire enclosure, a large tract of waste land on which were situated three corrugated iron hangars. The column surged into it, like sheep in a field. I had a good look round and it proved to be a disused army dump, two sides being fenced with barbed wire and the other two, walled. The hangars were built over the bare earth and were open to the elements by reason of missing doors and gaping shell holes. Patches of oil revealed the erstwhile positions of various motor vehicles.

It did not look very promising but I noticed that the hangars were beginning to fill up. The prisoners had realised that this halt might be a long one, although the Boche had described it as temporary. As night-fall approached, I was lucky enough to find an old tarpaulin, which I thankfully appropriated. Our hosts had not thought of providing latrines and the guests had elected to use the outside walls of the hangars for this purpose. As these were now full, those of us who had to sleep outside, found it advisable to get as far away from them as we could! Unfortunately it rained all night but although the tarpaulin did not provide much warmth, stiff as it was with dirt and grease, it was virtually waterproof.

Next morning I had a rude awakening. Suddenly, one of my friends shook me, saying:

'Wake up, old cock. The Jerries are on the war-path!'

German soldiers were dashing to and fro over the rows of sleeping prisoners, kicking them and bashing them with rifle butts to wake them up. First I wondered what was going on but I was soon to understand. They were sorting out the blacks. They collected all the West Africans in a corner – it didn't take long – and eight poor wretches were marched off. After a few minutes we heard a burst of rifle fire followed by eight single shots, and realised that our eight colonials had been executed. We could not understand why, but we very soon found out. That night four German sentinels had been found with their throats cut.

CHAPTER TWO

Toul Airfield

'Have your mess-tins ready. The Boche will dish out soup at eleven o'clock.'

This was our first camp rumour. At first it had an official ring about it, later it became unofficial and then it proved to be false. At 12.30 p.m. there was still no soup. Worse still, there was no water, either for drinking or washing, but the mess-tins were all cleaned up with tufts of grass ready for the long-promised soup.

Suddenly, a second rumour ran through the camp: 'The Boche are sending up field-kitchens.'

There were many variations on this theme. Some prophesied that they would arrive that night, and some settled for the next morning. Others said they were already on the way up from Nancy and that the Boche were calling for volunteer cooks to serve it out. It may seem that I am dwelling too long on this subject but nothing is so important as food to those who do not have it.

It was not until the third day, and then without any warning rumour, that three municipal water carts from Nancy borough drove into the camp and pulled up. This was it, the water ration but it turned out to be a free-for-all. Many of us could not get anywhere near the carts. I was one of the unlucky ones, but three days without food or water effectively taught me that for prisoners it is a case of each for himself and the devil take the hindmost.

Next day, the mobile cook-houses for which we had waited so long, made their way into the camp. This time I took care to be one of the first to be served! The soup was quite good but there was not enough of it.

Next morning a considerable body of German troops moved into the camp. We were ordered to fall in ready to move off. We realised that the Boche were by now much better able to cope with prisoners in an orderly and disciplined manner. We were marched off in the direction of Toul and learnt from the guards along the route that that was our destination. We were in fact led to the Toul airfield, a typically vast plain with two enormous hangars, and halted. We wondered why. It turned out that it was simply that we had to be counted, in the special German way. No other nation could possibly imitate them.

The order came:

'Fünf Stücke' (literally 'five pieces'). It seemed that we had now become pieces or objects instead of men. It turned out that we were expected to form fives and then, to our surprise, five Jerries fell in one behind the other to count us. They walked slowly down the column, each counting separately. At the end each Boche announced his total, with five different results! They conferred and argued violently. Then an order was issued. Five pairs of heels clicked loudly and they started all over again. The second attempt was no more conclusive than the first. They were all shouting at each other and some started to count the line the other way round, commencing from the other end. Yet more Boches arrived to assist the tellers. Of course, we could see the funny side of all this, particularly as Ramus put in his spoke with:

'They still won't know how many beans make five when they get to the Golden Gates.'

To make matters worse, some of us started to shuffle from one line to the next to throw the count out even more. When the Jerries realised what was going on, they waved their arms about wildly and screamed gibberish at us out of which we could only distinguish – *'Französiche Schweinerei'*, which we easily understood. I was to realise later that this scene would be repeated every time the Boches took a count.

At last after a couple of hours' hard work the total number of prisoners seemed to be established, 'errors and omissions excepted'. We were then ordered to march into the hangars. The corrugated iron walls of the sides were in good repair and so were the huge sliding doors in the front, but at the back they seemed to have been bombed, and as for the roof, more than half of it was missing. The cement floor was entirely covered with iron grids, the kind used largely at that time to form runways on grassed dromes. The grids raised the level of the floor by five centimetres at the most – just enough to clear the sheet of water stagnating beneath.

We were halted and formed into groups of twenty 'for soup distribution'. There was something to be said for it. The Boche was, at least, organised here. We had only been there for two or three hours and they were already mentioning soup and there was a cast-iron mattress for everyone! Everything had been laid on except for

straw and blankets. What was more, having contrived to get under
the roof, I was not going to move, come hail, come snow, unless of
course, they drove in at an angle.

First of all we organised our groups of twenty for the soup parade
because that was urgent, appointing a leader for each group. Then
we went off on a vain search for straw, but behind the hangars I
found some long grass which I collected in a heap and which was
better than nothing, especially with my tarpaulin above it. I lost no
time in making up a bed which looked comfortable enough. The rain
could still collect on the cement underneath without troubling me
much so long as the grass stayed dry. Future rheumatism could take
care of itself.

The soup was made by French cooks and consequently ought to
have been good, but it was not. It was poor and there was very little
of it. Of course standards are only relative. At a later stage, I should
have considered it good, so good in fact, that it would have made me
wonder if the Boche was trying to curry favour.

After eating (if you could call it that) I had a look round the camp
which was vast, as you might expect of an airfield. The machine
gunners' towers were very far apart, and the mobile cook-houses
were set up with all their gear in a great semi-circle, well-barricaded
ostensibly to keep the prisoners away from the provisions. It was
remarkable how quickly some men had seized the opportunity to
feather their nests. I walked over to look at the notice-board situated
twenty metres within the barbed wire. It said:

'Anyone crossing this line will be shot.'

This was far from reassuring. These posts were placed at hundred
metre intervals all round the camp. The watch-towers were situated
at the corners and in the middle of three sides of the camp, their
machine guns trained on the forbidden strip between the wire and
the posts. In the middle of the fourth side was a guarded gate leading
into a road built up on both sides for about two hundred metres with
the German administration buildings. The sight of this road leading
to freedom brought me the first inkling of escape, but I dismissed it in
the face of the insuperable difficulties.

However, three days later, a plucky little Frenchman walked
quietly out through that gate and passed the two guard posts and
their two hundred metres of cross-fire between them. A Boche on
fatigue, wearing denims had come into the camp with a hand-cart to
pick up twenty or so sacks of cement. When he came to leave, the
Frenchman, having stripped off his jacket, and wearing washed-out

overalls, started to walk behind the cart, making a pretence of pushing it, and sure enough, the doubly-operated cart made its way without any interference past the first post, along the deadly length of road, past the second post, and turned into the street leading into the centre of Toul. I hope his luck held.

That day the prisoners' roll-call was a farcical fiasco. It was bound to be because one man was missing and the Jerries refused to admit it. 'Escaped!' they said; 'Impossible!'

Impossible or not, after three hours of wrangling they had to accept the fact that we were one less, and at last we were allowed to return to our hangars.

These interminable periods of waiting were often the cause of sunstroke and other such ailments among the prisoners. During one of them, I passed out and when I regained consciousness I was stretched out on my bedding and heard that the German medical authorities had been notified. Soon two Jerry orderlies arrived and finding my temperature to be 40.6C (105F) they made me lie on a stretcher and covered me with a sheet, like a corpse. I didn't like that at all. I had no faith that their intentions were good. I wondered where we were off to, and it seemed a very long way, covered up as I was. When they lifted the sheet I found I was in a café converted into a rough field-hospital. There were beds ranged along each wall and on each bed a figure covered with a greatcoat or a blanket. I climbed off the stretcher with difficulty and was sent into the back room where I saw large bottles of medicine on the marble mantelpiece.

I was given a bed. I undressed and got into it. The orderly covered me up and spoke kindly to me. He was a Frenchman.

'How are you feeling?'

'I don't know. I passed out with a temperature of 105°'.

'Well stop worrying. You've got dysentery. They've all got the same thing. It's a shower – in more senses than one, but we'll get you over that in a couple of shakes.'

The orderly was right. An hour later I had the pain and all the characteristic symptoms of this horrible disease. Unfortunately, an alarming number of my fellow-patients became much worse and were taken off supposedly to the hospital at Toul but rumour had it that they were bound for the cemetery.

We received small doses of medicine tasting unmistakably of pastis[1] and as soon as the orderly's head was turned someone

---

[1] An apéritif very much appreciated in the south of France.

invariably proposed a round. One morning there was a startling rumour. It seemed that the camp was to be broken up. Everyone was to be removed by train.

'Never mind, boys, we'll all get drunk,' said someone, and then and there the entire contents of the big bottle were consumed. For my part the effect was not alcoholic but miraculous. I felt better and each hour that passed brought me one step nearer to total recovery.

By the afternoon the rumour had become more or less official. I was undecided what to do – whether to feign illness so as to land up in some hospital, from which I might have a better chance to escape, or to get back to the camp to face the future with my friends. The latter seemed the better course, and I decided to ask for an early discharge from the field-hospital so as not to miss the departure.

On my return to the camp, I found my friends Ramus, Lucien Lethessier, Roland Lemasle, Delrieu etc. in formation, ready to leave. This much was then definite, but rumour was rife regarding destination.

'It seems that we're heading for Sissones, according to the Germans,' was one suggestion, and another was:

'We're going to Versailles to be demobbed.'

I was most sceptical. On our way down to the station we passed through Toul and I noticed tears on the faces of the townspeople. We filtered on to the platform, alongside a train of cattle trucks. We were counted (which took most of the morning) then packed into the trucks as into the 'Metro' at rush-hour. Fortunately for me, I found myself close to one of the two ventilators, and could see out and breathe more easily than most of the others.

Then we were off and after a few minutes I cried out:

'We are going east.'

At this, a sudden fear gripped me, for the east meant Germany. Others, besides myself, were thinking the same thought, and it soon became evident to everyone that that was where we were heading.

'They are taking us off to their God-forsaken country, the bastards.'

What a weary journey it was! We were packed in like sardines in a tin. I was still weak from the dysentery and fearful of a relapse. However, when we stopped, the German Red Cross supplied us with some good soups.

After travelling for the rest of the day and the whole of the night, we crossed into Germany. The atmosphere changed. Onlookers no longer waved, but shook their fists and thumbed their noses. The children made as if to fire at us or slung stones at the train. The peasants glared at us balefully and even the cattle in the fields looked vicious.

The countryside was beautiful, the houses all clean and bedecked with flowers. No hint of war was apparent to disturb the peacefulness of the rural scene, neither ruined house nor crumpled steeple. As we studied the landscape we all realised the complete non-existence of our air power, both as combat support and for destruction behind the enemy lines. On all sides we could see gardens full of flowers, and swastikas flying at the windows. Children played soldiers and did the goose-step, while we travelled on and on towards an unknown destination.

Fortunately, French spirits are hard to crush (contrary to general belief) and soon, in our truck, all were vying to tell the spiciest story, and this was followed by a non-stop sing-song.

Suddenly, some time during the fifth night, the train came to a stop. This was nothing unusual, but on this occasion the halt lasted all the night and we realised that this was it. As soon as it was light enough to distinguish the name of the station we made out: LUCKENWALDE.

Soon we clambered out of our cages, painfully stiff, and straggled into the town, where most of the people ignored us but a few shook their fists at us. However, they did not pursue this as the German military seemed to have little time for civilians, considered by them to be privileged subjects, as indeed they were back in France.

Then, at the crest of a hill where the last house stood stark on the edge of the plain, we turned left into a camp at the entrance of which I could read: STAMMLAGER III A.

CHAPTER THREE

Stalag III A

This enormous POW base camp was situated in the shelter of a pine forest. It consisted of hundreds of identical wooden huts. On the right of the main camp there was an enclosure where many marquees were pitched, and it was towards them that we were sent.

After waiting half an hour we were allotted a place in one of the tents. Once inside, we were very pleased to find that it was light and that there was plenty of clean straw. I settled down and found that I was next to a friendly sergeant-major who had been a butcher in the town of Longwy in Lorraine. We were given soup, thin stuff but more plentiful than we had been used to getting in Toul. There was more bread and a little pat of ersatz butter. Apparently, this was a by-product of coal, but it was very much more like butter than our French margarine.

'They're a cunning lot of crooks!' observed Ramus.

Every morning we had to parade in platoons for roll-call and allocation of fatigue duties, followed by an attempt at PT. After that, our time was our own for the rest of the day. We were left alone except by the lice. There were all sorts of shapes and sizes. We engaged immediately in a campaign of extermination but soon had to capitulate to force of numbers.

Our only entertainment was to watch our coloured troops in an adjacent barbed wire enclosure, where Arab and Senegalese prisoners seemed to be receiving much harsher treatment. The Jerries, stick in hand, were continually rounding them up. The chief cause of the German displeasure seemed to be the petty trading which was carried on across the wire. The Arabs or Senegalese would throw over a little parcel of bread or some other rationed commodity. The Frenchman would open it, value the contents in cigarettes and throw back the appropriate number. In the last resort the French had to eat and the African could not do without tobacco. The effect of these transactions was to make machine-guns splutter and to unleash a mob of maniacs brandishing their weapons, with resultant panic!

On the eighth day there was a change in the routine. We were ordered to parade with all our gear, having cleared the tents. We were escorted into the main camp where each man had to place all his belongings, excluding leather goods, on a blanket in front of him. Then, stripped to the skin, we made parcels of all our possessions by tying together the corners of the blankets and handed them over for stoving.

While this was going on we were taken to the showers where orderlies daubed us with disinfectant. They shaved our heads, gave us a thorough shower, and there we were standing in front of our steaming packs, pleased to find that, with one stroke as it were, we were rid of the army of lice, and lightheartedly we got into our clothes, creased and shrunken though they were.

Once reassembled, we were escorted into another part of the main camp, where, in one of the huts, we were subjected to a search – the first of many. Our wallets were examined very closely and all our money, papers and pocket books confiscated. Photographs alone were we allowed to keep and even sheaves of cigarette papers seemed suspect. Any protests were countered with blows and shoves and we had to submit.

From there we passed through the photographer's department, where each man was taken full-face and profile, holding clearly displayed a slate on which was chalked his identification number.

These formalities had lasted all day, with no concern about feeding us. Now that they were over and we were installed in a new hut, we started to ask for food. To our dismay, we soon realised that no provision had been made and that we should have to wait till noon next day.

We thought we should be staying some time in that hut, but our guards had decided otherwise. Day had not dawned when we were already on parade, with what few possessions we had left. We were counted according to the usual ritual and there were about two hundred of us. We were marched off to the camp exit, no one knowing where we were heading and there wasn't even a rumour to give us an idea. All we could gather from the guards was the one word *'Arbeit'* which we knew to mean 'work'.

On leaving the camp, we turned left and walked the length of a hedge along a tarred road, and found parked there several smart coaches. No one supposed that they were waiting for us. It was not until the column halted alongside that we realised it was so, and read the words painted in Gothic lettering on their highly polished sides:

'HENSCHEL FLUGZEUGWERK'.

I understood and translated to the others: 'Henschel Aircraft Factory'.

The order was given to board the coaches. Ramus leant out of the window and shouted at the top of his voice, as did the touts on the Grands Boulevards in Paris:

'First race Longchamp!'

I soon realised that we were travelling north but that didn't enlighten us much as no one knew where Luckenwalde was on the map. We soon learnt, however, from a sign-post showing Berlin 25 km along the road we were following.

'Ah!' said Ramus, 'I've got it. We're going for a sight-seeing tour of Berlin.'

We travelled through a cheerless region of vast unbroken plains, bereft of trees except for those fringing the road, but soon we came upon the first houses of the suburbs, and this proved to be our destination for we stopped in front of an attractive little camp consisting of half a dozen brand new huts.

There we were met by an NCO and his men who took charge of us. There were also several civilians, probably factory officials, one of whom started to address us in excellent French. He informed us that this would be the camp for workers in the Henschel Aircraft Factory at Schoenfeld. Everything had been and would continue to be organised in the interests of our well-being; we should be joined by fellow-prisoners, all qualified tradesmen, to the total of six hundred. To facilitate the organisation and distribution of meals we formed the first company of two hundred divided into four groups of fifty each. There was no objection to friends being together as, according to this grinning spokesman, the German authorities of the factory were deeply concerned for our welfare and wished to see us installed so comfortably and happily that this would be a model camp of its kind. Entertainments would be arranged and we could ask through our own spokesman for anything we required. This would be granted as far as possible. Whoever was chosen would also be expected to transmit orders from the German authorities, and reciprocally to express the prisoners' demands which would receive careful and immediate consideration. A shop would be set up to enable us with our earnings at the factory, to purchase cheaply the small articles which we should need (and which, incidentally, they had just confiscated the day before!). We should be well-fed it seemed, and the cooking would be done by French cooks of our own choice. All in all, we should be living like fighting cocks. This was the will of the Führer, who, as founder of the New Europa, was eager to collaborate with the French, whose renowned culture he would respect.'

'Allons, Enfants de la Patrie-i-e'.

Ramus broke into The Marseillaise but the choir did not take it up, and in any case, it did not seem to please the Germans, except perhaps the interpreter who had just delivered the speech, for he was wearing a fixed smile (he always did).

Continuing his speech, as if he had omitted something, he announced:

'If by any chance an enemy plane *should* succeed in crossing our frontiers . . . '

But his words were lost in the ensuing laughter and his smile became even more fixed.

We were short of NCOs so I found myself elected head of my group. Furthermore, the Works Manager was wanting one of the prisoners to act as his personal interpreter, but he could not find anyone who spoke German. With the intention of provoking, I announced that I spoke English fluently. To my surprise, the Works Manager was delighted. He spoke English fluently too – so now I held a double office and had both to organise my group and pass on instructions from the factory management to the whole body of prisoners and make their requests known.

Although the first of these duties, that of Group Leader was to last for some time, the second fell into disuse, for except on the first day, we were not to see this Works Manager at all. So much for his interest in us and our requirements! They were only stage effects and a foretaste of German double-dealing.

We were given three days' grace during which we inspected with admiration the model lay-out and equipment of this camp. Six small huts were situated round a square which served as a parade ground. Each hut was bordered with geraniums and the usual two-tier camp bunks were fitted with mattresses, a most unusual luxury! We even had sleeping bags.

The canteen was light and spacious, whilst the kitchens were a model of their kind and electrified throughout. The sick-bay was fairly well equipped, and there was a fine recreation room, convertible into a theatre.

'It looks good', said Ramus, 'but I wonder what the rent is?'

On the fourth day, reveille was at five a.m. We were summoned to parade by the guards blowing their whistles at six o'clock. Of course, they had to start by counting us which meant that it was 7 a.m. before we got off. At a short distance from the camp we came upon the main entrance to Henschel Aircraft Factory, where there were territorial police on duty.

Soon we came to a building site, cluttered with materials, where we saw under construction a huge factory bay at least three hundred metres long. We realised at once that we had been brought there to help in the construction and not to work in the factory. We were to be employed on carting planks and rubble.

We were divided into teams under foremen. Mine was an old man, but he walked so quickly that I couldn't keep up with him. He was anxious to get a move on, but of course, for the time being, it was *his* war, not ours! Every fifty yards he had to stop and wait for us to catch up. In spite of his urgent cries of *'Los, los!'* (Hurry, hurry) it made no difference to our speed.

On the far side of the bay we came to a tools store from which the foreman supplied us plentifully. I should have preferred a shovel but I found myself with a pick. It turned out to be all to the good for there wasn't much call for picks but the shovel men were never without a job.

I had been sitting for some time in perfect prisoner posture on my upturned pick, when a German workman, passing close to me, slipped on the sly a small parcel containing three cigarettes and a snack of bread and sausage. A mid-morning snack was a luxury indeed and cigarettes were quite priceless as I hadn't had one for a fortnight, but I was even more agreeably surprised to see that even in this God-forsaken country there still seemed to be some kindness. This gesture and many other incidents which were to follow were to set up in me a conflict which grew more and more apparent throughout my captivity. How could a nation be composed of such good-hearted people capable of obviously disinterested kindness and at the same time of such evil-hearted blackguards?

The work of clearing up the site was to go on for quite a while, but on the second day, a foreman in a peaked cap called me out saying:

'Komm mit.'

Having wandered round the site with him, I found I was in a forge. There were two other prisoners there.

'Hullo!' I greeted them.

'Hullo! So you're the new locksmith?'

'I am?' I asked, surprised. 'I've never seen the inside of a lock!'

'What's that matter; I'm a *Wasserleitung*.'

'And what kind of a wild beast is that?'

'A plumber,' he replied.

'Do you understand plumbing then?'

'I know a bit about filling up holes.'

'Were you a plumber before the war?'

'No, a dentist.'

'And what does the other chap do?' I enquired.

'Fredo? He's the smith who forges the steel for the great German victory,' he informed me, ironically.

'Oh, I see, that's what they call putting the right man on the right job.'

'You've said it – when he starts to temper, the foreman loses his.'

Willy, the German in the peaked cap, was listening to the whole of this conversation without understanding a word but wearing a look of amusement. In fact, he looked quite a nice chap in spite of the swastika on his cap. He tried to tell me something in German, but I couldn't understand. Then he took a rusty bolt, dipped it in oil, clamped it in the vice and showed how to re-cut the thread. As the box was full of rusty bolts I grasped that this was my job for the day.

A workman came in to get his tools sharpened by Fredo, the blacksmith, and spoke to Willy with an accent which sounded like Cockney, so much in fact, that I could follow the general sense of the conversation. I conveyed to Willy that I understood this language and learnt that they both came from Hamburg and were speaking in dialect. This was a heaven-sent advantage to me, as from then on I made rapid progress in German. With the help of my knowledge of English and of Willy's dialect, I only took a couple of weeks to acquire a working knowledge of that language. I suddenly understood one of the phrases that Willy kept repeating on our arrival:

'In fünfzehn Tage, England kaput.' I now knew it to mean 'In fifteen days, England will be finished.'

I replied brazenly, *'Noch nicht'* (not yet) which made him burst out laughing.

I had finished the box of bolts by this time and was now occupied with filing down a piece of metal. After watching my efforts, Willy decided to try me out as an electrician, in spite of my protestations that it was all I could do to change a fuse. I found myself in charge of maintenance of the temporary electrical installations on the building site, where our days were now spent.

At night, we returned to camp, where some prisoners hoped to

spend the rest of their captivity, because, taking it by and large, this
was a pretty good camp. The huts were new and the guards were not
too strict. It was a great improvement on Luckenwalde. I shared a
six-bedded room with the other group leaders, but not for long. The
Germans discovered a sergeant-major among us and promptly
named him French camp commandant, with me as his second-in-
command. They gave us a separate office with a twin bedroom
adjoining.

Needless to say, our promotion caused a lot of comment. Some
suggested that we were collaborators. The sergeant-major's loyalties
seemed to me problematic, but for my part, I got on with the job to
the best of my ability. I organised a dramatic society which was able
to draw on professional talent from among the prisoners, a bridge
club, a chess section and all manner of sports. In view of this, the
Germans authorised me to run the canteen, where I could sell all
permitted goods. When their confidence in me was established, what
more natural than that they should offer me a trusted position in
their factory!

By order of the management I was appointed assistant to the
foreman of the inspection department. The hands were called
together and informed in my presence, that in the absence of the
foreman Rolf X, they were to take orders from me, a POW! In short,
the Germans could find at that stage of the war no one better to
undertake inspection in their aircraft factory than a French NCO!
What a golden opportunity! I felt sure that I was in a vantage point
but couldn't see how to make use of it. I realised that I had to be most
cautious as there were several Nazis about.

Learning the inspection procedure was easy enough. I had to tick
off the job sheets against the finished product and note the time spent
on the job. The foreman Rolf took to me and helped me with the
language. He was a most patriotic German at heart but had no time
for the Nazi Party. Naturally, he hoped for a German victory but he
didn't take offence when I said it was out of the question. He had to
admit that:

'*England ist genau wie eine Katze.*' (England is just like a cat, it has
nine lives.)

I gradually got more friendly with him and every day he would
bring me a snack prepared by his wife and would share his own small
weekly cigarette ration with me. He was certainly the best German I
ever met. Taken all round, I could count myself lucky to have fallen
into such a comfortable camp and on such a cushy job, but I refused

to be beguiled by these considerations, and did not lose sight of my right under the Geneva Convention, to protest as an NCO against being put in a work camp. The fact that I did not exercise this right was because I had come to realise that the work camp was a vantage point. At the very least, it offered a much better chance of escape, and now that I was appointed to the inspection department I was in a particularly privileged position with regard to obtaining information valuable to the Allies, on whom our hopes were now centred, if only I could make use of it. In fact, I knew that, given the opportunity, I could already make useful communications on output, for example, and on the prototypes of certain radio-guided planes, if only I knew how.

My first decision was that I had no right to consider escape. I believed that it was my duty for the time being to go on winning the confidence of the Germans.

By this time, all the prisoners including new detachments, were distributed throughout every department of the factory. Some of them were fully skilled tradesmen, others were unskilled labourers. I felt disgraced to watch them working (however little they might be managing to do) in the name of the Fatherland. Anything to hinder their progress was worth a try! I had an idea.

The men's conveniences were situated on one side of the factory in two large rooms, each divided into thirty or more closets. One room was reserved for the Germans, the other for the *Kriegsgefangene* (POWs) or KG as the letters in red paint on our backs clearly designated us. Neither batch of workers was allowed to use the other's quarters, which meant that it was only in the WC's that we felt at all at home! It became a sort of common room for a gossip during which, of course, production fell. I saw a chance to exploit this situation. I started off by installing a 'teleprinter' which consisted of a toilet roll on which I wrote up all the latest camp and factory news, both true and false, and, more important, bulletins on the progress of the war. Of course, my communiqués were never pessimistic. My foreman Rolf was an excellent source of information and kept me supplied every day with extracts from Goebbels' publications. I gave it an English flavour which made it very palatable, judging by the crowds it drew, and consequently the time it wasted.

Encouraged by my signal success, I felt it behoved me to make further efforts. I set about organising a grand tournament open to all POWs and entitled 'The Six Days of Schoenfeld' (an analogy with six-day bicycle racing, as practised in many European capitals). I put up posters about the factory announcing the event and invited prisoners to enter in pairs. The Germans assumed that it referred to some sporting event back in the camp and showed no interest. When I had secured entries from eighteen pairs, I made known to them the conditions of the contest. From first thing on Monday morning until 11 a.m. on the following Saturday, one member of each pair had to occupy the seat of their allotted closet during working hours, without a break. If at any time neither member was present, and the closet thus left empty for any reason at all, the time of such absence was recorded in minutes against the pair's score. To win the 'blue ribbon' in this tournament which carried a prize of two hundred and fifty marks (then about twelve pounds sterling) the winning pair had to keep their closet occupied continuously throughout the week without a break. Naturally, the teleprinter worked overtime to keep the rest of the POWs informed of the progress of the race. The venture was a fantastic success. The 'common room' was so crammed with sightseers that it was almost impossible to get in. The foremen came buzzing round after their prisoners, but couldn't get into the hive. The guards came to their assistance, pushing and shouting and the crowd would disperse momentarily only to re-form as soon as they had departed. The factory management was quite at a loss to know what was happening. They sent a protest to the German Camp Kommandant, who threatened us with reprisals. It made no difference. The contest continued and came to a noisy climax at 11 a.m. on the Saturday, as arranged. I had achieved my object. Production had fallen, and moreover the management were blaming the military for their lack of authority and the military were showing their resentment by refusing to allow any overtime. They were all at loggerheads and I was rubbing my hands.

My next effort was to have much more far-reaching effects. Whenever the German High Command decided to put into production a new batch of aircraft (consisting say of two hundred and forty planes of the same model) thousands of job sheets were issued from the works office. Every separate component, of which there were literally thousands, required as many of these job sheets as there were different operations to be performed on it. The operative concerned would read the appropriate instructions on his job sheet, and would sign it on completion, recording his time. In my department (of some fifty machines) component and job sheets together were then returned to me for inspection and recording. I then had to restore the job sheet to its progress folder and send this, with the components, to the next department concerned. The progress folders were therefore in my possession throughout the time during which my department was working on the job. For me to mislay any of our own job sheets would have been disastrous, but I thought that undetected I could do considerable damage at the final assembly stage, by destroying certain of the *intervening* sheets.

At first I sneaked a couple of sheets at a time and disposed of them down the lavatories, but as time went on, I grew bolder. Results were quickly evident. Components were being held up all over the factory through missing job sheets. The foremen were railing against the office and vice versa, but all to no avail. The job sheets were not recoverable!

After a lot of coming and going between works and office, the latter decided to issue 'priority job' sheets in an attempt to catch up the lost time, but after careful and conservative calculation, I estimate that the factory was delayed five days in the completion of each batch of aircraft.

For several weeks, I played this little game very happily, but I was under no illusion as to the risk involved, and soon spotted the two Gestapo investigators who had been planted in the works to get to the bottom of the business.

One day, my foreman was called to the manager's office and told that his prisoner was getting too friendly with his secretary, and that in order to separate them, one or the other must be transferred. My foreman replied that he would keep the prisoner! (By this time he was learning French from me.)

This was the first danger signal. The trap would surely be sprung. The secretary and I were under suspicion, and by removing us in turn, it would be easy to identify the one responsible. I slackened the pace considerably but not altogether so as not to compromise the secretary. I was on the alert and made numerous trips to the lavatories with empty pockets before risking another job sheet.

In the meantime, life was going on uneventfully at the camp, except for the arrival of two hundred more engineer POWs all skilled tradesmen, turners, millers, fitters etc. From them we were able to recruit a good deal of talent for our dramatic society. Thanks to the ability of a man called L'Homme, better known as René Marjac of Radio Luxembourg, this society was now able to produce shows worthy of a provincial theatre. Some of the plays produced were from the works of writers as well known as Courteline and René Dorin.

There was also a clever burlesque by René Marjac himself and several revues, including one particularly spectacular effort by Léhar called *Land of Smiles*, complete with a remarkable soprano.

The Berlin Newsreel came to film our show. We were gratified by this – but not for long. Those who had criticised our efforts from the beginning were right in this instance, as it turned out that the film was destined for use in Goebbels' propaganda machine. In the publication *Trait d'Union*, a rag which was circulated free throughout German prison camps of all nationalities, a front page photograph depicted a section of the audience laughing uproariously, bearing the slogan 'Prisoners who are not bored'. I was well aware what a demoralising effect this propaganda would have if it were published in France. We were faced with the problem of whether or not we ought to give up dramatic society activities rather than risk a repetition of this incident.

As it turned out it was not to be my decision, for my days at the camp were already numbered. I was summoned to the office of the German Kommandant, now a captain, who addressed me thus:

'I am most satisfied with the work you have done in this camp which has now become a model for the rest. The C-in-C of the Wehrmacht has decided to transfer you and your friend Levoy, to another camp which needs reorganising. You will be French Camp Commandant and Levoy will be your second-in-command. I congratulate you.'

'Thank you, Captain,' I replied, 'but I'm afraid I must refuse.'

'It is an order from the C-in-C.'

'Nevertheless, I must still refuse.'

'Refusing an order in war-time is punishable by death,' he threatened.

'I'm not a German soldier,' I retorted.

'But I am! You will be transferred tomorrow at 7 a.m. You will go by train under guard, and I advise you not to persist in your attitude.'

He clicked his heels to indicate in German fashion that the interview was at an end, and I went off despondently, realising that this meant saying goodbye to all my established friends, including Ramus, Prévost, Desquéroux, Marjac, Ort, Lethessier and many others.

Next morning, we left the camp at 7 a.m. with a double guard.

CHAPTER FOUR

The Hoodlums

At the station we entered a reserved compartment in a passenger train. Not dwelling too much on the future, we travelled like tourists, taking an interest in all aspects we could see of German life.

In spite of the distractions of the journey, I started to consider the events leading up to our transfer. I wondered whether this tale about taking over the command of another camp might not be an example of German double-dealing. Hadn't they promised our lads in the Maginot line, that if they surrendered they would not be taken prisoner? And, whereas they could have held out for six months, they had accepted this German promise at its face value, though it was worth no more than any other German treaty. In any case, I was in trouble as the disappearance of the factory job sheets would stop and the Gestapo could not fail to realise that I had been at the bottom of it, if they had not in fact already done so and organised my transfer in consequence. Things were getting so hot for me that I knew now that I had to escape at all costs.

There was no chance for an immediate attempt because of the two fellows who were watching us, so I decided to wait and see what the new camp was like but knew that I must take the first opportunity.

After about an hour and a half we reached a station called Ludersdorf. Our escort signalled to us to get out and we found ourselves by a level crossing from which the road ran straight up a long hill. The only thing in sight was a farm cart coming towards us. As we passed it, the driver hailed us in French.

'Hello, lads.'

'Hello,' we chorused. 'Are you French then?' I asked.

'You don't take me for a Jerry, do you?'

'Are you a prisoner too?'

'Like the rest,' he replied.

'So are we. We're on our way to some camp near here.'

'Oh, yes. That'll be at the top of the hill on the left. You must be the two hoodlums, then!'

'The hoodlums?' I queried.

'Yes, we heard say that a couple were coming.'

That was all we could elicit, because our escort was impatient and kept hurrying us along with loud cries of *'Los, los!'*

So now we were to be treated as hoodlums. Levoy's thoughts could almost be read on his face. I thought I probably had more to worry about than he had, but I wasn't to know this. However, to say the least of it, this had not been a reassuring conversation. We were beginning to have the mentality of the Germans weighed up. We knew that it was dangerous to get oneself branded as *'Gesperrt'* or 'Outcast'. Towards those whom they regard in this light they develop a collective spirit of inhumanity. One Boche on his own might be friendly, and so might a couple of the same rank, but a group of them would turn into barbarians on the slightest provocation.

We arrived at the camp early in the afternoon. There was no question of being made leader here. We were put into a huge hall as lofty as a theatre, with two-tier bunks along three sides. In each corner was an open brazier, but the fires were out when we got there. We had only had time to glance around when a French sergeant came up and made himself known.

'I am Sergeant Thomas, French Commandant and liaison officer of this disciplinary camp.'

He received us with the warmth we should have expected from a fellow countryman, and we never had anything to complain of from his treatment. He was a retiring sort of a man, happy to do as little as possible. He did not throw his weight about or fraternise in any way with the Germans.

He recorded our names and showed us our beds. We were separated, Levoy slept on a top bunk with the advantage of being near a brazier, and I, on a lower one in the middle of one of the walls. The mattress and pillow were made of rough sackcloth, meagrely stuffed with straw. There was a blanket and under the bunks a couple of enamel wash-basins.

The rest of the inmates were out, presumably at work. I went over to Levoy in his corner. We were far from reassured. This great empty hall, with its wretched attempt at amenities, so different from what we had experienced up till now, contributed to our misgivings. The double doors stood open all the time, providing the only light in this windowless mausoleum. Instinctively we got up together and went out to have a look at the rest of the camp.

On the right was the guard-house through which we had entered,

and on the left a small building which we recognised immediately as
the cook-house. Behind stood a small padlocked shed and the
latrines. Round the perimeter of this small camp was a single barbed
wire fence and no sentries in sight.

'I say,' said Levoy, 'It ought to be easy enough to get away!'

'There must be some snag somewhere,' I replied. 'Possibly a high
tension cable or something like that.'

The cook was a Frenchman. We could see that through the
window pane. He was writing as we went in but he got up and,
throwing a shovel full of peat on to the fire under his steaming boiler,
he asked what we wanted.

'To know what you are cooking in your boiler,' I said.

'You must be either barmy or newcomers. There's only one thing
on the menu here, all the year round – boiled carrots – and consider
yourselves lucky, because last year we fed on boiled mangels six
months on end.'

Having thus completed our tour of the estate, we went back to our
palliasses to straighten them up a bit and have a rest after our
journey, but we had no sooner settled down than we heard French
voices outside and straight away five or six POWs straggled in. We
realised that they had reported sick and were coming back from
seeing the doctor, for one had his arm in a sling and another had a
bandaged head.

We got to know them straightaway of course, and they started
immediately to enlighten us as to life in this disciplinary camp, or
Kommando as it was called. We learnt that all inmates except the
Jews,
of course, had charges recorded against them. The charge was
generally 'Refusal to work', but there were more serious ones too.
For instance, the man who slept in the bunk above mine, had just
simply shoved a guard into a dung heap on the farm where he was
working, and, grabbing the fallen rifle, had turned it against the
German NCO who was leaping to the rescue. Some were there for
striking officials but less spectacularly than he, others for stealing
from the Germans, or for having sexual relations with German
women. There was one in particular, whose offence was that while
employed on odd jobs at the German Camp Kommandant's home,
he had contrived to put the officer's wife and daughter in the family
way at the same time.

We learnt that reveille was at 4.30 am and that we had to leave for
work at 5.30 am. This was to dig irrigation canals across a plain
swept by the east wind where the temperature was thirty degrees of

frost. Fortunately for me, my English wife, who was now back in her own country and safe, I hoped, had been thoughtful enough to send me a thick pullover.

Suddenly, we were summoned to appear before the German Kommandant who turned out to be a *Feldwebel*, or sergeant-major. He said little but took pains to make it very clear that it would pay us best to lie low, saying that if we made any attempt to escape, we should be shot down like rabbits.

When we were back in the hall we watched the workers return. There were about sixty, all in very poor shape. The condition of most of them was pitiable but their spirit was indomitable. They all greeted us with a smile and a handshake, and made us welcome. One group adopted us personally and we gave them a hand to break up wood for the brazier in our corner. A fire was only allowed in the evening at this camp, so any sick prisoners, excused from work, only gained the privilege of shivering throughout the day.

When we received the carrot soup, it turned out to be a bowl of hot water with four or five thin carrot rings floating on the top, but they also gave us a hunk of bread and a piece of German sausage. We should have made short work of this if one of the lads had not warned us in time that this was all we should get until this time next evening.

I began to realise for the first time in my life that I had my back to the wall.

We spent the evening talking over our prison camp experiences, and discussing the rumours that were going round about the new Russian front. News had now filtered through of the RAF's heroic defence of Great Britain and the lads were beginning to take heart again in spite of the spectacular advance in Russia.

It was then time for evening roll-call. We all had to fall in, five deep down the centre of the hall. A fat German entered, saluted and counted us carefully. He seemed satisfied, for he saluted again with a click of his heels, about turned and went out, shutting up the double doors behind him. We heard him fix in place an iron bar and then lock two or three padlocks.

We were now shut in completely without ventilation, but in spite of the stoves, which were by now dying out for want of fuel, there was plenty of air for us in this vast building.

Before I went to sleep, I had a chat with the fellow in the upper bunk who had pushed the Boche into the dung heap. He swore to me by what he held most sacred, that if any German came bothering him while he was working, he would strike with whatever tool he had in his hand (as there were picks, shovels and axes, and I was convinced he was in earnest, this was no empty threat!)

In spite of the discomfort and cold, I slept quite well and woke up with a start to cries of *'Aufstehen! Aufstehen! Raus, Mensch! Los!'* (Get up with you . . . and be quick about it – or untranslatable words to the effect.)

A dozen guards were dishing out punishment with their rifle butts to the prisoners lying asleep. I was just quick enough to avoid a blow but Levoy was unfortunate. He took one which left him limping for the rest of the day.

We were issued with a 'sock rotting' brew of coffee, and then found ourselves trudging silently through the snow on a black icy night, towards our place of work. The snow was driving in squalls, making our dispirited party even more miserable. Our destination was at least five miles away and we reached it as dawn was beginning to break on the horizon. We came upon a wooden hut standing out against the snow-covered plain, where we queued up to receive our implements. I got a pick and Levoy a shovel, which was a bit of luck because we then had to pair up with picks and shovels.

As it got lighter, I could make out several civilians standing with the guards. They appeared to be in charge of the work, and one of them who seemed to be the foreman allocated the tasks for that day. With iron pegs, he marked off eight paces for each pair to trench.

My first blow glanced off the frozen soil, making no impression and the blow that followed made little more – hardly to be wondered at since it turned out to be frozen solid to a depth of one metre, as we discovered by midday for it took up till then to dig that far! It was said that the camp thermometer registered 38 C degrees below zero. No wonder we could not feel our feet in our army boots, that our breath froze on our lips, and that our eyes clicked with ice as we blinked.

All at once we found water collecting in the bottom of our trench and the old hands urged us to stand in it so as to warm our feet! We were reluctant at first but they insisted and showed us that they were doing so themselves, so we tried dubiously. At once we realised that they were right for although ice formed continuously round our ankles, it seemed like putting our feet into warm water by contrast with the minus 38° we were experiencing on the ground.

We kept on working like this all day long, not daring to stop for fear of being frozen stiff. We even managed to increase our pace not only in the interest of keeping warm, but also because the old hands

shouted to us that as soon as we had completed our job we could wait
for the slower workers in the shelter of the hut. Unfortunately, we
found we were the last to finish, unused as we were to this kind of
work, but some of the others came and gave us a hand.

Night was closing in fast when we set off again on the long snowy
road back to the camp. We were soon marching silently by the light
of lanterns as we had done eleven hours earlier, and by the time we
got back to our bowl of stewed carrots we were completely
exhausted.

One day was exactly like the next. I doubt whether the galley
slaves had a worse life. Moreover, a deep foreboding hung like a
cloud over this dread camp. I sensed that sooner or later a blow
would fall. Fellows like the one in the bunk above mine would only
put up with so much and then revolt given half a chance. If then,
through sheer weight of numbers, the prisoners might succeed in
overcoming the guards, the consequent reprisals did not bear
thinking about!

While I was hacking away at my trench, I was racking my brains
and could only come to the conclusion that it behoved me at all costs
to escape rather than let myself get caught in the ensuing holocaust,
and this was not the only consideration to influence me.

The fact that Levoy and I had been transferred to this disciplinary
camp was tantamount to having been charged. I was only too well
aware of the nature of my offence, sabotage, and that if I remained
here, a trial before a military tribunal and my execution must
inevitably follow. Only one course was open. At all costs, I must
escape without delay.

I knew nothing of Levoy's offence and did not ask him about it as I
had made a point of telling no one about my own nefarious activities.
Nevertheless, I felt sure that it was equally in his interests to escape
and I told him what I had in mind. I found him in complete
agreement and it now remained for us to find a way out.

Every night in the hall, we got together on our own to talk over the
subject. We were forced to admit that on the surface, it looked
impossible. Contact with the outside world was absolutely non-
existent, so there was no hope of getting hold of civilian clothes or
money (other than camp currency, worthless outside).

It was evident then that we should have, perforce, to escape in
prison clothes without money and that we could not get far like that.
We could only get money by attacking someone, and clothes by
breaking in. The idea did not appeal to us, inexperienced as we were

in this kind of pastime. I couldn't see myself coshing someone with a blunt instrument as the reporters say! It seemed a bit beyond me.

For the time being we were stuck. We realised that in any case we should be risking our lives and that we must hit on something that held at least the semblance of being feasible. We were devoid of ideas and time was going on. We had now been here for two months, and every time a guard came into our sleeping quarters, I felt sure it was for me. My anxiety was so great that I was not sleeping, but this brought compensation, for after one wakeful night I said to Levoy:

'We'll go on February the 6th.'

'Right'o. Got an idea?' he asked.

'Yes a smasher!'

That day, the work went much more easily. All the time I was plying my pick, I discussed with Levoy the details of my plan, which we found practicable providing luck was on our side. We shook hands on it, hardly hearing the foreman shouting, *'Los, los!'*

However, in spite of my inspiration, the very next day we were to have a stroke of bad luck. One of the prisoners, a sergeant-major so it was said, had also had enough of this place. Consequently, he had taken French leave and, at the same time, the *Feldwebel*'s (German Kommandant's) car. None of us realised that he had gone, and as he had cunningly chosen a Sunday for his disappearing act, the Germans did not miss him until the evening roll-call.

We were laughing heartily and wishing success to his venture, when suddenly, in burst the *Feldwebel* firing half a dozen shots with his revolver.

'French swine,' he shrieked, his face scarlet with rage. Then followed a long tirade in German, clearly on the subject of exterminating us all.

From the following day we were subjected to much stricter vigilance and every act of malice that our guards could think up. We could put up with the malice, Levoy and I, but the tightening of the guard, in the circumstances, was not at all to our taste!

The next few days were uneventful, but we spent the evenings getting our clothes in good repair, and briefing the five or six accomplices essential to effecting the first part of my plan, the actual departure. This, I considered, must take place in the interval between the time when the guard taking evening roll-call gave the OK and the moment when he shut our sleeping quarters for the night. I knew that it was essential for us to have a whole night ahead of us, after being checked in, in order to get clear of this desert area.

On the day of our departure, misfortune struck again. There was a deep snowfall, a catastrophe indeed since our route had to take us across country. Levoy tried to dissuade me and one of the accomplices came and told me it was madness. I felt that he might be right but I was even more certain that it would have been madness to stay, so in the face of all opposition, I stood by my decision to go.

By nightfall our luck changed. The snow stopped before it was more than two feet deep, and when I got back from work there was a British Red Cross parcel awaiting me from my wife. This contained, among other things, some chocolate which was to prove invaluable on the trek ahead. We gave the carrot soup a miss that night and supped off English canned goods. The time was getting very close. I could see Levoy looking a bit green and I expect I was too, by the feeling in the pit of my stomach. During the last five minutes, I went over the final instructions with our accomplices. Then I set the stage by putting a couple of pails of dirty water near the door, and with bated breath, we waited for the curtain to rise on our adventure.

'*Appell!*'

A fat guard had arrived to call the roll. By pre-arrangement, Levoy and I took our places right at one end of the front rank, with our accomplices placed at intervals along it. The count proceeded and almost immediately, it seemed, he gave the word, '*Stimmt*' (OK).

Stepping forward and closing in on the guard until he was completely surrounded, our accomplices bombarded him with questions.

'Are we working on Sunday?' he was asked.

'Please give us shoes.'

'What about our mail?'

These and like requests were painstakingly put into halting German. Meanwhile, we casually turned away and went one after the other towards the buckets. We picked them up unnoticed, and slipped out into the darkness. Once outside we got rid of our encumbrances and made off in the direction of the latrines. Within a few seconds we heard the guard come out and padlock the doors carefully behind him. We knew that before going back to his quarters he would turn the dog loose. It was a magnificent Alsatian police dog, and realising that he could betray us at the outset, I had spent a good deal of time making friends with him, often giving him bits of sausage which I felt would have done me more good than they did him! We did not have to wait long for our friendship to be put to the test. Rex, as he was called, came straight up to us. It was a moment of crisis, but he didn't bark and was pleased with the special fare I had been able to offer him out of the providential food parcel.

We lay low for about an hour, letting the dog roam freely round us, then when all was quiet, we decided that it was time for us to climb over the wire. We arranged for Levoy to go ahead while I entertained the dog with more tit-bits. Then, making sure that there was no sign of alarm, I went forward with the dog following. He watched me climb up and over then started to growl. He was, in fact, just on the point of barking.

'Rex!' I hissed at him, and remembering his manners, he stifled the bark in mid-throat and trotted off!

Now that we were outside it was absolutely imperative that we should put as much ground as possible between us and the camp without delay, a formidable task in the deep snow, which clogged our footsteps and made the pace slow. At times, we were cut off entirely by drifts and forced to make detours, but after about two miles of this hard going, we were lucky enough to strike a road, which we recognised by its double row of trees. There was even a trace of a path which two or three passers-by had already trodden down.

'Wait a minute!' I whispered, producing from my pocket a precious compass which I had providentially bought from a fellow prisoner at the first camp and managed to retain in the face of all subsequent enemy searches.

I checked the direction of this road and found it ran north and south. This was excellent for us as my plans all along had been to make north for the village of Schoenfeld and to hide there in the camp of the aircraft factory, unsuspected under the noses of the Germans. There we knew that we were certain of finding dependable allies who would take care of us while they did their utmost to secure us civilian clothes, essential to our ultimate bid for freedom. Our only obstacle now was that Schoenfeld was thirty-five miles off, of which we still had thirty-three to do before daylight!

Although the path was not straight it did enable us to keep up a reasonable pace. We went through the blackness of the night for a considerable time without seeing any sign of life, but eventually a village loomed up in front of us out of the darkness against the background of snow. We wondered what to do. We had planned to by-pass all villages, but doing so meant we had to risk getting lost in a snow-drift. We also realised that time was most important so we decided to take a chance and walk straight through.

As we walked along the street, a dog barked but no-one stirred
and we were soon out in the open country again. We went through
three more villages just as uneventfully, but at the next one we got
our first scare. A light was showing from one of the houses and as we
approached it, we heard sounds of laughter. Just as we drew level
with the door, it burst open, disgorging a party of about half a dozen
noisy couples. We had no choice but to walk along with them. I was
in terror that they would recognise our prison uniforms and
wondered if the KG painted in red letters on our backs, would show
up in the darkness. We both instinctively realised without recourse
to words, what we had to do. We dropped a little behind, moved over
to the far side of the street and then quickened our pace till we had
left them behind.

'Whew!' breathed Levoy. 'That was a near one!'

'Let's hope we weren't spotted and that no one's busying
themselves to ring for the police,' I said.

'They may not bother to at this time of night,' added Levoy.

'Why? What's the time?' I asked.

'Past midnight,' replied Levoy, looking at his watch.

'Already! We must speed up. If we don't get to Schoenfeld before
daylight, we're done for.'

The path grew narrower so we walked in silence one behind the
other till we came upon another blacked-out village. It seemed a
place of more consequence but it was too late to turn back. There was
no sound, not even the dogs were disturbed by our muffled footsteps.
In spite of its eeriness we were thankful to be so much alone. All at
once, on my right I spotted a glowing cigarette and caught Levoy by
the elbow. He had seen it too, but had the presence of mind to keep
walking. The strength seemed to ooze out of my legs but we went on
and after about twenty yards, I risked a quick look back, only to see
that the cigarette was still with us.

We came to a fork in the road with a sign-post but we dared not
stop to look at it.

'Keep going and take the right fork,' I said. 'It doesn't matter if
it's the wrong road so long as the cigarette doesn't overtake us, and
keep going faster.'

We came out into open country again, but we still hadn't shaken
off the man with the cigarette. By now, we were almost running, and
as there was practically no path trodden at this point, our going was
very heavy. Levoy peered back.

'It's all right. He's given up,' he announced.

'Press on all the same,' I retorted. 'How do you know he hasn't chucked the butt away?'

We fell over our feet in our haste, but after about a mile we were too exhausted to keep pace any longer. However, it seemed that we were no longer followed and I suggested that we ought to stop to check our bearings.

We scooped out a hollow in the snow, in the shelter of which Levoy shone his lighter onto the face of our compass. I was relieved to see that we were still on course and heading north.

'Have a bit of chocolate,' suggested Levoy.

'That's just what we need,' I agreed, 'We must keep walking though. We can't afford to waste a minute, and let's hope that we get through the next village all right. If the chap behind the cigarette was a 'copper', he may have telephoned.'

'Look here,' Levoy retorted shrewdly, 'if he has telephoned, we've had it. If we've got one on our tail and half a dozen ahead, there's nothing we can do about it, so why worry?'

He was right, but I was aware that it was his exhaustion that was speaking. He had not yet got his second wind – not that I could talk! My feet felt like blocks of lead.

The critical moment was coming. We struck an isolated house first, then a couple together, a barn and then we were in the village street. We made our way between snow-covered houses, silent and sinister in the darkness. How long could a road seem? Not a mouse stirred. My nerves were so taught that I jumped when the church clock struck once.

'What's that?' I asked.

'Three-fifteen,' replied my friend.

After what seemed an eternity, we found we were clear of the village and that our fears of pursuit had been misplaced. Our road widened and started to ascend. We came to a crossroads and a roundabout with a sign-post in the middle. I shook off the snow and climbed up to read what it said: BERLIN 23 kms.

We were heading in the right direction for Schoenfeld was the outermost suburb of South Berlin. The road kept rising and we saw that we should have to cross over or under a railway line. We could pick this out in the distance by the green signal lamps and its row of regular lights. Suddenly, a sharp 'click, click!' halted us in our tracks like a couple of pointers.

'Listen!' I hissed.

'What was it?'

'Someone's just loaded a rifle,' I said.

'That's what I thought it sounded like,' Levoy whispered back.

We listened a second or two in silence. We needed to stop anyway, and used the pause to take stock.

'I'll go on my own,' I suggested. 'Then if I'm captured, you can slip into the woods, but if you don't hear anything just keep following a hundred metres behind.'

We shook hands, in case this meant separating indefinitely, and I went forward with the utmost caution, fearing at every step a call to halt. The road ran through the railway embankment almost like a tunnel, so wide was the railroad above. The darkness was oppressive but I eventually reached the far end without incident. I continued to advance another thirty metres without stopping, completely at loss to know why I had not been challenged by a sentry, and when Levoy caught up we were still wondering this. All at once, however, we heard the noise again, the very same double click, and realised now that we were at close quarters, that it came from the changing signals.

Although it was a false alarm it had taken its toll of our energy and when we came to the next obstacle, we simply had not the nerve to overcome it. It was about half an hour after the 'signal' incident when we sighted the lights of a signal box perched above an illuminated level crossing, and decided that in our prison uniforms, we could not afford to attempt to cross the line at this point. We elected instead, to make a detour to the left through deep snow. At first the going seemed impossible but we said nothing and struggled on. It took us quite twenty minutes to do three hundred yards and this brought us on to an open stretch of line on a slight embankment, fenced off by a formidable barbed wire fence. We realised that the snow–covered track was electrified and experienced a nasty moment when we hoped we should put our feet down in the right place!

We reached the other side without mishap, and found the countryside still bare and lacking in landmarks, so we bore to the right thinking that this would bring us out on the main Berlin road again, north of the level crossing. However, it did not work out like this at all. We could not find the road again and kept getting held up by drifts, until it was borne in upon us that we were hopelessly lost in the fields.

At this point, I felt that we must fall back on the compass, and was reassured to find that we were still following the right course; so we struggled on slowly and with great difficulty, anxiously aware that the precious hours of darkness were slipping away, until we stumbled on what seemed to be some semblance of a path and decided to follow it. We were soon to realise what a lucky chance this had been, for the path came out at a cross-road where, to our delight and astonishment, we were able to read on the sign-post: SCHOENFELD 15 kms.

We were sadly in need of this bit of encouragement, worn out as we then were by the hard going. By this time, we were in such a state of exhaustion that the slightest impediment was enough to make us stumble or fall, so much so that on one occasion Levoy would not get up again.

'You go on without me. I can't make it,' he gasped.

'Come on, up you get. Cut out the dramatics,' I said roughly, pulling him to his feet. But a little later it was his turn to be doing as much for me.

Eventually, we came to another cross-road, this time with a street lamp by which we were able to read the sign-post clearly; it showed us that we were only five kilometres off our destination. Soon we should be facing the trickiest part of our undertaking – our entry into the Schoenfeld camp.

We heard voices coming towards us. This was far from reassuring as we realised we must be looking pretty rough. Soon, we were able to make out dimly the figures of two men, probably workers on early shift, muffled up like eskimos.

'*Heil Hitler!*' they greeted us.

I was momentarily thrown off my guard by this form of address though I had heard it passed often enough between Germans. Fortunately, Levoy managed to maintain his presence of mind and gave them a '*Heil Hitler*' in reply.

As we went on, we came upon more passers-by and found the same greeting always acceptable, and hoped it would always prove so simple a password. At last we found ourselves in Schoenfeld. We passed along the village street and by a group of folk so deep in discussion that they took no notice of us. Now we felt an added anxiety, for ahead of us we could see the camp guard-room already lighted up near the gate, and we had been counting on arriving while it was still in darkness. Perhaps this was all for the best, however, as we were now able to pin-point the sentry's position.

'Reveille must have gone,' whispered Levoy.

'Never mind we'll turn off to the right along the side of the camp and make for the corner furthest from the gate, near the stores.

There's no lighting there and it will be the easiest spot to get over the two lots of wire.'

We reached the camp itself but turned right at the corner and crawled in the snow so as not to be seen from within. The snow was so thick in this open field that it cut off our vision completely. All we could make out was the top of the wire, but of course we could not be seen either – the biggest advantage that the snow had given us yet.

What we did not realise was that since our departure from Schoenfeld camp, an ack-ack battery complete with searchlights, had been installed in this very field, only approximately three hundred yards away. About ten yards from the far corner we stopped.

'This'll do,' I whispered. 'You climb over first and wait for me when you have crossed both lines of wire.'

Levoy got across without difficulty and lay in the snow. When it came to my turn, however, having crossed the first lot of wire, I got caught up on top of the second, and in trying to get free, I must have attracted the attention of the nearest searchlight crew, for at once its beam was switched on and started to rake the wire from end to end. Before it caught up with me, I tore myself free with a supreme effort, sacrificing my clothes in the process, to land sprawling headlong in the thick snow, which concealed me from the searching beam.

When the light finally switched off, we picked ourselves up, still considerably shaken and crept stealthily round the nearest hut. No one was about in this part of the camp and we slipped into the stores, where, as we had expected, we found the store-keeper lying asleep. He was the good old type of French peasant and we knew we could count on him. I shook him gently by the arm. We had arrived.

CHAPTER FIVE

Bébert from Belleville

Maurice, the storekeeper, had good cause to goggle at us. He really must have thought he was seeing things. We were not a pleasant sight. We had popped up straight out of the snow and were still covered in it. Our forage caps were pulled right down over our ears and our scarves were stiff as boards from wind and snow, while our breath had formed frozen spume around our mouths. My coat was in tatters from the barbed wire and the snow had piled up round our feet and ankles and our trouser legs so that they had turned into solid lumps of ice.

'Hello, do you know who we are?'

'Yes, but you *do* look a couple of scarecrows. Where've you come from?'

'That can wait. Get up as quickly as you can and find Lucien and Ramus,' I said, and as he got up and dressed hastily, I added, 'whatever you do, don't say a word about us to anyone except Lucien and Ramus.'

'All right,' he said, trembling like a leaf with what might have been fear, cold or excitement, and rushed off to get our friends. A few moments later, there they were shaking us by the hand and slapping us on the back, till large lumps of snow began to pile up on the store-room floor.

'I see you have brought us some good weather,' gibed Ramus, but Lucien, who was more responsible, frowned and said:

'This won't do, chaps, you can't afford to hang about here, for one thing a German might drop in at any moment.'

'No,' added Ramus, 'or we'll soon have to lay on a pump to get rid of the water.'

In the room temperature, we were literally melting. Lucien had thought out a hiding place for us. Maurice held the key to the room where the straw used for palliasses was stored. It was another hut and was stuffed with loose staw from floor to ceiling. We thought this was an excellent place and went there straightaway. Maurice opened it up and in we plunged like a couple of rabbits burrowing into the middle where we hollowed out a little cave for ourselves.

'I'll be back in half an hour with some good hot coffee,' said Lucien, who was one of the camp cooks. 'That's what you need!'

Ramus had already made himself scarce to report for roll-call, no doubt. Maurice locked up again after Lucien had gone and we were so deeply engulfed in the straw that all sounds were muffled, and in any case we fell asleep immediately. We stayed in our straw igloo for five days and nights, and most of that time we slept. We got our strength back very quickly thanks to our friends who kept us constantly supplied with plenty of food. Ramus proved to be a tower of strength. From all round the camp he scrounged various articles of civilian clothing which one would never have expected to find in such a docile camp. He got hold of an overcoat to fit me and a lumber jacket for Levoy, plus a couple of shirts and ties. This was not enough to let us pass as civilians under an expert scrutiny but at least we had got rid of the incriminating KG from our backs.

Lucien had a whip-round among his most trusted friends and raised enough German money (although it was forbidden to hold this in POW camps) to buy us two tickets to the Swiss frontier, with a bit over in case of need. So much for POW solidarity, and my heartfelt thanks to our unknown supporters!

Moreover, Ramus was able to procure a railway timetable, and to pass on some most interesting information. For some time, certain camps, selected by the German High Command as meriting preferential treatment, had been declared 'open' on Sundays and their inmates were given temporary liberty, on parole, and allowed to walk about town. Furthermore, according to Ramus, within the precincts of a certain ordnance factory (consequently under guard) there was a camp of French civilian workers, one of whom, a man called Bébert, was willing for a consideration, to perform services for the prisoners.

'You might get hold of the rest of the clothing you need through him,' suggested Ramus.

'We must have a try! Where is the camp?' I enquired.

Ramus gave us details and drew us a plan. We decided to leave next morning at 7 am during roll call. This would give us a double advantage, that the Germans were busy and that it would still be dark. Our best way out was the way we had come in, providing we could avoid drawing attention to ourselves again on top of the wire. With this in mind, it was agreed that either Ramus or Lucien would get it cut for us beforehand with wire cutters.

Lucien had prepared a special supper for us by way of celebration, and Ramus arranged for several of our closest friends to come and say goodbye to us. We felt completely recovered and ready to tackle the next phase of our journey, when Lucien, back from a walk round the camp, informed us, to our consternation, that we had been betrayed.

'The Germans know you are in the camp and have already searched all the huts. The only reason they haven't been here is because this place is always kept locked.'

'Are you quite sure about this?' I asked.

'Absolutely certain. It was one of the Germans who told our Spokesman.'

'Who is the swine who has given us away?'

'I don't know, but we shall find out and then he's for it. In the meantime, though, they've got the story all right. They know you are leaving at 7 am tomorrow during roll call! Needless to say, they'll be waiting for you.'

We were all silent for a few minutes, except for an occasional expletive. I was livid to think that there was such a treacherous reptile born who could betray his comrades to the enemy. I got hold of myself quickly, realising that this was a time for action, not recrimination with danger on the doorstep.

'We'll leave at 2 am and the Germans can cool their heels at 7 o'clock,' I decided.

Ramus agreed to cut the wire at 1.55 am and we checked dials. When we had arranged all details, we decided to snatch a couple of hours sleep to prepare ourselves for what lay ahead. The storekeeper kept watch to make sure that we did not oversleep, while Ramus promised not to go to bed at all. There was nothing else to do but sleep until we were awakened.

Levoy started snoring straight away. I admired his composure. He seemed to me like a piece of flotsam entirely at the mercy of the current, be the sea rough or calm. He just let himself go with the tide. He had contributed no initiative and no constructive suggestion, either in the planning or execution of our escape, but on the other hand, he had remarkable self-possession and I fell asleep on the thought that together we made a good team with some hope of success.

'Hey! Get up!'

The storekeeper was whispering urgently in my ear.

'What! Already?'

'Yes. Ramus has got back and everything's in order.'

I rubbed my eyes and saw that Levoy was fastening his jacket. I got into my overcoat and started to make my way through the straw followed closely by the others, towards the door where we waited while Maurice reconnoitred. When he had given us the all clear, we set off in single file with Ramus in the lead to show us where he had cut the wire.

We soon found out that Maurice had made himself scarce. No doubt he was only too pleased to have got rid of such compromising visitors. I value this Alsatian's contribution to our escape effort the more highly for his timid nature. He must have had to summon up a great deal of moral courage to overcome his natural nervousness, so different from Levoy's phlegmatic composure!

Ramus had done a good job. There was a gaping hole in the wire. He whispered a hasty 'Good luck' to us and we hurriedly thanked him for his help. There was no time for talk. We crawled through the two rows of wire with ease and reached the road in a few steps.

We had to pass before the main gate but we did not think that this would be very risky on such a dark night. There was no particular reason for the guard to take any notice of us, as we might easily have been civilians coming home late. Nevertheless, I felt my heart miss a beat as we passed in front of him. However, all was well, but much later I was to discover that the Germans had put a special guard all round the camp from 4 am onwards (on the assumption that we were proposing to leave at 7 am). When they found the gap in the wire they took reprisals on the whole camp.

We did not hurry for we knew that we had four hours in which to do six kilometres. According to Ramus, it would be best for us to get into the civilian camp at the Ordnance Factory when the workers were going into their shift. We surmised that as civilians, they would come and go freely, not in military formation as prisoners, and that this would enable us to filter in.

It was still snowing when we came in sight of the camp. We could see the entrance plainly illuminated and knew that as a camp within the precincts of a war factory, it was guarded by security police. We saw people beginning to come out of the camp and realised that it was now or never.

'Shall we have a go?' asked Levoy.

'Yes, we daren't wait till it's light.'

'Shall we go together because separately we may lose each other inside?'

We walked shoulder to shoulder towards the light, neither of us feeling very confident, and feeling even less so at the sight of the guards. Though they were in the shadow, the faint beam from one of the two bulbs was enough to show up their jackboots! We dared not falter for fear of calling attention to ourselves. For me, it was the worst moment of the whole adventure.

'*Morgen,*' I said on a momentary impulse.

'*Morgen,*' replied the guard.

That was all there was to it. We were through! In spite of the black-out we could make out the outlines of several army huts. We opened the door of the first one to make enquiries. We found ourselves in sleeping quarters just like those we had at Schoenfeld except that there were about sixteen single beds, not the two-tier variety.

There were only about four or five occupants and they were late for work, judging by the way they were scrambling into their clothes.

'Is there anyone called Bébert here?' I asked.

There was no reply but one of them turned and looked at me.

'Do you know someone called Bébert?' I asked him.

'I'm Bébert. What d'yer want?'

'You are? Well that's lucky, because I want to have a chat with you.'

The man I was addressing was a typical ponce of the kind to be found in Paris, rue de Lappe. He was slight, not very tall. His black hair, sleeked back with brilliantine showed signs of thinning. He was wearing a dark blue T shirt with a kerchief knotted round his neck.

'You'll get the bloody boss after me if you hold me up, so let's have it quick.'

He took us to the far end of the room near the snow-blocked window.

'Sit on my kip, mates,' he said. 'and spill the beans. Hold it! I know what you're going to say; you're a couple of escaped POWs and because your clothes still give you away, you need a leg up?'

Before admitting this, I looked around to see if anyone was listening.

'Don't get the wind up, mate, they're used to it. You aren't the first to come looking for Bébert de Belleville. Which part of France do *you* come from?'

'Both from Paris.'

'Good show. We'll get on all right, we three, but I must be off and do my bit for Adolph. I had yesterday off *krank* (sick) and it's laying it on too thick if I'm off today too. You batten down here, you two, you'll be safe enough as long as you stay inside. I'll come back at midday and find you some grub.'

The others had gone already and Bébert rushed after them.

'What do you make of it all?' Levoy asked me as soon as we were on our own.

'Well, he's a queer fish whichever way you look at it. He certainly looks a ponce, but I think he's on the level. Anyway, we've burnt our boats and there's no going back. We've got to trust him and hope that he and his pals turn up trumps.'

Levoy was dubious.

'They seemed in an awful hurry to get to work, almost as if they were concerned for the boss. Voluntary workers! The dirty rotten lot of bastards – skimmed from the gaols I bet.'

'Well we don't know anything one way or another, and this is certainly no time for us to get involved in politics. All we want is for them to give us some clothes and for the time being we had better lie down as if we were off sick, in case any Germans look in.'

We took off our shoes and picked a bed apiece. I took Bébert's and was able to lie down and watch the daylight come up for I was too nervous to sleep for fear of someone coming in. I kept turning over in my mind the events of the last few days and the unknown difficulties ahead.

As it was now broad daylight and the factory was obviously close at hand, since I could hear the drone of the machinery clearly above Levoy's snores, curiosity caused me to look out. The window was pretty well snowed up so I could not see much, but by flattening my nose against the pane I could just manage to make out the camp entrance and the two civil police on duty there. They wore armlets displaying swastikas on their grim uniforms, the sight of which made me shudder and withdraw in repugnance for this type of guard had a very bad reputation.

I picked up a detective story which was lying on the table and for want of something better to do, I tried to lose myself in a story even more sensational than our own.

Shortly after midday the workers came trooping back. They could only shove through the swing door one at a time, and as he burst through, each man made a dash for the head of his bed, grabbed his billy-can and fought to get out again against the stream. This resulted in a series of comic collisions, to the accompaniment of curses. The most humorous of these took place when one 'old soldier' who had conspired to take his billy-can to work with him in order to get priority at the cook-house tried to keep his dish upright against impossible odds.

'Hullo, lads,' Bébert hailed us on arrival. 'I'll get you fixed up in a few minutes when we come to the second helpings.' With which he went off to the cook-house to collect his own, and a much better meal it was than we had seen in POW camps. It started off with a good slice of boiled bacon and a canful each of mashed potato. In the lid they received beetroot sliced up in oil and vinegar and there was bread and cheese all round to finish with. Bébert and one of his cronies collected second helpings for us which proved almost as big as the originals!

After this feast, Bébert took us aside into his corner and asked who had put us in touch with him.

'A friend of ours from Schoenfeld,' said Levoy.

'Who? What's his handle?'

'Ramus.'

'Dunno 'im. No matter. I can see you've packed up your traps and you're short of your holiday gear.'

'That's about it. Ramus told us you might help?'

'Got any brass?'

'Some,' I said cautiously.

'Good. I'll see what I can do. I've nothing suitable myself, but perhaps we can pick up what you need here and there. Let's see. Two pairs of shoes – what size? Eights and nines, good. Two pairs of trousers, one jacket. Your jerkin'll do, but you'll need some kind of mac. Then you'll need a titfer to be ready to push off. That'll be about four hundred marks. Is that OK?'

'Yes, but we haven't got enough civilian money,' protested Levoy.

'Never mind, this firm takes POW currency,' Bébert replied.

'We haven't any,' I was obliged to admit.

'Well, one of you must have a ticker?'

'Yes, I have,' said Levoy. 'But it's a gold one and valuable.'

'Don't worry about that,' said Bébert. 'We'll square it later. This firm has a reputation for honesty. You stay in this joint through the day. Don't go outside.'

The afternoon was uneventful, but for some reason or other, one of the workers did not go back, and we had the opportunity of getting him to put us wise about the kind of work they were doing here, and camp life in general. Levoy had been right in guessing that they were voluntary workers. We got to know quite a lot about the inmates of that room and particularly about Bébert.

'He comes from Ménilmontant,' the worker confirmed.

'He's one of the tough guys then.'

'Yes, he's a ponce.'

'A ponce?' said Levoy, simulating surprise.

'Yes, a ponce. He had several women on a beat around Pigalle till the Jerries came and scattered his herd. To make the best of a bad job, he volunteered to come here. He's all right – a nice guy – you can trust him.'

Now that we had been so confidently reassured of the integrity of our protector, we were able to relax enough to settle down to a game of cards on the corner of the table while awaiting the return of this paragon of virtue!

When eventually Bébert came in he announced:

'It's going to be all right. I've been talking to the Poles in the next camp and they'll hand out the stuff, but it'll take them three days to get it.'

'Three days!' we exclaimed together.

'Yes, why not? aren't you doing all right here?'

'Yes, but we're in your way,' I protested.

'Don't worry about that, mate. You're not in the way at all.'

Supper was much the same as the midday meal, but with more bread and the addition of margarine, German sausage and beetroot jam. It was hardly over when in walked a young woman who looked like a tart. She said hullo to the room in general and sat beside one of the men already at the table.

I asked Bébert, in an aside, who she was.

'She's his girlfriend. She comes from near Tours.'

'But how did she get here?'

'From the women's camp, three kilometres away. They work with us at the factory.'

Soon more girls came in, all young and not bad-looking. In the end there were about fifteen of them. The room was quite full by this time and all were chatting and laughing among themselves. Someone from another corner produced an accordian and dancing started up in the middle of the room and even overflowed between the beds, interspersed with a singing turn from a big-bosomed full-voiced brunette.

The time was passing very pleasantly and Levoy and I were enjoying looking on. Bébert came up to us and said:

'Well, lads, how're you doing?'

'So far, so good.'

'Your luck's in,' he went on. 'Two of the boys are on leave, so there are a couple of spare beds.'

We were glad of this bit of information as we had just been discussing the prospect of having to sleep on the floor.

'We certainly are in luck,' agreed Levoy.

'Yes, but be prepared to share beds.'

'Share beds?' I enquired.

'Yes, you see all these girls? Well, some of them are attached but the rest come here for a good time, for a night out. When it is time for them to go back up to their camp, they can't be bothered to walk three kilometres. They'd rather turn in with the lads here and be on the spot for work next morning, d'yer get me?'

He added with a wink, 'Take my tip! If you fancy any particular bird more than another, get your spoke in straightaway.'

It was all put so plainly that Levoy and I could only exchange ironical glances. After a moment's thought, I made up my mind. It was all a part of the escape and a much lighter sentence than fourteen days' prison. To the starving man, any dish is a banquet, and after all, it is surprising what one can do for one's country!

'You never can tell,' said Bébert. 'With a bit of luck and a little know-how, you might be able to combine business with pleasure. These birds'll take any risk for someone they fancy, and there's nothing like 'em for pinching identity papers off some civilian or other.'

From then on I inspected the women more carefully. I was not very enthusiastic on the whole, but there was one who seemed quite attractive. She was a tall girl with a wistful look in her eye. She was pretty, and, unlike the rest, she didn't look a tart. Her good figure was no detraction.

I decided to approach her straight away before old Levoy had a chance to cut me out. I was not certain that she wasn't one of those whom Bébert had described as 'attached', but chancing this and for want of a more original line of attack, I sat down on the form at her side, saying;

'I believe I have seen you somewhere.'

It didn't sound like me talking. After two years in prison camps, I felt I had lost my touch and was thoroughly ill at ease.

'Do you think so?' she replied.

'Aren't you a Parisienne?'

'Indeed I'm not. I'm from Nantes.'

'Are you married? I asked her.

'No.'

'You were writing a postcard just now. Was that to you boyfriend?'

'No, to my little girl. She's nearly five.'

'I wouldn't have thought to look at you, that you were the mother of a family.'

'That's perhaps because I'm an unmarried mother.'

We chatted for some time and I learnt that her name was Nicole. All at once she rose.

'Where are you going? What happens next?' I asked her but she was already out of earshot.

I noticed that some of the women were making for the wardrobe lockers standing at the head of every bed, and saw them get inside, leaving the doors ajar. The rest of them were filtering through the swing door out into the night.

'What's going on?' I asked, making quickly for Bébert.

'It's the nightly German inspection,' he told me.

'German inspection?' I echoed, fearfully.

'Don't worry, mate. They don't bother about us, and they won't even notice you. They're only concerned about the birds. Their orders are to chuck them out at lights-out. That's why those that are staying have hidden in the lockers, which are our private property. The Jerries have no authority to make us open them up if we refuse.'

'Look out!' shouted someone near the door.

The lockers were all locked up at once and the keys removed by their owners. A guttural *'Heil Hitler!'* announced the arrival of the two German black-uniformed and jack-booted guards as they charged noisily in through the swing door. One looked under the beds and the other went up to one of the lockers and started sniffing at the keyhole. He turned round to its owner with an interrogative:

'Mademoiselle?'

'None here.'

'Ja, ja.'

'Nix, nix.'

The German let the matter drop. He knew that under the privileges granted to voluntary workers he was not within his rights to demand that the locker be opened. In true German fashion he believed in avoiding complications. He realised he was on a good wicket in this camp and meant to stay there. He had done what duty demanded. He had carried out an inspection and had seen nothing. His orders did not require him to smell!

'Gute Nacht!'

It was all over and they had gone. The lockers were opened up and out stepped the girls.

It was bedtime and all got undressed, men and girls alike in one grand strip-tease. I had chosen one of the two spare beds and returning from a little necessary trip outside, I found Nicole already in it. I slipped into the narrow bed alongside her and the last man in put out the light.

*

The next day Levoy and I occupied ourselves with reading the books which we found lying about, and having a hand of cards now and then until evening, when the workers returned bringing with them another selection of girls, including of course, the 'regulars' but not, alas, Nicole. So after all I didn't get the identity papers which she had so faithfully promised.

I spent the evening watching Bébert taking part in a lively poker game, and when bedtime came, I was in a way relieved to see that only seven girls had stayed on and that I was to be the odd man out.

On the third day we were very pleased to find Bébert had collected all our vital equipment, and we tried on the new clothes. They were just right, giving us exactly the air of Germans got up in their Sunday best. We enquired what we owed him.

'Your ticker and a hundred marks,' he stated, uncompromisingly.

'That's only allowing three hundred marks for the gold watch!' Levoy quickly protested. He was a bank clerk in civilian life, and no fool in mental arithmetic.

'That's all it's worth to me mate, and I've still got to find the customer.'

Levoy made a gesture of acceptance. He had no doubt taken into consideration, on the credit side of the deal, the provision of unexpected entertainment. We were now all set for the next phase of our escape and decided to leave next morning. We spent so long talking it over, that I forgot to choose a partner until it was too late to make any overtures and I had to leave it to chance by getting into bed first.

What turned up proved to be a woman of about thirty-two with a good figure but not too pleasant an expression. She must have fancied herself as a lady, for in the very act of sidling up to me in bed, she announced:

'I trust you will treat me with respect, *Monsieur*.'

As I was just thinking how little she was to my taste and how much I would have preferred Nicole, my little friend from Nantes, I readily agreed.

'Certainly, *Madame*.' And with relief but some difficulty in this narrow bed, I turned over and went to sleep.

Next morning I found I had earned myself some very black looks and she went off disdainfully with an indignant toss of her head. Levoy, who had just spent a third night with the same girl, was still asleep. I woke him up, feeling that it was time we got down to business, and remembered that we were still on the run. Now was the time for us to leave this haven and face again the hazards of the storm. Our intention was to take the underground from a nearby suburban station, to the centre of Berlin. There we hoped to find railway maps and timetables which would enable us to pick out a roundabout route of minor branch lines to get us to a point near the Swiss border.

We got up with the factory workers so as to pass the guards in their company. Once safely outside, we shook hands with Bébert and went our way.

CHAPTER SIX

Unter den Linden

We soon found the underground station and had a look at the map. We picked out 'Friedrichsstrasse' knowing it to be central and near the seat of Hitler's Chancellery.

'They say he's been taking a walk down the Champs Elysées, why shouldn't we do a bit of sight-seeing? Let's take a stroll along Unter den Linden as far as the Brandenburger Gate,' I said jokingly.

We laughed at the prospect till we remembered that one of us would have to go to the booking office to get our tickets.

'I think you ought to do that, Levoy,' I suggested for he spoke German without an accent.

'But how should I ask for them?' he asked. 'Ought I to state the destination or should I just ask for two tickets, as we should in Paris?'[1]

We watched the procedure of a passenger going through the ticket office and realised at once that we must ask for Friedrichsstrasse. We were soon on the platform, and while we had to wait about, each could see that the other was showing signs of strain. I had the feeling all the time that people were staring at us and was relieved to see the train pull in.

There were a good many people in our coach and we stood in one corner. At each station, more got in and by the time we heard 'Friedrichsstrasse' announced over the loud-speaker our passage towards the door was completely blocked by the crowd. I was on the point of calling in French *'Laissez descendre,'* but stopped in time and forced myself to say repeatedly:

'Bitte, entschuldigen Sie.' (Excuse me please) as we made our way through the door.

We found ourselves on the platform and carried along with the crowd bound for the exit, among whom were a large proportion of soldiers but whose presence did not unduly disturb us. On the other hand I felt an overwhelming panic when we had to pass a policeman

[1] Metro tickets in Paris are of a uniform price.

near the turnstiles at the exit. I felt sure that he had his eye on us, but it was only imagination, an unnerving sensation which is part of the apprenticeship of every man on the run. Friedrichsstrasse was very busy as were most of the streets in this part of Berlin.

'Don't let people notice you gazing at Hitler's windows like that. You'll get us picked up!' I scolded Levoy.

'That must be the Chancellery,' he replied.

'Oh, to hell with the Chancellery. Look at that policeman; he'll be getting suspicious. Take the next turning on the right.'

We came out almost at once on Unter den Linden and walked along it, as I had jokingly suggested earlier, as far as the Brandenburger Gate. At this point, I came to the conclusion that I had seen all I wanted to and suggested that we should look out for a little café where we could have a cup of their ersatz brew, and hope to get a chance of seeing an up-to-date railway timetable as I did not feel we could rely on the one Ramus had given us.

We found a quiet place in a nearby street which seemed eminently suitable. Inside, to our dismay, we found lots of people, most of them soldiers. We had the coffee as planned but dared not ask for the timetable. That having misfired, we had to look for another one, and that time we were lucky, for they had a current timetable. I was able to verify the times we had already picked out before we set out in the direction of the station.

As we were walking, we talked over how we should set about buying the tickets. Neither of us was keen to be the one to go to the booking office, which was a risky business. We were well aware that ticket clerks at major stations could press a button to call the Gestapo if they suspected any passenger. All at once I remembered Rolf's address (my boss at Schoenfeld).

'Let's go and see him first; he lives quite near here,' I suggested. Levoy was doubtful – 'How do you know he won't give us up?'

But I insisted, for I trusted Rolf without reservation although he was a German.

'There's no risk of that, he's a fine chap and he will tip us off about travelling in Germany and tell us if we can safely go up openly to the railway booking offices.'

My companion gave reluctant assent and a few minutes later we found ourselves on the pavement below Rolf's apartment. We were satisfied just to identify the house with a view to coming back in the evening, because we were well aware that he would still be at the factory. Then we went off to explore the district, and visited among other places of interest, the well-known Karstadt, supposed to be one of the biggest department stores in Europe. We noticed that its counters were no better stocked than the rest of the shops we had passed, where the only goods not in short supply seemed to be mangel-wurzels.

All at once we found ourselves in a little square where we came face to face with a most heart-rending scene. A little boy, wearing a big yellow star, was doing his best to shield his face from gravel with which half a dozen older boys were pelting him. His tears only made him a general laughing-stock. His only crime was that he had been born a Jew.

A little further on we stopped to have a look at a fatigue party of POWs under military escort. If they had only known that two escaped comrades were watching them! Perhaps we would have been better advised to keep walking, for one of them, taking us for privileged Germans in reserved occupations away from the front, shouted without hesitation:

'There's a couple of shirkers, keeping their heads down.' And then louder in pidgin German so that we couldn't help knowing that it was meant for us, 'Off to the Russian front you dirty . . . ers.'

This bit of gratuitous advice decided us that we had better go back to Rolf's house. It looked like many others in Berlin. From the outside it looked like a mansion, but in the porch it was clear that the house had been divided into four or five flats, one or two on each floor. Over a row of letter-boxes was the name of the occupier and the location of his aparment. This system suited us very well for we were in no way anxious to come up against a concierge as we should have done in Paris.

We rang Rolf's bell and his wife, a pretty little woman, answered the door. She was somewhat puzzled. She didn't understand what was going on but invited us in. Her husband had not yet returned but she politely suggested that we should make ourselves at home while we waited for him. She was reassured when I could tell her that it was to me that she had sent a snack every day by her husband, for such a long time, and that I had come personally to express my gratitude. She was obviously pleased to meet me, having so often heard Rolf speak of me, but her smile gave way to a look of anxiety when I explained our escape and the purpose of our visit. She knew that we left in our wake a threat of death to any German helping us in our attempt, but nevertheless, she did not let her mind dwell on this, but was quick to make pleasant conversation.

Rolf was astounded to see us, but immediately took the situation in hand and asked his wife to lay two extra places for us. We had not come anticipating a meal but were overwhelmed with gratitude, for we hadn't expected to eat that night at all.

Rolf listened to our account and discussed our plans with us. He told us that there were frequent passenger controls on the trains and that we should be taking a big risk. As far as getting the tickets at the station was concerned, he would come with us and take them for us himself!

Time passed only too quickly in the company of these incomparable friends, and we had to leave to catch a night train on which we hoped to pass unnoticed. Outside it was pitch dark on account of the stringent black-out. There were only occasional blue lights here and there. We all four linked arms to avoid getting separated. Madame Rolf insisted on coming with us to the station and kept a lookout while her husband got us two tickets for Leipzig.

All went well, thanks to their invaluable assistance and we were soon installed in opposite corners of an empty compartment. If we could only have stayed like that! Unfortunately, other passengers got in.

'*Heil Hitler!*'

'*Heil Hitler!*' we chorused.

Aware of watching eyes, I glued my nose to the window to avoid them. On the other track I saw painted on an engine in enormous letters: 'RADER MUSSEN ROLLEN FUR DEN SIEG', which I recognised as 'The Wheels must turn for Victory'. Their victory I hoped never to see, but I wished our wheels would start to turn, for I was beginning to feel very much on edge again. I realised that waiting was the most trying part of an escape. So long as progress is being made, no matter how slow, courage is forthcoming, but it is the periods of enforced delay which strain the nerves to breaking point.

Levoy was asleep or pretending to be. He was doing the wise thing, avoiding being drawn into embarrassing conversations. I decided to follow his example while keeping my ears open for anything going on on the platform. At last, after a couple of blasts on the whistle, the train pulled slowly out and I went off to sleep in earnest.

The sound of the brakes roused me from the depths of unconsciousness. I had just been dreaming that the Germans had come out on top. We slowed up as the train drew into a gloomy station. By chance, our compartment came to a halt level with a

Myself as a young man.

(Above) During my military service, 1926.

(Left) Myself, on the left, with my lieutenant and a corporal the commencement of hostilities 1939/40.

platform lamp on which was inscribed the name: 'LUDERSDORF'.

My heart turned over. It was the name of the place from which we escaped through the snow – the very station at which we had alighted under escort on our way to the punishment camp!

I hardly had time to recover when I got a second shock. The door of the next compartment slammed and who should pass along the platform under my very nose, but that self-same German *Feldwebel* who, only a fortnight previously at Ludersdorf Camp, had threatened to shoot on sight, any prisoner trying to escape. Whew! I looked across at Levoy to see if he had noticed, but he was fast asleep, and a good thing too! Such shocks are bad for the health.

However, the rest of the journey went off uneventfully and we came to the blacked-out station of Leipzig. We got through the barrier without any hitch and soon found ourselves in the streets of a very imposing town with massive stone buildings which were gradually revealed in the light of dawn.

We had time to kill, for we knew that our Nuremberg train did not leave till 9.5 am and that it was wiser not to loiter near the station, always a well-guarded spot. We strolled to and fro along the main streets gazing at the half-empty shop windows. We noticed some impressive buildings but on the whole we were not very taken with this large provincial town. However, in a big square we came upon one of the wonders of this hostile country. By chance we were crossing this square at the exact moment when the world-famous clock of Leipzig struck the hour. The whole front of an elaborately sculptured building suddenly came to life. Every little statuette in its own niche started to move or gesticulate to a background of tinkling music from innumerable little bells. It was a pity that there were no other curiosities like this to help us pass the time, but we could not resist the temptation to return to this square an hour later to watch and hear this remarkable clock a second time.

At last it was time to go back to Leipzig station, reputed to be one of the grandest in Europe, and out of all proportion to the size of the town it serves. In spite of all our fears we managed to get tickets without hitch, and were soon comfortably installed with a compartment to ourselves. It was an interminably slow stopping train, and as folk got in, it soon filled up.

We had foreseen that at that time in the morning we could not convincingly pretend to be asleep, so we buried ourselves in German newspapers, although the propaganda of exaggerated reports, loaded with lies, stuck in our throats. We read, for instance, that in the POW camps, French prisoners were joining the Pétain League *en masse* at the rate of at least 80% in every camp. (On the other hand we had just left a camp where we knew that there were no adherents to the League, and in Schoenfeld, Ramus told us, as we passed through, that they had succeeded in raising only one recruit!) We also read that POWs in Germany were treated like lords while their brave counterparts in the hands of the British barbarians, were chained together in defiance of international treaties so scrupulously observed by the Führer!

Throughout the day, we did not manage to ward off all attempts at conversation, and towards evening, I found myself having to read out the latest official bulletin to a garrulous old chap with a long moustache.

'You don't come from these parts then?' he probed.

'I'm from Berlin,' I replied, adding to justify my civilian status. 'I work in an ammunition factory and have a few days' leave, I'm off to see my wife in Nuremberg.'

'This train doesn't go to Nuremberg,' he announced. 'For nearly a month, it has only gone as far as Plauen. Didn't your wife let you know?'

Ignoring his last question, I asked why the route had been cut short, and to my satisfaction, he showed me with a gesture that the line had been bombed. I looked at Levoy and then at my ticket – it was made out for Nuremberg right enough. This put us in quite a spot. I took the chance and asked the old fellow what I ought to do.

'You have to get a train from Plauen to Eger in Czechoslovakia where you can pick up a train back into Germany to Nuremberg.'

I realised that this might mean disaster. We did not know whether the German-Czech frontier was open. If not, and there was a control, we could not avoid re-capture.

At this moment the train pulled into Plauen. There was a shout of 'All change' and we realised that this would at least give us a chance to talk it over privately together.

The old man had been quite right and a porter confirmed that there was no train in the direct route to Nuremberg until the afternoon of the following day, and this involved doing a detour of the bomb damage by bus. Alternatively, as the old man had said, we could get a train via Eger in a couple of hours.

We decided that it was less risky to proceed to the frontier in two hours' time than to remain so long at a station. We should have been very much on edge while waiting, had it not been for the fact that two men on a seat nearby, judging from their ill-assorted garb, were obviously on the run. It was reassuring to us to realise that as long as they could go about with impunity, we were not likely to be the first couple questioned! It is always a comfort to see people worse off than yourself. Nevertheless, the period of waiting was anxious enough.

Railway stations were always dangerous spots, liable to Gestapo controls, and two hours under this strain left me feeling very nervous. Levoy did not have much to say, but I knew he was feeling the same. Our fears, however, were groundless. We left without anyone approaching us and crossed the Czech frontier without even realising that we had done so.

At Eger we did not leave the station, for the Nuremberg train was due to leave. There were only four of us in the compartment, and as it was night, we were able to settle down as if asleep. After about half an hour, when I was telling myself that we must now be back over the frontier in Germany, the door opened suddenly and a German in uniform appeared in the doorway.

'*Heil Hitler!*'

'*Heil Hitler!*' we answered in chorus.

If it had been the Gestapo we should have been lost for neither of us had seen him coming, and we were without papers or travel permits and with no chance to make a get-away. Fortunately, he was only a ticket-inspector, but we learnt our lesson and took it in turn after this to keep a look-out.

We travelled all that day and it was night again when we reached Nuremberg. We met no obstacle when we got out of the train and none of the onlookers, corpse-like in the faint blue light of the black-out, stepped forward to question us. We found ourselves once more in the black streets of a strange city.

We quickly made our way as far from the station as possible as we knew that there was no train that night to Stuttgart, the next stage in our journey towards the Swiss frontier. We had to wait for one till the following day, but were at a loss where to spend the freezing night. The station waiting-rooms were out of the question and we had been warned against air-raid shelters. We thought of looking for a convenient bit of waste ground, where if we did not escape the rigours of the weather, we should at least be untroubled by police controls. We were still looking for a suitable spot when a group of noisy young people came towards us. To our astonished delight we realised that they were speaking French and that they were no doubt workers returning to camp. Two of them hung back for a moment to

light their cigarettes out of the wind, and I took this opportunity to
approach them.

'You are French!'

'Yes.'

What risk could there be in asking our fellow countrymen to help
us? The worst they could do was to refuse.

'So are we. We're POWs on the run. Do you know where we could
spend the night?'

They looked at each other with hesitation as if I were asking the
impossible. Then one of them took a decision:

'Come back in an hour,' he said, offering us a cigarette.

'We will, and thank you.'

We were certainly in luck, not only to avoid sleeping out in a
temperature well below zero, but to escape the risk of being picked
up by the police; so we set out lightheartedly to walk round and
round the block (to avoid losing ourselves) until our deliverer turned
up at the appointed time.

'I didn't want the other fellows to get a look at you just now,' he
said. 'We're in a very queer camp, where there are plenty of stool-
pigeons. I'll help you as long as it is on the quiet. I don't want to land
up in a concentration camp! Cigarette?'

'Thanks, you don't know how grateful we are to you.'

'Never mind about thanks. This is no time to hang about here.
There may be other chaps from the camp coming this way. Come
along with me. I've got a small room in town which I share with a
friend who is all right. He won't give you away. There are only two
beds but we'll manage.'

This was wonderful. We couldn't have hoped for anything better
and we followed him through the back streets and alleys of this
mediaeval city. The room was very poor and was almost filled by two
double bedsteads with antediluvian iron frames and broken springs,
but this did not worry us. We were only too glad to be under cover as
far as the *Schupos* (German civil police) were concerned, and to let
tomorrow take care of itself.

We had to be up in good time as our two new friends left early to be
in time for work and were anxious to lock up behind them, but we did
not have any fault to find, we were only too grateful for services
rendered.

We made our way back to the station and got on the Stuttgart
train, a slow one which took all day to get there. At every station
there was shunting to take on coaches or drop them off. It seemed as

if we were going backwards more than forwards. The occupants of the compartment changed several times in the course of the journey. At Waldorf the train was full up, when an attractive blonde got in. She took my eye to such an extent that I forgot myself sufficiently to offer her my seat! I found myself repeating the word *'Bitte'* until she finally accepted it. All eyes were upon me! I had made myself conspicuous and remembered too late that German men never give up their seats to ladies. To all present, I was branded as a foreigner.

However, there were no repercussions and what the Germans lack in gallantry, they make up for in disinterested generosity. One of them brought out a big packet which he opened on his lap to reveal a huge fruit tart. He divided it carefully into as many portions as there were passengers and gave everyone present a piece. In silence Levoy and I blessed this good Samaritan who all unwittingly gave us our first food for two days.

As a result of simulating sleep so realistically, in the end I dropped off and did not waken until we reached Stuttgart and I heard: *'Alles aussteigen!'* (All change).

It was night and just as at Nuremberg, the station was in darkness except for the few blue lights. We followed the crowd and got through the barrier without trouble. Once out of the station we .stopped in a corner to consider how best to spend the night. We decided that if we could we would get a night train on our way towards the Swiss frontier and thus avoid the necessity of hiding in this large strange city.

We could not see to read our pocket railway-guide in the darkness, so I suggested that I should go back into the station to look at the timetable on the board. We agreed that it was useless to risk both of us going and arranged that Levoy would not move from the place where I left him. I went inside and soon found the timetables displayed in an inner room. I was just looking at them when I heard about ten yards behind me: *'Heil Hitler! Papiere!'*

I glanced over my shoulder. To my horror, it was Levoy, who in spite of what we had arranged, had follwed me and been pounced on by a Gestapo agent. My first instinct was to get away, but to do this I had to pass close to them as they were standing in the doorway and there was no other way out. I moved casually towards them, but Levoy glanced at me as I was going by and the German was smart enough to spot it, and grabbed me by the arm.

'Papiere!' he repeated.

'Nix *papiere.'*

'Komm mit.'

It was all up, to use the expression of those on the run. For a moment I thought of making a dash for it into the darkness but I had not the energy. The strain of the last few days had used up all my reserves. It was almost with relief that we abandoned this ill-fated attempt and gave ourselves up as POWs, feeling nevertheless, that an important lesson had been assimilated – that an escape, however well-conceived, must not be allowed to become too long-winded. The quickest route is the best, as delay is in itself an enemy.

The agent marched us off towards the police station in a firm grip. I was screwing up my courage to make a bolt but was taken unawares to find the Gestapo post was actually in the railway station. The officer on duty made us empty our pockets and proceeded to interrogate us. He was frigid but correct. He kept us waiting for an hour on a bench and then handed us over to two armed police, who escorted us outside, where to our disgust, we were put into a Black Maria.

The journey in this notorious conveyance took about ten minutes. We arrived at the city gaol of Stuttgart where we underwent a further questioning and were forced to strip and submit to all the indignities of an intimate search. They confiscated a few odds and ends, and then shut us in an observation cell with the light on, where we found a couple of doubtful types already installed.

The cell was clean. It had cream walls, a lofty ceiling and a bitumastic floor. There were two hinged shelves which could fold flat against the walls, but were being used by the two inmates. One of them, with a strong Alsatian accent, asked what we had done to get brought in. We said that we were re-captured POWs and asked why they were there. One of them refused to comment except by shrugging his shoulders, but the Alsatian claimed to be there for expressing his political opinions too freely.

For want of anything better, we stretched out on the floor, and in spite of the lack of comfort, I managed to go to sleep. The noise of the door opening at four or five am roused me. The guard with the keys came in and signalled to us.

'Get up.'

In the corridor outside we were given into the custody of two military guards who took us back in the Black Maria to the station. We thought we were being taken to the police depot, but we were wrong. A compartment had been reserved for us on a train that was just about to leave and we found ourselves on the way to an unknown destination, each in a corner with a Boche facing him.

Some time that morning we arrived at Ludwigsburg, a residential town. Under the watchful eyes of our guards we marched along its fine avenues until at the top of a hill we reached the gates of Stalag VA where a small but fierce little sergeant-major was waiting for us.

Once again we were searched and this time with some brutality. Police dogs, held at chain's length, were on the watch for the slightest excuse to sink their teeth in our defenceless bare bodies. The guards moved us to and fro at their pleasure by adjusting the length of the chains to which these snarling brutes were attached. All our possessions were confiscated. With bitterness we watched the passing of all our gear, supplied by open-handed Ramus and supplemented by Bébert. We had to put on instead an assortment of unbelievably ragged garments. There was only one relic of our short vacation left. None of the prison boots fitted me and consequently, I contrived to get the Germans to leave me my civilian shoes.

Once dressed, we were registered, interrogated, sworn at and beaten up. Then we were escorted further into the camp to an enclosure within which stood a low brick building. It was obvious that this was the prison both from the narrow barred windows and from the sentry posted in front of the padlocked door.

Our cell was very small and already contained one inmate. We each had a blanket, but no bed, not even a shelf. When the three of us lay down we took up the whole floor space. I was lucky to be in the middle, for Levoy could not stretch out without putting his feet in the WC (which was an open soil pipe flanked by footrests and fitted with a flush). Our cell-mate could not have been described as congenial. He was the only one of us who had any cigarettes and he kept on smoking them without offering us one. However, there were excuses. His story was a particularly bitter one and other people in the same circumstances might have been just as inconsiderate. He was a POW who had made a successful escape, and who on reaching Paris, had been betrayed to the Germans by his own wife. This despicable woman had a Boche lover and the return unannounced of her husband interfered with her plans. Every time he ground a stub underfoot, it was with the vow – 'I'll kill her!'

CHAPTER SEVEN

The Black Hole of Willingen

On the third day of this incarceration we were taken out of the cell and once more escorted under close guard to the railway station. We wondered where we were off to next and tried to get some information from our guards.

'*Wohin?*'

But the guards remained silent. The train was going south and soon we found ourselves again encircling the rim of the hill basin in the bottom of which lay Stuttgart. The scenery was magnificent, snow-covered and bathed in sunlight. All the time we were travelling, vast acres of pine trees were flashing by and when we finally came to a halt at Willingen we were still in the midst of them.

A short, but fantastically beautiful, walk through the snow brought us to the gates of Stalag V B and there, abruptly, the beauty faded into brutality as we were faced with the unnerving sight of a suffering Russian POW. He was emaciated to such an extent that skin hung on his frame like a coat flapping on a peg. His face was white as a corpse, and his eyes so crazed with torment that they looked like bursting from their sockets. He could no longer walk properly but proceeded with a mechanical waddle like a dancing doll, to the jeers of his escort and to the derision of some sadistic Teuton onlookers.

This was not a hutted camp of the kind I had had experience of before. It was constructed round an existing brick-built barracks and its concomitant buildings into the nearest of which we were escorted.

In the passage, I was able to interpret various signs: *Revier*, *Archiv* and *Küche*, for instance, which meant 'Sick-bay', 'Records' and 'Kitchens'.

An NCO asked our names, numbers and the names of our original Stalags. Then he took us both to the end of a corridor where the sentry on duty unlocked a door. We were then hurled through it into a room already containing many other prisoners.

When we answered the inevitable questions about what had

brought us here, we started to have a look round our new quarters. We found we were shut up with eighty other French prisoners in a room 20 × 25 feet. There were two sealed windows which could never be opened because they were barred and nailed from the outside and covered with wire netting as an extra precaution. As a result the atmosphere was suffocating. In the middle of the room was an enormous three-tiered wooden rack which served as a communal bed. The remaining floor space was so crowded that it was almost impossible to move about.

Though the air stank foully from a hugh open sanitary tub, continually overflowing, which stood in a corner near the central rack, the atmosphere of the place could not have been more friendly. We felt at ease immediately among these comrades in misfortune. They all told their stories of their various escapes and discussed plans for the next. In spite of present hardships, morale was high and all were waiting impatiently for the chance to take off again on what they were certain would be a successful venture, aware as they were through past experience of the dangers to be avoided. The real value of these discussions was that an appreciation of each man's past mistakes was gained by everybody. It was, in effect, a finishing school for escapees.

There was a very small soup ration (and nothing else) but I must admit that it was much better in quality than what I had received in other camps. This was because we were supplied from the kitchens which catered for the Germans themselves and for the sick-bay somewhere above us.

Levoy and I secured a corner on the top shelf of the rack. Next to me was a bearded portrait painter from the Savoy district of France. I found his professional skill very interesting, for painting had been a favourite pastime of mine in the good old days. We formed a firm friendship and often vied with each other to see who could produce the best likeness in pencil sketches. This was my only distraction apart from watching the continual movement caused by the arrival through the door of recaptured prisoners and the corresponding departure of others. But there was one form of entertainment for which there was always competition to get near the two windows. These overlooked a courtyard where newly apprehended prisoners were escorted. We called them the 'Tourists'. They came in about every half hour, and many of them were disguised very convincingly as ordinary civilians. Many others, however, were more imaginative and these supplied the entertainment. Among them was a glazier, with his panes on his back, and he was followed a little later by a couple of the Hitler Youth Brigade in shorts and swastikas. Then came a priest, a couple of nuns and on another occasion, two attractive young ladies! We also saw a window-cleaner marched in complete with his ladder and bucket. We greeted each arrival with peals of laughter and bursts of clapping to show what we thought of their disguises. We were particularly impressed by a master sweep and his mate, both wearing top hats (still the mark of this trade in Germany) and carrying their rods and brushes, but we awarded the laurels for the most ingenious make-up to the herdsman who was leading behind him a cow, emaciated by the rigours of a very long journey throughout which she had kept him supplied with fresh milk.

The prisoner who slept on the other side of Levoy seemed familiar to me but I could not place him. He was very opinionated on all subjects, and politically professed to be a follower of Karl Marx. This gave me a clue to his identity, for back at Ludersdorf (whence we had first escaped) I had heard similar views from a fellow with a big beard who said he had been a ladies' hairdresser somewhere near the Champs Elysées in Paris. I felt quite sure that this clean-shaven communist was none other than the bearded Figaro! I confided my suspicions to Levoy, who was inclined to agree but wondered what had become of the weasel-faced individual who had always been his inseparable companion. We decided to ask him outright.

'I think I have seen you somewhere before?'

'Oh? It must have been my double,' he replied.

'Possibly. But weren't you at Ludersdorf?'

'Me? No.'

'You have never seen us before?'

'No. Never.'

'Perhaps I came across you somewhere in France before the war? What did you do?'

'I was an accountant.'

I could not get any further, but we were quite certain he was the same man even without his beard. Three days later, however, when the door opened, in walked the man we had known as his mate. The only difference was that he was the one who was wearing the beard! He could not make it very convincing like his friend and soon gave up the pretence. Putting their cards on the table they told us their story.

They made their escape from Ludersdorf the day after we had left. They somehow managed to break away from the work gang on its five mile journey to the frozen drainage site, without being observed by the guards. Still in prison uniform they made their way to Berlin. The first step in their very subtle scheme was to get themselves arrested there. With this intention they accosted a policeman on point duty and greeted him in perfect German with:

'We are escaped POWs,' but without the effect they had intended.

'Move along there!'

They persisted:

'We've escaped from a prison camp.'

'Clear off!'

They could not make any impression. The policeman thought they were pulling his leg and our two fellow-prisoners had to think again. They went into a military canteen, and picking a table already occupied by a German officer, they lost no time in getting into conversation with him.

'Excuse me, *Herr Kapitän*, do you happen to know the time of the next train to Paris?'

'To Paris?'

'Yes, we've escaped from a POW camp, and we want to get to Paris.'

'Ha, ha, ha. That's a good one. You Frenchmen always like a joke!'

He refused to take them seriously and was quite convinced they were having him on. In the end these two smart Alecs had to cause a commotion in a police station before anyone would pay attention to their story. They gave their names and then came their cunning.

'What's your base camp?'

'Stalag V B,' they lied (in reality it was III A).

They calculated that the police would hand them over to the military authorities who would be obliged to return them to their base camp, in this case Willingen which was only about twenty miles from the Swiss frontier, whereas Stalag III A at Luckenwalde would have put them quite four hundred miles deeper into Germany. Before their subterfuge came to light through the Records Department, they were counting on getting the next phase of their escape under way. This was to get themselves admitted to the sick-bay together from which they had planned a joint escape. A few days later, they must have managed it and we heard nothing more of them.

When we had spent about two months in the 'Black Hole' we were assembled one freezing morning near the camp entrance and forced to undergo a particularly tedious roll-call. Most of the inmates had been claimed by their respective Stalags within a week of their capture. Yet Levoy and I were still there after two months. The only possible explanation we could think of was that there had been some mix-up or other in the German organisation, and that we had simply been forgotten. This, of course, was very fortunate as I had no desire at all to be taken back to Stalag III A and its disciplinary camp at Ludersdorf.

We stood shivering while a brow-beating speech was delivered by the lieutenant in command of this God-forsaken camp, where the Geneva Convention was never observed in respect of elementary hygiene, Red Cross goods distribution, or the common right of every prisoner to write home. At the end of his communications he issued an order to the troops to march us off to the station.

We made the journey in cattle trucks and it was only our common morale as escaped POWs which prevented us from sinking into the apathy of the beasts they had been built for. For us any prison was only a passing phase between attempts.

We were retracing a route which we had taken by passenger train to get to Willingen but this time, of course, more slowly. It was already well into the afternoon when we found ourselves slowly winding back round the rim of the Stuttgart basin. We still had no idea where we were bound for, but we were not at all sorry to be getting away from the Black Hole of Willingen.

It was night before the train stopped and we were all ordered out, but, nevertheless, Levoy and I recognised the station as Ludwigsburg and we realised that we were destined to revisit the Stalag where we had spent three days in a cell two months before.

The trip from the station was uneventful and the public ignored us completely. Our reception at the camp gates was no better than it had been the time before. The guards screamed at us, the dogs barked and the same sergeant-major fired off his revolver in the air by way of impressing us.

We were marched across the camp to an inner enclosure bearing the sign 'GESPERRT', which implied that we had forfeited all rights. We were to be considered as 'banished'.

We found there several wooden huts, mostly already occupied by escaped POWs who had been recaptured and were now being assembled here. We were herded in like sheep, and neither our shepherds nor their dogs came in after us. We did not have to work and we passed the time as best we could, thinking ourselves very lucky if we had a chance to read a book or have a game of cards. The only regular fatigue was the collection and distribution of the daily soup ration, which was so small as to be hardly worth picking up.

I found myself in a different hut from Levoy and as a result we drifted apart somewhat and I became friendly with two men sleeping near me – Lucien Tarsitano and Gino Campi. They were both Frenchmen but Lucien was of white Algerian stock and Gino's family had originally come from Italy. We had two main topics of conversation, the good meals we used to have before the war and a minute investigation of all possible methods of escape and crossing the frontier.

One day there was great excitement in the Gesperrt Compound and the inmates were all milling round a notice that had been posted on one of the huts. Over their heads I could read the title: RAWA RUSKA.

We wondered what these outlandish words meant and thought they sounded Russian. Eventually, I got near enough to decipher that by order of the Führer, a reprisal camp had been set up behind the Eastern Front near the town of Rawa Ruska in Eastern Galicia (which had been Polish until overrun by the Russians earlier in the war, and had subsequently been recaptured again, this time by the Germans). This camp, I read on, would receive POWs guilty of repeated attempts at escape. It was surrounded by dangerous swamps and situated at a great distance from any frontier, thus discouraging any who might not understand their duties to the German armies defending the New Europe and who might be tempted to take to the roads in a false hope of reaching their homeland, thus causing confusion in a country where order and discipline were revered.

There was a ring of doom to me in the sound of the words Rawa Ruska and from the comments I heard round the notice, others must have felt it too.

'What price the swamps?'

'The b.....'

'Where on earth is Galicia?' asked someone, and the laconic answers came:

'In Russia'.

So long as we were in Germany we felt we were within reach of France, but if we were to be taken off to Russia we knew that we would be exiled indeed. We all wondered how we could avoid this fate. Immediate escape would have been the obvious solution but it was out of the question from our '*Gesperrt*' enclosure. We were far too closely guarded. Lucien, Gino and I decided that our only hope was to escape from the train during the first night, by cutting a hole in the floor of our truck, and with this in mind, we set about looking for a suitable tool. All our efforts were unsuccessful and we still had nothing several days later, when a second notice informed us that our departure had been fixed for the next day.

CHAPTER EIGHT

Journey to Russia

Next morning we stuck close to our friends in an effort to keep together on the journey, but the Germans were well aware that this was a convoy of prisoners dedicated to escape, and consequently they took drastic measures to foil any attempt at the outset. From the beginning friends were separated, for our guards knew from experience that prisoners seldom tried to escape alone and usually depended on companionship to support their courage. We were therefore escorted under a heavily reinforced guard to a large field near the camp where we were shuffled like a pack of cards. However, thanks to counter tactics on our part, they did not manage to break up our little trio, nor did they discover our only penknife despite a particularly thorough search.

Once these tedious preliminaries were over, we marched in closed ranks to the station where a train of cattle trucks stood ready. The Germans had taken special security precautions here too. As we walked up the platform, the first thing that we saw was a large roll of barbed wire attached to the back of the hindermost truck. Lucien and I exchanged glances, realising that this was designed to discourage would-be floor piercers! Then we spotted machine-guns posted on roofs overlooking the station. Our last discovery was that every single truck carried a raised look-out box complete with a flight of steps, and was to be manned by an SS sentry with tommy-gun.[1]

'That's just a reminder that nobody travels faster than bullets,' commented Gino.

An order rang out and we clambered into the trucks, where we found we were too many to lie down altogether and had to sleep by rota. No sanitation was provided at all, not even a bucket, for the Germans considered we were only beasts or what they called 'Schweinhunde'.

At last the train departed rapidly gathering speed. After nightfall, Lucien took out his penknife and moved away to get on with his job

[1] Type of trucks usually used at rear of goods trains.

of gouging through the floor boards in spite of the hazard of the roll of barbed wire trailing down the track behind the train. However, he was soon back, saying:

'Why bother? A couple of the lads are at work on the door already, and they've got much better tools than mine.'

I went over and had a look at this clandestine undertaking and saw a little chap drilling a hole about three inches across, just beneath the spot were the truck's sliding door was padlocked on the outside. He was using a pivot tool that looked something like a pair of compasses. I made up my mind to get to know him for I was filled with admiration both for his job and his composure.

'When do you mean to make your break?' I asked.

'Tonight, of course!'

'About what time?'

'Oh, about two o'clock, when the guards are a bit dozy.'

'I'd like to come along too, if I could bring a couple of pals.'

His reply surprised me but amused me:

'My mate and I are jumping first and after that we don't care a damn. The whole bloody truck can follow if they like.'

'Good, that's on then, but I'd like to lie down for a bit first, if one of you wouldn't mind giving me a shake?'

'We'll do that, you can count on us.'

I groped my way back to Lucien and Gino over the bodies of would-be sleepers, to tell them about it. In the meantime they had had second thoughts about the trailing barbed wire and decided against the attempt.

If I listened too long to them, I knew I should lose my resolution so I stretched out in the small space allotted to me alongside them, and went to sleep.

I did not have much time to dream for it seemed that I had no sooner dropped off, than someone was shaking me urgently and whispering in my ear.

'It's open.'

I paused for one second, like a diver on the top board screwing up his courage, and said:

'OK. I'm coming.'

I hurried, not so considerately this time, I'm afraid, over the sleeping forms, and could feel the draught from the partly opened door. I got there in time to see the first man stepping gingerly over some remaining strands of barbed wire which festooned the doorway from outside. He stood poised for two seconds then disappeared into

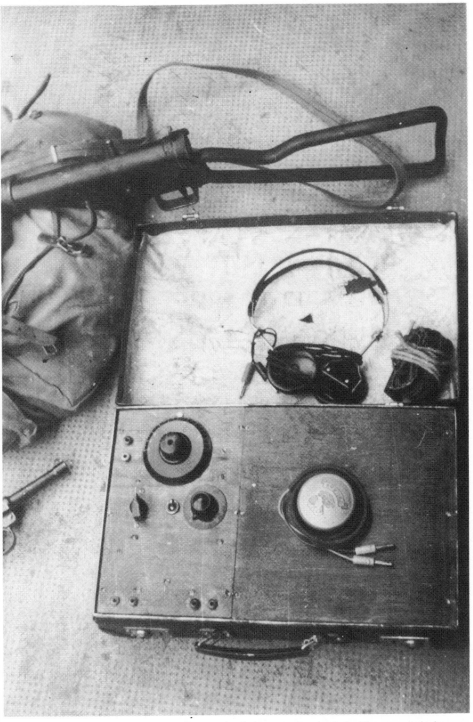

The small wireless with which Roger, the baker, communicated with our people in Switzerland, mainly to announce the crossing of an agent at such and such a point and at what time he should be met.

Philippe Allemann on his way to Switzerland to have the wireless repaired. It is in the small attaché case.

the night. The second one followed him immediately without even looking back.

It was my turn then, and nothing but fear stood between me and freedom. I had a momentary panic, and realised I could still back out without losing face, but I mastered it, negotiated the barbed wire and stood in the doorway bending over backwards to balance myself. The train was travelling fast and the wind seared my face. It was pitch dark and I was more scared of hitting the piers of a bridge or some other object than of the aim of the guards, but it was too late to turn back and, shielding my face with my arm, I hurled myself forward in the direction the train was taking, trying to put into practice the rolling tactics which I had found on the sports fields to have great effect in breaking a fall and so avoiding injury.

In these conditions, I made a comparatively easy landing and rolled along the side of the track like a ball. When I came to a stop, I was still under the lee of the running boards and so close to the wheels that they sounded like thunder in my ears, but I realised, with relief, that I was too close to be a target for the guards.

Then, I bethought me of that rapidly approaching coil of barbed wire, and speedily did a sideways roll to clear the track, landing up in the gutter at the side of it. All in a moment I realised that I was now an excellent target as the train went thundering past for what seemed an eternity. Suddenly, I was bathed in a brilliant red glow which I realised almost at once to be the train's rear light now receding rapidly into the distance. I could not believe that there had been no firing and suddenly, it was as if I had awakened from a nightmare, to the realisation that I had succeeded. I was free!

I got up quickly, climbed up the embankment and was over the fence, without any trouble, to find myself on a tarmac road. I walked back along the track in the hope of coming across the other two. As I walked I realised my hand was hurting me but the sizeable cut on the palm which was bleeding freely was the only injury I had received.

'Psssst!'

A low signal came from someone very close at hand which took me completely by surprise. Even in the dark, however, I could place him as 'Shorty' from the train – the one who had jumped first.

'We're under cover, over there.' he explained as he took me over to his mate who was crouching in a ditch.

'Are you all right?' he asked me.

'Yes, I'm OK.

'But you're bleeding?'

'I cut my hand when I landed on the track, but it's nothing much.'

'Good, well, let's get organised. One of us must find water to fill the bottle, and one must go on to the nearest marshalling yard. Nothing else would be lit up like that in the middle of the war. Will you go?' he enquired of me. 'Then Shorty can go and find the water, as it's his bottle, and I'll stay here and keep a look out for both of you in the dark. Try to find us a nice truck, direct to Rouen while you're about it – that's my home town.'

'All right, I'll see you later.'

I set off towards the lights, keeping to the road which ran alongside the track, for as long as I dared. After walking just over one mile I could see that his guess was correct, and that it was a marshalling yard of considerable importance. I climbed over the fence and darted down the embankment to take cover in the shadow of a stationary goods train. I could make out a good deal of movement between trains on the tracks and heard noise and shouting, but realised that this only came from the railway workers and not from troops. Then I started to search meticulously, darting from truck to truck to examine their destination labels, but found nothing going in a direction that would be at all suitable for us.

Suddenly I had to crouch down between the wheels because someone was coming. Unfortunately, I was not to know that this was a policeman or that I was not properly hidden. When he came alongside he drew his revolver with one hand and flashed a light on me with the other.

'Come out!' he gave me the guttural order.

I do not know what prompted me, but on the spur of the moment my hand closed over a stone and, aiming at the revolver, I hurled it with all my might and ... shattered the torch! With one bound I was out on the other side and off down the track at top speed. When I had left the train behind me, I realised that the Boche was still after me, and how lucky I was to have kept my own shoes at Ludwigsburg and not be wearing heavy army boots. They gave me an agility along the track which enabled me to gain so much start over my jack-booted pursuer that I found, since he had made no use of his revolver, I could take it a bit more easily and then put a spurt on with the hope of discouraging him altogether. Looking back over my shoulder, I caught a glimpse of him under one of the shaded lamps and realised he was one of the deadly black-uniformed security police, and he still held his revolver at the ready. I wondered whether he had no ammunition or whether he was anxious to take me alive. In any event, I decided to put a good deal more ground between him and me! It was imperative that I got out of the railway cutting but to do this, I had to climb up the embankment and get over the fence before the policeman overtook me.

I was still seeking the answer when I found myself at a station and ran the length of the platform at top speed, gathering a couple more pursuers as I did so. They were fresh for the chase and I had now done a good mile. One of them nearly caught me but lost his wind and gave up.

I was weighing up my chances as I ran. Fatigue was causing me to stumble and I knew I could not keep going much longer. But I realised that after each track lamp had cast its pool of light on the line, the following stretch was swallowed up in contrasting blackness. Immediately after passing the next lamp, I dived off the track into the cover of this obscurity. Providentially, at this point there was a large coffer on the embankment, the kind of box where platelayers keep their picks and shovels. Behind this I hid, and as calculated, my pursuers did not realise that I was still not running on ahead and the chase passed me by a few paces away. The big policeman was still in the lead and I was surprised at the number who had joined him.

My ruse having succeeded, there was nothing to stop me from climbing the embankment and getting right away, but I was so exhausted by the chase that I began to have second thoughts about my chances of ultimate success. I had nothing to eat or drink, no money and I was at least one hundred miles from the frontier. I reasoned to myself that the train must by now be a long way off and consequently, that I had achieved something; I should not now be taken off to Russia. If I gave myself up, I suspected that I should be sent to some camp in Germany from which I could prepare an escape under much better conditions.

I felt that this was the only thing to do and decided to hand myself over to the first person who should come along, and with this intention I walked back along the track towards a lantern which someone appeared to be swinging at arm's length. I decided to let this workman have the credit of my arrest and when he was about twenty yards off, I showed myself.

He stopped dead, held up his lantern to get a better look at me and then took to his heels! I was astounded but could see the humour of the situation. In fact, it brought home the saying that a German by himself is never very bold. They need mutual support to bolster up their courage, and only show their arrogance when they have superiority of numbers. So in about a quarter of an hour, I was not surprised to see a whole batch of little bobbing lanterns coming towards me.

This time, I was arrested and taken off, but I must say in favour of these railwaymen that none of them treated me badly. In fact, they took me to a little hut where they made a telephone call to notify the authorities of my capture, and while they waited for the armed guard they gave me water and a cigarette. One of them even noticed my injured hand and looked after it for me by cleaning it and putting on a dressing from the first-aid kit which was installed in the hut.

'*Krieg grosse malheur.*' (War is great evil), he said in a mixture of French and German.

I had heard this platitude before, usually in the mouths of those guards most prone to double dealing and I would not respond to his overture. I preferred to sit in silence on my seat near the stove, thinking of my fellow prisoners in the train on their way to an enigmatic future somewhere in the Ukraine.

After about an hour, a policeman arrived to take me in charge and we set off down the track in the direction towards the spot where I had jumped off the train. In fact, we went even further and arrived at a large important railway station called Aschaffenburg, where we went straight into the police post.

On entering I found myself confronting an officer of the Military Police, whom I saluted, for I was determined if possible to make them respect my military status. It proved a good tactic for the officer responded with a smile and offered me a seat. He was proceeding very correctly with my interrogation when a sudden interruption made us both look up. The big policeman with the revolver had caught up with me at last! He hurled himself at me and grasped me by the throat.

An order rang out like the crack of a whip. The officer had come to my assistance and I then witnessed a reprimand from superior to subordinate which could surely only happen in Germany. For three minutes the officer shouted in his face (which was still red from the exertions I had caused him). This interlude over, the officer resumed my interrogation but the formalities were quickly completed and I was taken off again under guard.

As I was marched along the platform, I was conscious of the curious stares of the passengers in a train alongside. Then we turned down a flight of steps and went by subway to another platform.

I then received the shock of my life. I was grabbed by SS guards, struck in the face, shoved and kicked all along the train standing there, which to my horror, I recognised. They had been kept waiting for me for four hours and the SS guards were beside themselves with fury.

I was hurled at the feet of an officer, but pulled myself up and saluted him in an effort to replay my previous tactics, but this time they were less successful. He did not return my salute but gave an order which had the prompt effect of giving me a rifle butt between the shoulders.

As I swerved to avoid another, I was brought down by a violent blow which I failed to see coming. A series of kicks brought me to my feet again and I was pushed on along the platform, with the guards deliberately treading on my heels to make me stumble and each time I did so, making this an excuse for punching me in the back or kicking my behind.

We came to the only passenger coach on the train, which was obviously reserved for the Boche guards. They signed to me to get into one of the compartments and several followed me. They started to take off their jackets and belts and I realised that I was in for a rough passage but I had had already enough of their blows. Finding myself at the far end with nothing between me and the other exit, I decided that come what may, I would send my first SS attacker to hospital.

At that moment, however, an order behind them had the effect of making these savage fanatics fall back a moment to make way for their officer to come through. He was a short man, but he grabbed the collar of my tunic and shook me by it, to my momentary astonishment.

'You French swine, when did you escape?' he demanded in fairly good French.

Feeling I had nothing left to lose, I cast aside all caution and shouted back to this bumptious little upstart:

'Swine yourself. A couple of miles back, if you must know.'

Thunderstruck, he let go and drew back. I was astonished at the effectiveness of my insolence, which resulted in his ordering his men out of the carriage. Then he turned to me and said mildly:

'Two miles back the train was travelling at speed. You didn't jump then. You got away as we slowed up to come into this station.'

'No, I jumped long before the marshalling yard.'

'Where are your friends?'

'A long way off, I hope.'

'You've only done what a soldier should, but I warn you that if you try it on again, I shall shoot you like a rat.'

As he uttered this threat, the officer stepped back, clicked his heels and saluted me! I shall never understand his change of attitude, whether it was prompted by the audacity of the escape or by the impudence of my tone. Whatever the cause, however, he ordered two of his men to search me and then to return me to my original truck. They confiscated my only weapon, a tooth-brush, and then led me back normally to the truck where, a few seconds later, I found myself once again with Lucien and Gino.

I soon learned what had happened after I had jumped into the night. About a mile further on the train started to slow down and finally came to a halt in the station of Aschaffenburg. When the German guards got out to stretch their legs, as was their custom at all stops, they caught sight of the hole in the door. Immediately, a general alert was sounded. The door of the truck was flung open and the herd of prisoners within, still half asleep, was driven out on to the platform. They were fallen-in five deep for a count, and as my friends described this, I could well picture the complexities of the scene. Of course they found they were three short, which was the signal for the Germans to whip themselves into a frenzy, and I was dismayed to hear that most of the lads had been knocked about for something of which they had not even any knowledge. Not that they were concerned about this punishment. As prisoners who had all attempted an escape, they even derived some satisfaction from it. What was much harder to bear, though no one reproached me, was the two days without food or water imposed on the truck by the Germans.

The door was slammed and the hole in it nailed up with planks. We were also given an extra dose of barbed wire over the ventilators. In spite of all the hardships, morale was good and the general comment was:

'Let's hope the other two pull it off.'

A further long wait brought no signs of them and it looked as if our wishes might not be in vain. During the eight hours that the train was detained there we feared for them but our rejoicing knew no bounds when eventually the Germans had to admit defeat and the train pulled out of the station.

We spent most of the day singing our way through our whole repertoire of bawdy army songs, while the train made very slow progress. From time to time it would get up speed only to lose what had been gained at a prolonged shunting match at the next marshalling yard.

From what we could see of the lie of the land, we had no idea where we were, only that we were travelling relentlessly towards the East.

At about 8 am on the third day we drew into a large station, the name of which we recognised. It was Krakow (Crakauwitz). Here we had a foretaste of German base cunning. Right opposite a platform with waiting Polish men and women, the SS flung open the truck doors, made the occupants get out and offered them for the first time the opportunity to relieve themselves. After three days and nights in moving cattle trucks, and with stomachs already upset from prison-camp conditions, it was more than we could do to restrain ourselves when the opportunity was offered. One of the less fastidious set the ball rolling and the rest followed suit. It was obvious that this exhibition was contrived in the sadistic minds of the Germans to debase the French in the eyes of their friends the Poles.

We were soon away from Krakow, but had to wait till the following evening for the doors to be opened again. This time we were told it was for a soup issue. None of us had a mess tin, but provision had been made. We were marched off to a large heap of used tins, rusty and dirty, and told to take one each for our soup. Then we were lined up in the dark outside a German Red Cross hut and moved forward towards the single light where each man received his portion. This was dished out by two white-coated women, supervised by a civilian Red Cross Official and two SS guards. Starving as they were, the prisoners made haste to get started on their soup as soon as they received it and then, flung it away! I tasted mine on my finger and understood. It was made of unpeeled and unwashed potatoes, boiled in their dirt to a mush, a half of which was thick black mud. Not even a dog would have touched it. Eventually, one of our guards, realising it really was uneatable because everyone was spitting it out, complained to the Red Cross people. Their reply was enlightening:

'What do you expect. We were told it was to be train-load of Russians.'

The train drew out into the night and never was the saying *'qui dort dine'*[1] more true. However, next day we received a loaf of bread

---

[1] He who sleeps doesn't need to eat.

and a hunk of cheese to be shared among eight men, and our spirits rose immediately.

Those of us by the ventilators could look out at the countryside. We saw that scenery was monotonously flat, without tree or grass-land, the plains being partly flooded and partly bespattered with patches of dirty greyish snow. There was nothing you could call a road, and such tracks as we could see were seeped in a layer of deep slush from the melting snows. The sparsely scattered dwellings were built of very dark timber, almost black, with their shutters, however, invariably painted light blue, the one touch of colour in the drab undertones of this grey landscape. We could see that some of the huts were still blanketed with a thick layer of straw on the outside, held in place by planks nailed to the wooden walls. In the distance we could see high mountains which we knew must be the Bohemian Mountains or the Carpathians.

In all this scene of desolation no life stirred, animal or human. We had to wait till the train slowed down to pass through a small station before we were able to get a look at any of the inhabitants of this God-forsaken region, and then we could see that they were all of a piece with their background, sombrely clad peasants with shabby caps and no coats, their women folk swathed in black shawls.

They watched the progress of the train as if it were a funeral cortege and they, the mourners. We called out to them as we passed and made friendly gestures, but drew no repsonse whatsoever. We wondered if they were merely indifferent or whether their fear kept them silent, these unhappy Poles.

Some time during the eighth night, our train stopped at a station and, when daylight came, we could see that, at last, we had reached Rawa Ruska.

CHAPTER NINE

Rawa Ruska

We all got out and fell into a column, four deep, on the platform. Then we filed out of the station and went up what seemed to be the main street but it was little better than a swamp. In fact, I was in danger of losing my shoes so deep and sticky was the mud. On the other side of the track we saw wooden hovels and, standing at the doors, were a few emaciated inhabitants clad in tattered rags. From the cast of their countenance they were obviously Jews and, as we proceeded, it became ever clearer that we were penetrating into one of their ill-fated ghettos. We were not yet to know that Rawa Ruska was later to become notorious as a reprisal concentration camp for French POWs.

Soon we came to a large open space, a sea of mud across which ran a gangway of planks, raised up on wooden piles, which led to the main gates of the camp over which we saw inscribed Stalag 325.

On the right was a large red brick building marked 'Block 1' and on the left a similar one marked 'Block 2', both served by two narrower branches of the pontoon. We were marched on towards Block 2 and found we had to enter a barbed wire enclosure to reach the building, which had the effect of putting us in a camp within a camp.

Block 2 was a massive building and lofty although only two storeys high, with an adjacent wooden outbuilding which I surmised, rightly as it turned out, to be the latrines. Outside the building we were halted for a few moments and I had a chance to get an idea of the general lie of the camp through the barbed wire. There were four identical blocks altogether and one more under construction. In addition there were four long, low buildings, quite different in style. I could not discern them clearly as they were several hundred yards away, but could make out that they were light in colour and guessed they were whitewashed.

We began to move into the vast Block 2 building through its narrow doors, one at each end, and found ourselves jostling for position as if anxious for our incarceration! Lucien, Gino and I contrived, with some pains, to keep together. The sleeping racks

were built on the same plan as the one at Willingen but were quite
twenty times as large and spread with an ample supply of fresh straw
(no doubt, here in the Ukraine there was no shortage of this).

We staked our claim for a sleeping space and tried it out,
luxuriating in this new-found comfort after the rigours of the cattle
trucks. We had a walk round to locate our friends and then made a
reconnaissance of the latrine accommodation which we found far
from adequate for eight hundred inmates. The Teutonic technique
seemed to indicate a preference for exhibitionism in these matters
and certainly implied that the most primitive methods were most to
be desired. The latrine building was open inside and was equipped
with a huge trench about six yards across and running the full length
of the hut. Along either side was fixed a telegraph pole, the only
seating accommodation over an open cesspool. All users were
exposed not only to full publicity but also to the constant danger of
falling into the pit.

We spent the first two days in Block 2 having a look round and
enjoying the odd game of cards with those who were lucky enough to
have them. On one of these occasions, I met and made friends with
Benny Berthet, the well-known tennis player and Parisian couturier.
But these interminable card games were soon to pall on an empty
stomach and food to become our only objective.

The Germans ignored all our protests and we began to think they
intended to leave us to starve. Tempers rose and spokesmen began to
emerge from the crowd which was turning savage. A committee of
representatives was formed to present a petition to the Camp
Kommandant. His reply was forthright.

'No supplies have come through yet. You're not in Germany any
longer. You're in occupied territory. What's good enough for our
troops is good enough for you. *They* eat when they can and when they
can't they go without! Deputation dismissed!'

It was not until the following day that we were told we were to
have a soup issue, which meant that, counting the last two days in
the train, we had been entirely without food for five days.

The problem now confronting us was that we had no receptacles
of any kind. The queue moved towards the kitchens but with the
inevitable result, the distribution could not take place. This was
obviously a bit of German spite and the starving men raised an angry
clamour. However, one bright lad held out his makeshift feeding
trough, a red ridge-tile. It did not take the rest of us long to realise
where that came from and in no time at all my own tile was receiving

its ladleful of hot water and uncooked millet – canary soup, we called it – which I proceeded to lap up. On the way back to Block 2, I glanced up out of curiosity at the building under construction. It had no roof left.!

Lack of food was not, unfortunately, our only trouble. We were totally unable to keep ourselves clean. There was a fine washroom in each block but none of the taps were running, and as we could not wash, our nice straw was soon infested with fleas and lice. Henceforth, our chief sport was hunting. We made a protest to the Germans about these conditions, but were told that, for reasons unstated, the water could not be turned on. This was another piece of German malice. But they did concede that we might get water from a solitary tap outside the kitchens when they were not drawing water within.

There were already two thousand five hundred of us using that tap, and every day saw trainloads of new arrivals in the camp. We were soon to be fifteen thousand using one tap, and that only about eight hours a day. Admittedly, every morning we were given a large ladleful of brown liquid, unwarrantedly dignified by the name of tea, a repugnant infusion of pine-wood chips. Not only did this serve as the daily drinking ration but also as hot water for those of us who tried to keep up some semblance of civilisation by shaving and giving our faces a wipe over.

As time went on, this exiled community established its own economy. Those still without mess tins could go to tinsmiths who would manufacture excellent utensils for them at a charge of a few marks, from used cans retrieved from the German kitchens by those employed there on fatigue. People wanting the cobbler, the tailor or the watch-maker, would find 'shops' of every trade in various parts of the camp. One of the most prosperous was the laundry, with ten employees. The boss was a smart Alec. He had worked up his business by cashing in on shortages. He bought up all the soap he could lay his hands on, however exorbitant the price, bribed someone in the kitchens to supply water, paid his hands to do the washing and pocketed his profit. As a result, he could buy bread at twenty marks (equivalent in 1941 to £1 approx.) a small slice, in the blackest of markets which operated behind the camp kitchens.

There was also considerable intellectual activity in this remarkable camp. Among the prisoners were numerous teachers, schoolmasters, engineers, chemists and technicians of all kinds, who founded a 'University of Rawa Ruska' which was later to be given

official recognition, examinations up to the Baccalaureat standard
being subsequently confirmed by the University of Paris. Another
aspect of the cultural achievement of this community was the cooperation which took place between Roman Catholics and Pro-
testants. They set to work together to transform the bare hall,
allocated for the purpose by the Germans, into a beautifully
equipped and decorated chapel, which was then used by both sects
in turn.

However, although most of the prisoners managed to keep
themselves occupied, some could not adapt themselves to this way of
life and took no interest in anything. They let themselves sink into
melancholy and despair and their health declined along with their
spirits, so that eventually, they constituted the biggest proportion of
sick-bay patients. The remainder of these were foolish fellows who
had dissipated their energy in interminable games of football,
stripped to the waist in the scorching Ukrainian sun, which is fierce
enough to ripen two wheat crops each summer. It seemed to me that
these foolhardy sportsmen were encouraging pulmonary troubles
which were quite incurable in this environment, and that it was
much better to reserve one's strength while at the same time, keeping
one's mind fully occupied. Gino, Lucien and I organised a camp
casino, taking good care that the odds were always slightly in our
favour. This was not so remunerative as some other camp
enterprises but it was good enough all the same.

We three also set up and organised 'The Water Board', this time,
on principle, as a non-profit making company. In the unfinished
block, Gino had come across a beautiful big cask – a *demi-huis*
(holding roughly 110 gallons). We hit upon the idea of making a pair
of shafts for it which would enable a team of four to carry it over to
the tap during the day. This 'company' proved an unbounded
success to the satisfaction of its members and the envy of the rest of
the Block.

After about two months, Rawa Ruska began to improve. The food
ration was still scanty but it was supplied daily. Postal services were
instituted and some of us began to get parcels from home. We were
among the first of the lucky ones, thanks to Madame Tarsitano,
Lucien's mother. These parcels often contained food which needed
to be heated up or even cooked, and wood was so rare as to be
practically non-existent. With typical ingenuity, however, the
prisoners soon had their various brews on the simmer over jealously
guarded little fires all round the camp. Just as these cooking smells

began to stimulate our appetite, the sight of our fires stimulated the wrath of the new German Kommandant, a stout little captain who sought to inspire terror by firing shots into the air. He made up his mind to put a stop to this culinary festival, jumped on his bicycle and pedalled furiously towards the part of the camp where fires were thickest on the ground.

'Look out, here's Tom Mix!' cried somebody, and there was a general scramble to disperse, with steaming mess-tins in hand.

To the discomfiture of one of these 'cordon-bleus', the very one who had raised the alarm, the *Kapitän* was too quick and the dish too hot. The furious officer kicked over the precious stew and thrusting his revolver against the trembling prisoner's stomach, demanded:

'What did you call me?'

'T-t-t-tom M-m-mix.'

This answer seemed to satisfy him, for giving the mess-tin another kick, he jumped on to his bicycle again and made for the administrative block where he burst into the office which had been allocated to our elected French representative, a barrister from Tours called Mercier.

'Who is Tom Mix?' he asked.

Mercier, quick-witted as befits a barrister, took in the situation at once and his reply was a masterpiece of diplomacy.

'A great American, a saviour of humanity, a redresser of wrongs, famous for his kindness...'

This was quite enough to re-establish the fat fellow's self-importance, and henceforth the Boche seldom interfered with the French when they were practising their favourite national art, the preparation of tasty dishes.

Unfortunately, the parcels were few and far between and the prisoners' health deteriorated all the time. Tempers were ragged with far-reaching effects on all aspects of life in the camp. An example of this was the exaggerated ritual of the bread distribution. The ration was one small loaf (12oz) of heavy black bread among six men. Before dividing it, the six would draw lots to establish which of them should have the right to perform this delicate task. Then, under the watchful eyes of the other five, the man on whom the lot had fallen would cut the loaf into six parts, weighing and adjusting them against each other until they were exactly equal in weight, to the last crumb. He did this by means of a primitive but accurate balance, made from a stick, three strings and two bent pins. Even after all these safeguards they would then draw lots among themselves for each individual part, so important had one crumb more or less become to these starving men.

A number of working parties were now being sent outside the camp, on a variety of jobs, which encouraged a break-out of black market activities among those opportunists who managed to turn such excursions to their advantage. A few eggs made their appearance at exorbitant prices, and when a map of the region turned up for sale, Lucien bought it so that we could set up an 'Information Bureau' for would-be escapees. This was now much in demand because escape fever was rife and we were to witness some spectacular attempts, of which one only, to my knowledge, managed to succeed. He was the portrait artist from Savoy, whom I had got to know in the black hole of Willingen.

A few were recaptured but the majority were shot down while breaking away. Their number was small, however, compared with the toll which death was now claiming daily in the sick-bay. Here they were continually reporting sick with acute pain in the chest which doctors called 'pleurite'. Two or three days later their breathing would become very difficult and painful as pleurisy set in. Without proper attention, and suffering as they were from malnutrition, this quickly degenerated into a virulent form of tuberculosis, from which there was no hope of recovery.

One day, to my dismay, I found myself suffering from the dreaded symptoms, and Lucien took me along to one of the doctors. He examined me and ordered me to be admitted at once to the sick-bay. Then, on hearing my name, he asked:

'Do you happen to be the son of Dr Rieul from Le Hâvre?'

I told him that I was.

'I was once a pupil of his in Paris!' he exclaimed.

Owing to this remarkable coincidence he was from then on to take a particular interest in my case. I was taken into the sick-bay in Block 1, which was an exact replica of Block 2. Here we had the advantage, however, of being spared the continual searches and outbursts of German spite to which the other blocks were subjected (except on one memorable occasion when the whole of the sick-bay, even the dying, was shamefully ordered outside to enable the Boche to conduct a minute investigation of the buildings). We also had the services of a very few French army doctors, who did their best with no drugs or equipment at all to look after the poor wretches sprawled on the bed racks. I must pay tribute to these true men of medicine who had come there voluntarily to do what they could to relieve the suffering of their fellow countrymen.

Despite all their efforts, I quickly became much worse, for I had a very severe form of 'pleurite'. One day in his anxiety for me, Lucien took a decision which I subsequently realised saved my life. He put my name down, along with Gino's and his own, to go to a work camp the very next day. It was a rash decision, suicidal according to the doctor, but Lucien would not be put off.

'If you stay here,' he said, 'you will rot to death like the rest of them.'

Feeling terribly ill, as I now was, I knew that he was right. What did it matter to me where I died? Here, or anywhere...

Next morning, I managed somehow to drag myself to the place where the working party was being assembled and was soon bundled into a cattle truck, even more closely packed than those that had brought us here from Germany. To make matters worse, the truck stood still throughout the whole August day with the full force of the Ukrainian sun beating down on it. At one point, I thought I was going to die. I could not breathe and felt I was going to collapse, but was saved by a shower of rain. I managed to catch the drips from the roof in my cupped hands through the ventilator, and though the water was black and sooty, it certainly did me good.

At sundown, the train pulled out on its three-day journey, which turned out to be much worse than the last one although shorter. When we reached our destination, there were six corpses taken out of the next truck to ours, but they were all Russians and probably in worse shape than we were when they started.

We stopped on an embankment in open country, overlooking a civilian camp where we were surprised to see both men and women. We could hear shrieking in the air as German soldiers used whips to scatter a large crowd of the ragged inmates drawn by curiosity to have a look at the train.

Alighting, we skirted this disquieting camp and turned into our own quarters which were adjacent. By contrast, this Kommando (or work camp) had a pleasant aspect, with two large trees in the middle. The sleeping quarters were much like those at Rawa Ruska but with the addition of ablution rooms equipped with running water. Needless to say they were invaded immediately, such a luxury it was to clean up in comfort! A further pleasant surprise was to follow, a distribution that evening of Pétain comforts[1] including

---

[1] Food parcels from the Vichy government to show that they cared for the French prisoners.

cigarettes, a good supply of army biscuits, chocolate, beans and rice. Lucien and Gino got down to cooking without delay, and saw to it that I received generous portions to build up my strength, even handing over their own share of the chocolate and biscuits to give me a better chance.

The civilians we had seen in the adjoining camp were undoubtedly Jews, but there was also on the other side of us a camp of Russian POWs, mostly Mongolians. We started to fraternise with them at once through the barbed wire but when we got too near, the sentries from their look-out towers would open fire. However, some of us managed to throw cigarettes over, which were passed round at once by the Russians, each one having a draw in turn.

In the evening we saw that they were assembling on their square near our boundary. We wondered what was going on and then, all at once, we understood, when a hundred or more melodious Russian voices broke out in perfect unison into an old folk-song. This was followed by many other tunes and they concluded this touching gesture made in honour of our arrival with a rendering of the 'Volga Boatmen!'

We had appointed as spokesman a priest known as Abbé Pierre, and he reciprocated at once by getting us all to sing a number of well-known songs in return, which were received with great enthusiasm by our Slav allies. This display of Franco-Russian solidarity incensed the German guards, who set about with clubs to break up the gathering while the look-out fired off token volleys.

Next morning we were assembled for duty. There was nothing for me to do but to report sick, and I joined some twenty sufferers in a group aside. Up strutted the German sergeant-major shouting angrily that he would inspect the sick parade himself.

Stopping in front of the first man, he bawled:

'*Zunge 'raus!* (tongue out). *Arbeit!* (to work).'

He went right along the line like this and in the end he passed three only as unfit for work, of whom I was one. Even he had to admit that I was genuinely ill. The rest went off to work and we three were escorted to the sick-bay and put in charge of a German-speaking Russian doctor, with whom I was able to carry on a conversation. He told me that this camp was situated just outside the fortified town of Deblin and was only about thirty miles from Warsaw. I learned from him that during the previous winter 80,000 Russians had died in Deblin, and he swore that the Germans were lying when they said that this was due to typhus, and asserted most vehemently that they died from starvation and exposure. This doctor was not only friendly, he was also efficient and treated me so skilfully that I was soon able to go to work with the rest.

Every morning we left the camp and passed under a bridge round which a gang of young Jewesses were working, ranging I should say, from sixteen to twenty-five years of age. They were widening the bridge to enable a second line to be laid, using pick and shovel and laying concrete under a slave-driving overseer, who abused them noisily and whipped them incessantly, so that their rags were hanging in shreds revealing a blackened and bleeding flesh beneath. Always, as we went by we made our protest, but though we shouted him down, it had no effect whatever on the overseer and we only got hit with rifle butts for our pains.

We too were put to work on this same railway widening but a bit further down the track (than the bridge). Our job was to construct an embankment of sand to take the second line, and further on still, gangs of Jews were doing the plate-laying. I shall always carry with horror the memory of these wrecks of humanity, emaciated and lacerated as I saw them every day, stark shades against the rising sun, staggering along the embankment, stumbling under the burden of a rail far heavier than they, and savagely urged on with kicks and blows.

One day at the site, two of our gang who were boxers by professsion, asked leave to go and get their handkerchiefs which they had left in their coat pockets at the foot of the embankment a little distance off. There were a number of sentries posted every six yards and two left their posts to act as escort to the two prisoners. A train was approaching, no doubt returning from the Stalingrad front, where the battle was in full swing. All of a sudden, these two ex-athletes were up the embankment in a bound and across the track just in front of the buffers of the oncoming train before the guards had time to take aim. All this happened so quickly that the guards were cut off from the fugitives for the length of time it took for the whole train to pass. All they could do was to lie down and fire abortively between the wheels as they flashed by.

As soon as the train had gone, a number of guards took up pursuit and to our disappointment, brought back the two intrepid fellows an hour later, and not before they had given them such a beating up as would have demoralised any but a prize-fighter!

We were not surprised at this treatment for we knew by now, having seen their bestialities towards the Jews, that we were in the

hands of sadists. We learnt, for example, that the Jewish wounded
were virtually abandoned in a damp underground passage of a
ruined fort, which the Germans had the shameful audacity to
describe as a sick-bay. Here they received no attention whatever
except from rats which some of the inmates were too weak to prevent
from attacking their flesh. We were also appalled to learn, and
indeed to confirm with our own eyes, that the sergeant-major's
favourite sport was to stalk the Jews with his rifle round the corners
of their huts, like a man potting rabbits in the undergrowth.

The weather was now rapidly getting colder and the sun already a
mere token of its former self. We began to worry about the prospect
of having to endure the rigours of a Polish winter, for our clothes
were scanty and some of us were bare-foot. The snow began to fall
but we were still taken off to work. We could not sit about during our
breaks any longer, but warmed ourselves, as children do, by playing
vigorous games while the sentries stamped their feet in a vain effort
to keep them warm. The Polish civilians began to prepare their
winter quarters by nailing the straw cocoons around their huts. They
managed to pass word to us that during the previous winter, the
temperature had dropped to −48° centigrade which is equivalent to
−54° (or 86° degrees of frost Fahrenheit), but as events turned out,
we were not destined to spend the winter there after all.

One morning before leaving for work, we noticed an unaccustomed
mustering of the Jews in their adjacent camp. I was able, as it
happened, to throw some light on this:

'Oh, they're off today,' I told the lads. 'A woman was telling me
about it yesterday through the wire, while I was giving her kids a bit
of chocolate. She was explaining that they were all very happy
because the Germans had announced that all Jews were to be sent
home!'

When we were all lined up ready to leave at the usual time, we
heard a burst of firing not far off, but this was nothing uncommon so
we took little notice. When we were on our way to work, however, the
meaning was soon made all too clear. Sprawling at random at the
bottom of a ditch lay the bodies of the Jewish girls who had been
building the bridge. We gazed at them speechless and appalled. We
were stricken with horror and grief for the girls whom we knew so
well by sight, from passing them four times a day for six months. One
man near me spoke their epitaph:

'So they've finished the bridge!'

When we got to our work already much shaken and nauseated by what we had seen on the way, we were surprised to notice a nearby company of some eighty Jews, men, women and children, herded together by SS guards in black, who were compelling them by a noisy display of force to get into separate groups, the children in front, their mothers behind and the men at the back. In this formation, the guards drove them to within thirty yards of where we were working. Then eight children were pushed forward to the edge of a ditch where the guards forced them to kneel down. An order rang out, followed by a burst of tommy-gun fire. Eight small bodies plunged into the trench while the air was rent by their mothers' shrieks.

For a moment we were all rooted to the spot in horror, and then, as one man, we screamed out abuse at these despicable murderers and even pelted them with whatever rubble came to hand. The SS retaliated by threatening us with their arms, while their chief approached us and in excellent French, said:

'If you don't like it, you can take their places!'

We went on shouting but with no effect. After the children, the women were dragged by hair or foot to the edge of the pit, where the same fate awaited them. Then it was the turn of the men and they went forward eight at a time without putting up any resistance, doubtless because they knew it was useless and wanted nothing but to make an end. Their Rabbi alone remained, and he made no haste but walked slowly forward with head held high, and knelt of his own accord at the brink. His body failed to fall and was kicked into the grave by a German boot.

We felt devastated by this experience and worked on in silence. The ache in the pit of our stomachs persisted all the day and came not from our hunger but from the intensity of our revulsion. We could not even face our soup that night.

That unforgettable day marked for us the beginning of the end of the *Kommando* of Deblin. The pit had been filled in that evening and we only visited the site two or three times more, but on one occasion, I picked up a half buried handbag. Seizing my opportunity, I had a look inside. There was nothing of any consequence except two photographs. One was a group of Jews with their Rabbi, whom I felt sure was the one I had seen shot. The other, I recognised at once in spite of the fact that it had, no doubt, been taken before their captivity when they were still healthy; it was the photograph of the two little Jewish children to whom I had given the bar of chocolate the day before they were to die. As we were subsequently to learn, an order had been issued by the German High Command for the extermination of every remaining Jew in Poland.

Within a few days we were despatched again in our cattle-trucks to Rawa Ruska, all of us, that is, except our two boxers who had managed to escape again, this time without recapture.

CHAPTER TEN

Christmas at Furstenburg

During the months of our absence at Deblin, Stalag 325 at Rawa Ruska had become better organised (but there was still no running water in the wash-room taps). Roll-call, every morning, was followed by a PT session which always culminated after the German fashion, in community singing. The Germans were within their rights in imposing this regime, ostensibly 'to make the prisoners fill their lungs', and to some extent it had a beneficial effect, but we were somewhat cynical about their concern for filling our lungs while leaving our bellies empty! – and even more so when we had to sing about it. However, we got our own back by rendering at the top of our voices, in French, the popular song 'They'll never get Alsace and Lorraine!' Perhaps it was as well they could not follow the words!

Fortunately, we only stayed long enough to undergo the formalities of inoculation and in a few days, passed once again through the now empty streets of Rawa Ruska Ghetto in the company of some three hundred other prisoners on our way to the cattle trucks. This time the train ran at top speed towards Germany because, as we soon realised, our guards had Christmas leave and it was already 23rd December.

Our destination proved to be Furstenburg-on-Oder, the site of Stalag III B. We had hopes of getting absorbed inconspicuously into this vast camp, but our hopes were soon dashed when we were escorted once more to a special inner barbed wire enclosure labelled *'Gesperrt'*. There we found we were to be subjected to all the usual indignities imposed on us by the Germans. Above all, not only did we continue to have starvation rations, but there was no form of heating at all in spite of the glacial conditions. The wash-basins were frozen solid, but fortunately there was no shortage of snow on the ground. To keep our circulation going at all at night, we had to double up and sleep huddled together, two to each narrow bunk, thus gaining an extra blanket. All day we kept on the move inside our huts in an attempt to keep from shivering.

We spent New Year's Eve all together listening to a rousing

address given by Maître Mercier, the barrister who had been our spokesman at Rawa. His words heartened us and rekindled the spark of our patriotism which had been sadly dimmed during the last few days by what we had seen going on in the outer camp. There we had watched French prisoners demonstrating their allegiance to Maréchal Pétain. This they did in numerous forms but one which was permanently visible was the decoration of mock gardens around their huts with pieces of coloured glass, no doubt salvaged from a nearby glass factory, by reproducing Pétain's profile and his hatchet emblem with various propaganda slogans.

One day a notice was posted on all huts in the *Gesperrt* enclosure. All POWs were asked to come forward, whose civilian work was in any way connected with building. A proviso was added that all candidates must be prepared to relinquish voluntarily their right under the Geneva Convention (this was the first sign, to my knowledge, of any recognition of that treaty) not to be employed on rescue and demolition services.

Rescue and demolition services would only be needed in bombed areas and that suggested to me the Rhineland, just across the border from France. As a result of this, escape fever flared up and became rife once again throughout the camp. You could not avoid hearing such pertinent remarks as:

'Are *you* in the building trade?'

'Not really, but I could put in a pane at a pinch. How about you?'

'Well I'm quite a dab hand at daubing, until it comes to the ceilings.'

By some remarkable coincidence, almost everyone was a builder; but the Germans, unimaginative though they were, did not show credulity to the point of taking our word for it, but subjected us to an individual screening.

'What is your trade?' I was asked by the officer in charge of the interrogation board.

'Electrician,' I replied.

'And yet according to the details supplied by our records department, you are described as being connected with the wholesale stationers' trade. How do you explain this discrepancy?'

'I did declare being in the paper trade, in hopes of getting out of having to work, I didn't think there would be any call for stationers.'

'That's a lie! As an NCO you were not compelled to work anyway!'

'No, it isn't. I didn't understand anything about the Geneva

Convention then.'

'Well, you understand now! Why do you want to work as an electrician?'

'To get my hand in, ready for a job in civvy-street,' I replied, thinking to myself how well this expressed my true motives!

After a momentary consultation with his colleagues, he told me that I was accepted.

We left Furstenberg in a passenger train, which by now was quite a novelty. A whole coach was reserved for our party of 75. Lucien Tarsitano was not among us since, as a North African, he had learnt that he was to be repatriated. We crossed Germany going in the right direction, towards, France. Morale was rising all the way. Every mile represented one less when we came to escape.

'Karlsruhe! Everybody out!' came the order, to our disappointment; a few more miles would have seen us in Alsace.

We went through the town in formation, and it gave us plenty of opportunity to view the good work done by Allied planes. Instead of the fine houses and lovely gardens we had witnessed when we passed through these parts ten months before, there were only piles of rubble.

'They've had it coming,' said the man next to me.

The *Kommando* to which we were taken bore a strange name: DACHDEKKER BATT. V (or battalion of Tilers Number 5), but it was just on the same pattern as the other work camps. It was already occupied and we represented reinforcements. The original occupants, however, were completely apathetic and submissive. No escape had ever been made from this camp. The food was good and Red Cross parcels arrived with great regularity, with the result that although these prisoners were so near to France, their motherland, they were contented with their lots and preferred to wait undisturbed for the day of liberation rather than venture out on hazardous undertakings. But we were going to be able to bring about some changes here by rousing them out of their stupor.

My abilities as an electrician were soon put to the test, when I was ordered to repair an overhead electric cable. I had to fit iron grips to my shoes to enable me to climb to the top of the pole, but a false step quickly landed me at the bottom with my hands full of splinters.

My next job was to wire up a canning factory but fortunately we were working in groups and I was able to shelve my responsibility on to more competent shoulders, to the benefit of the installation.

This job lasted a few days which enabled Gino and me to study the possibilities of escape, and watch a very successful one, carried out by a friend of mine named Dary, but our plans were upset before they could come to fruition. The town of Stuttgart, some hundred miles further back into Germany, was very severely bombed and we were to be sent back next day to clear up the rubble, and to do urgent electrical repairs. We were also told that we should not be returning but that Stuttgart would be our base in future.

Early next morning we were assembled near the camp gates for the Germans to check our numbers before leaving. Twelve men were missing! The German Kommandant was furious and told the perplexed guards:

'I'm certain they are still here, hiding in the camp.' (I could have told him that he was right, for I was one of those in the know. They were, in fact, all twelve huddled between the double floor-boards of the stage in the camp theatre.)

'Make an exhaustive search,' he ordered. 'Tear up the floor-boards and pull down the huts if you have to,' he continued, and turning to us, added, 'The train will wait until your friends are caught, you French *Schweinerei!*'

But the search was unsuccessful. Lots of woodwork was demolished, but never in the right place. Meanwhile, the Kommandant received urgent appeals from the station that the train could not wait any longer. He had to admit that he was beaten but not without a parting thrust.

'We are leaving because the train must go. Don't think your friends will get away with it. I'm throwing a cordon of guards round the camp for as long as necessary, until they're driven out by hunger.'

He proceeded to carry out his threat and we moved off with a reduced guard. Those of us who were in the know realised that our twelve friends were in a tight fix, and we could see no way out for them, but a friend of mine called Royannez had a reassuring thought:

'Don't worry, they've got that cunning old fox Barrault with them and it's his sixth escape. He'll get them out of it somehow!'

The journey was uneventful and we alighted at a suburb of Stuttgart. We were surprised to find that this *Kommando* was quite different from any we had known before. It was set up in a modern school building. The dormitory to which Gino and I were assigned was on the fourth floor with a panoramic view of the town over the roof-tops. The whole place was well appointed, with an excellent dining room, showers, individual WCs not to mention that there was central heating actually functioning.

We were all from Rawa Ruska in our quarter, which soon became a centre of conspiracy. Escape was the order of the day despite our new-found comforts. Gino and I agreed to take the earliest chance we could, influenced by the fact that we had just been put back a hundred miles.

The next day was Sunday and in the evening we had the satisfaction of seeing the detachment of guards which had been left behind at Karlsruhe on the Kommandant's order, returning empty-handed. When we had a chance, we asked one of them what had happened and learned to our great satisfaction that the *Franzosen* had all escaped during the night through a hole they had cut in the barbed wire.

On Monday morning, we were taken to a bombed site and put to work in groups salvaging equipment. It was a pleasure as much as a duty for us to make sure that we sabotaged much more than we saved. Gino was kept on this work, but Royannez and I were drafted out to electrician duties. Actually, my knowledge of electricity was amateurish and theoretical, but by comparison Royannez's was non-existent. Fortunately, one man in our group was a qualified electrician and he showed us how to go about things.

I picked up the trade quite quickly, however, and soon found myself allocated as a solitary POW to a small private firm in the city. The proprietor called for me every morning at the camp gates, and having signed as responsible, took me off to his shop. He explained at the beginning that if I escaped from work he would be liable, not only to a substantial fine, but also to imprisonment. He asked if I would give my word not to take advantage of the latitude he gave me and I agreed to this.

First thing in the morning, I usually found myself with a pile of household articles to repair, irons, kettles, fires, bed-warmers and the like which had been deposited at the shop by customers on the previous day. As soon as these were cleared up, I went off, with two apprentices (duly warned to take good notice of whatever the 'French electrician' told them!) to people's houses and sometimes to factories in the town, to carry out repairs, usually caused by recent bombardment. I must have managed to give satisfaction somehow or other, because my employer kept on coming to pick me up every morning.

Meanwhile, we spent our nights at the camp discussing various

escape projects, but none of them appealed to me. In the middle of
one such discussion, the door opened and the Kommandant came in
followed by four of the twelve POWs who had made the mass escape
from under the stage at Karlsruhe.

We crowded forward to shake hands with them, but the
Kommandant called for silence:

'These friends of yours thought they could escape and get right
away. Understand once and for all, that escapees are always
recaptured here. These men will await their sentence, then they will
go off to solitary confinement and then when the time comes, back to
Rawa Ruska.'

'What about the other eight?' came an insolent enquiry.'

'Out of twelve, eight have been taken. These are four of them, and
four more are already safely locked up in a Stalag in France.
Needless to say, the last four will be recaptured before I'm much
older!'

As soon as the Kommandant had withdrawn, the newcomers
were bombarded with questions from all sides, and we were thus at
last able to hear what had really happened to the twelve prisoners
after we had left the Dachdekker camp. None of the Germans had
thought of investigating the double floor of the theatre stage, and at
nightfall, the cordon of guards was thrown round the camp as
ordered. In the middle of the night, Barrault, the wily fox, emerged
stealthily from the communal hiding place by himself, and crawled
in the shadows right up to the barbed-wire, proceeded to cut through
the double fence with wire-cutters, and then made his way back to
the hiding-place as he had come. At dawn, one of the guards soon
spotted the breach and immediately raised the alarm, concluding
that the French had gone!

The Germans held a conference round the gap in the wire, and in
face of such conclusive evidence, the corporal in charge withdrew the
guard and brought his men on to Stuttgart. As soon as the coast was
clear, the twelve artful dodgers had split up into three groups of four
and gone their separate ways.

A few days later another man was recaptured and brought in. It
was my friend Dary (whom I had seen escape from Karlsruhe). He
was not at all despondent. On the contrary, he was already talking
about the next time.

'I shall pull if off when I try again,' he told me. 'I know an
excellent route now and I shan't make the same mistake again.'

I found this most interesting, as I had not yet been able to hit on a feasible way myself, so I asked him what his mistakes had been.

'I was caught in a goods truck on the railway,' he explained, 'because I had not known that after it had been sealed it would be searched again and weighed at the frontier. But now I know and next time I shall make a point of throwing out goods equivalent to my own weight and I shall see that I'm properly hidden.'

As I listened, my mind was made up.

'If you agree, I'd like to have a shot at it over your route. I should want to go with Gino, and if we didn't get caught, you'd know that it would be safe for you.'

Dary had no objection, which was what I had expected since we were good friends. He said we should have to make our own way to a little village near Freiburg where there was a forced labour camp of French civilians. There we should find a man called Roland, who would put us on our way. There would be no charge for this service. He would help us out of disinterested patriotism.

Two armed guards broke up our interesting conversation to take Dary off to prison.

'Goodbye, and watch your weight!' he shouted as he went.

CHAPTER ELEVEN

The Black Forest

Having come by this valuable information, Gino and I worked out a plan. We still had to consider the vital question of the break-out and realised that this must be organised to the finest detail to avoid disaster. Whereas a man once clear of his camp might be re-arrested and find himself again in prison, one who bungled the break-out might well find himself in the cemetery! We also had to decide how we proposed getting to Freiburg which was about a hundred miles away, on the far side of the Black Forest.

We contrived to get hold of a map of the region and discovered that there was no railway line running across the Black Forest in the right direction except to Strasbourg and we felt that it would be foolhardy to show up on the main line to France. We decided to take a branch line to Freudenstadt on the edge of the forest and to make the crossing on foot, a formidable walk of some forty kilometres.

For this, we realised that it was essential we should have a compass, civilian clothes and cash. I undertook to provide the compass. It was a simple matter for me, the electrician, to construct one at work and in no time we had a little gem that worked perfectly in a match box.

Adequate mufti was a more difficult proposition but there were about thirty other men in our room, all from Rawa Ruska, and they undertook to do their best to scrounge around and raise the necessary clothing from the places where they worked. I was lucky enough to lay hands on a black suit, brand new, in the house of a German lawyer. Nor was this my only acquisition. I managed to whip out an impeccable white shirt from a pile of freshly ironed laundry. I was easily able to get hold of a tie but to find the right sized shoes was much more difficult. In the end, I had to make do with a pair several sizes too large and fill them up by wearing three pairs of socks.

Gino too, had managed very well and our friends had a whip round and raised enough money for our needs from their own treasured and totally illicit escape hoards. All was ready. Zero hour was fixed for 13.00 hours on 14th May 1943 at the foot of the town gasometer.

Every day at noon, I was brought back to the camp by my employer to eat, but Gino had a snack at work, so we agreed to leave separately and meet later. As a precaution, we divided the cash and made a parcel of what food we had raised (bread and chocolate) in which we cunningly concealed the compass.

On the morning of 14th May, Gino put on his uniform over his civilian clothes. I checked him over for safety and found nothing showing, so off he went to work with our little parcel tucked under his arm. I spent the morning on tenterhooks and would have been sorely tempted to break my parole by dashing off in working hours had I been suitably attired in advance, even though it would have entailed my friendly German employer getting into serious trouble. I much preferred, however, to time it so as to compromise the guards, especially as the one on duty happened to be particularly offensive.

When the lunch hour came at last, I let myself be taken back to camp as usual. As soon as I reached my sleeping quarters, I undressed quickly, got into my new suit and put my POW uniform on top. Then I rushed downstairs, delaying only to shake hands with a few good friends, and presented myself, in an apparent state of panic, to the guard on the gate, explaining vehemently with much gesticulation, that I had come away from the house where I had been working just near the camp, and left my lunch packet behind. I told him it would only take me a minute to go and fetch it.

'*Nein, nein!*' he objected, but I went on pushing past him and waving my arms till I found myself outside the camp. He was obviously undecided what to do, and I made a great play of turning my back on him and going off towards a particular house. At first I was afraid he would shoot but he let fly with nothing but protests and I must have covered fifty yards under the threat of a bullet in the back, before yielding to the impulse to break into a run at the first corner.

As I ran, I could just imagine all hell being let loose behind me and made at top speed for the cellar of a half-built house which I had singled out beforehand. There, I tore off my prison garb and stuffed it into a corner out of sight, emerging a moment later as a smartly dressed citizen, hurrying to board a passing tram.

Once in my seat, I felt most self-conscious and was sure that everyone was looking at me. The conductress loomed up before I could even get my breath, and I didn't know where the tram was going. I took a chance and asked for the station.

'*Bahnhof, bitte*' ('Station, please').

To my relief it worked. I was handed a ticket and some change for my proffered coin, and a little later she called out '*Bahnhof*' as we came to a big crossing. I got off and found myself confronting the main Stuttgart station of which I had such unhappy recollections. The sight of it took me back to the abrupt curtailment of my first escape and the incredible round tour which had followed. I realised that this was to be no time for reminiscence. The place had brought me bad luck before and the best thing was for me to get as far away as possible. In any case I was just about due to go to meet Gino at the gasometer. I made my way towards it through the side streets and was glad that we had chosen such a conspicuous landmark for our rendezvous.

One o'clock came and went but Gino did not show up. I found this very worrying, feeling that I was much too near to the camp and yet must wait about for him. I even spotted one of our work teams proceeding under escort. I had been waiting an hour when I was forced to face the fact that he wasn't coming. Either he had backed out or else he had been prevented. Whatever the reason, I realised that without our parcel, I had no food and no compass, and was only thankful that we had split the money.

Before being prepared to go off on this venture alone, I felt I must know what had happened to Gino, one way or the other, and at the risk of being captured, I approached one of the prisoner demolition squads (keeping well clear of their guards) and hissed into the ear of one of the lads as I went past:

'Tell Gino – tomorrow, same place, same time.'

Then I got as far away from them as possible, making my way to the centre of the town simply to kill time. I then walked along the main shopping street opposite the station, gazing into shop windows and studying the cinema posters, always with the feeling that all eyes were upon me. I wondered if this was merely imagination or if my lack of a hat really made me conspicuous in a town where everyone seemed to wear one. I was trembling with anxiety when it came to passing a policeman for the first time. It was all I could do to behave normally, but he did not seem to notice anything out of the ordinary. However, this gave me food for thought and I decided that it would be unwise to parade about in broad daylight for fear that the police had already been alerted, so I plunged into the obscurity of a cinema which was showing '*His Son*' with Emil Jennings.

During the film, I had a chance to think about immediate problems and realised that I must get hold of a hat, some food and somewhere to sleep. My first need was easily fulfilled. As I left the cinema I heard French being spoken behind me. I looked round and saw two men whom I took to be members of a forced labour camp, and as such, probably willing to help me. I followed them till we came to a quiet spot and then approached them.

'Good evening, do you by any chance come from Lille?' (I had recognised their northern accent).

'No, I'm from Arras and he's from Douai,' came the reply naming two towns in the same region.

'I come from Le Hâvre, but at the moment I'm escaping from a POW camp and I need a bit of help. I'm so conspicuous without a hat that I'm sure to be picked up. Could one of you please sell me some kind of cap?'

'Here you are, try mine. If it'll do you, you can keep it,' said one of them straight away.

I did my best to express my heartfelt appreciation and then went off in search of food but it took me longer to solve this problem. In the first place, all food was rationed, even the restaurants, but I knew that in certain eating houses known as *Stammessen* vegetarian dishes were allowed to be served off the ration. After searching for about half an hour, I managed to locate one of these places but found there was no service for another hour. I had to content myself with studying the menu outside until I knew it by heart. As I turned away to take another walk round before opening time was due, I spotted one of the guards from my camp, a German interpreter called Bols whom I knew very well. He was in the act of rushing towards me to pick me up!

He could not have been more than fifteen yards off, but between him and me stood a German officer, holding an Alsatian dog on a lead. As he passed him, Bols, acting under the compulsion of his military training, turned his head and gave him a salute! This gave me my chance and at exactly the same moment I rushed straight at him, having caught sight of a turning just behind him. I managed to dodge his tackle with a speed and agility which I had thought I had lost long ago, and darted round that corner before either of them could take aim.

I raced off at top speed, glimpsing over my shoulder that Bols, but only Bols, was giving chase; not the officer, and luckier still, not the dog! Passers-by tried unsuccessfully to trip me up, but I turned round

another corner and went right across a big square, easily out-
distancing Bols who was a fat man, and getting myself swallowed up
in the back streets of a poor quarter of the town until I came
providentially upon a tram.

This gave me a chance to review the situation and I decided to
return later to the *Stammessen* which I had so laboriously found and to
partake of the meal at the appropriate time, calculating, as it turned
out, correctly, that they would certainly not look for me again at the
same spot.

As I sat eating the horrible vegetarian concoction which was set
before me, I applied the same line of reasoning to the next problem
confronting me, which was where to spend the night. I eliminated
the idea of going to a hotel where I should have to produce identity
papers. I rejected the bench in the park where I should certainly
have been picked up for vagrancy. I could not stomach the prospect
of returning to that ill-fated station where in any case, the waiting-
room would probably be continually checked by the Gestapo since
they had an office in the station itself, as I knew only too well. I had
also to put aside the idea of looking for an air-raid shelter as I had
been forewarned by the old hands of Willingen and Rawa that they
were fatal. But I came to the conclusion, on the other hand, that if I
went right back to that half-built house just near the camp, they
would never think of looking for me again in that neighbourhood.
Moreover, I anticipated that I should be able to slip back into my
prison uniform which I had hidden there, to avoid sleeping in my
precious new suit.

At about 10pm I made my way to the half-built house and took
good care that no one saw me go in. I went straight down into the
cellar only to find that my prisoner's uniform had disappeared. This
made me stop and think. I knew for certain now that the Germans
had searched this place already, presuming therefore, that they were
most unlikely to come back. To be on the safe side, however, I
thought it best to climb right up into the timbers of the unfinished
roof. The only thing I had to worry about now was how to avoid
getting my suit covered in plaster. I solved this by sleeping in it
inside out, so that none of the dirt would show next day.

I knew that I had to get away very early next morning before the
workmen arrived and I went off to sleep worrying about whether I
should wake in time. As it turned out I kept on waking up with the
cold all through the night and was very relieved at dawn to turn my
suit again and quit this perilous district.

I still had about eight hours before I could hope to see Gino and I started off again on my interminable walk round the town. The feeling that people were staring at me still pursued me. It was only an illusion but it reminded me that I could not afford to appear in public unshaven, because the Germans as a race were most particular about this and a growth of stubble would have been most conspicuous.

I found a barber's shop open, and, at last, plucked up my courage and went in. I was relieved to see that I was the only client, and the barber set to work at once. He was most garrulous, chatting away all the time about all manner of things, including current events about which I was dangerously ignorant. To add to my nervousness, other clients arrived, including two German soldiers, but I managed to confine my side of the conversation to appropriate monosyllables presumably without compromising myself and I was most relieved when the barber applied his final whiff of talcum.

At the appointed hour, I went back to the gasometer but Gino was not there, nor did he come and I was forced to accept the fact that I should be making my bid for freedom alone, without the little parcel of food containing the compass.

According to plan, I went back to the centre of Stuttgart and took a tram to an outlying suburb where I knew that the train to Freudenstadt on the edge of the Black Forest would stop. On arrival at this station, I learnt from the timetable that this train was due to leave in an hour. Disliking station waiting-rooms, however small, I took my ticket and went for a walk, arriving back just before the train was due. The station was crowded but from the door I spotted the trap that was laid for me. Standing discreetly behind a pillar were two armed guards and near the ticket inspector I could see a couple of doubtful looking civilians.

I moved away instinctively, thinking to myself:

'So you thought you were going to get me here, you bastards, but you can wait for a bit. You may get me later on, but this is one place where you won't.'

It seemed best to take the road which ran alongside the railway line on which I hoped to travel, and soon I had the disappointment of seeing my train go by without me. However, I was consoled by the thought of those Gestapo agents waiting there empty-handed. In the face of their presence, I could only walk on to the next station and see what the position was there.

It was a superbly beautiful day and to have spent it in freedom walking through this lovely countryside would have been sheer delight had it not been for my ever present anxiety. But this time, luck was with me. I came upon a halt with one official only in the booking-office. Consulting the timetable I found out that the next train to Freudenstadt (due in half an hour) did not stop at my halt, but chancing to look at the 'up' trains, I noticed that one was shortly due which would get me back to the station where the Gestapo were patiently waiting for me, two minutes before the next train to Freudenstadt was due to leave. I went over to the ticket office and booked to Stuttgart so as not to make the clerk suspicious by asking for the very next station. Everything worked out as I had hoped and I only had to slip across the platform into the Freudenstadt fast train to be comfortably installed in a corner seat, from which for two minutes, I had the pleasure of watching the two soldiers and the detectives checking all on-coming passengers at the station barrier.

The journey was uneventful except for a glorious sunset which I saw to full advantage as I made my way on foot up the hilly streets of the little town, which backed on to the depths of the famous Black Forest. Where the houses ended, the road ascended through a wooded tunnel following the bank of a mountain stream which cascaded far below. I remembered that I had to follow this road for a certain distance (about twelve miles) before plunging into the forest itself.

It was a fairy-tale landscape with long winding ravines, a steep cliff on the one side of the road and a sheer drop into the torrent on the other, giving me no chance to skirt prudently round the villages as they came along. There was no choice. I had to go straight through and risk being questioned.

I was on my way through one particularly straggling village, passing the inmates who were undoubtedly surprised to see a stranger in his Sunday clothes so far away from a town at nightfall, and had come to within sight of the end of their houses, when I became aware of three people standing talking in the middle of the road and realised to my dismay that one of them was a policeman. My instinct was to turn tail but I knew that would have been fatal. I had to keep going and look as unconcerned as possible.

'Good evening,' said the policeman, turning to take a look at me over his shoulder.

I had never heard any member of a police or other military force in Germany use this form of greeting, and I did not fall into the trap (if trap it was!).

'*Heil, Hitler!*' I answered, raising my arm in the well-known salute.

'Where are you going?' he asked me in German.

Casually, but taking great pains to simulate a German accent, I replied:

'I'm just off for a walk to pick a few flowers. What wonderful weather we're having.'

'Yes, it's very good.'

Giving him as friendly a smile as I could produce, I added:

'Good night.'

I did not presume to think I had managed to bluff him, but I had had a good try and it was up to me to get as far away as possible before he thought better of it. Glancing cautiously over my shoulder, I realised that he was still on my trail when I was well out of the village. For want of a better idea, I did, in fact, start to pick flowers and had gathered a sizeable bunch before I became aware, to my relief, that he had abandoned following me. Surprised as I was, it bore out my previous experience, that one German on his own is seldom very resolute, but I could not afford to take a chance. He might easily have telephoned the next village and arranged a trap for me to walk into.

Up to this point the road had been climbing all the way and thirsty as I was by this time, I was relieved when it began its long descent towards Bad Peterstal, but I had not realised that I still had to go through yet another village encased in the ravine, until I spotted a sign-post bearing the name Bad Griesbach. I could not remember having noticed that name on the map and I felt I could not again risk being stopped and questioned, whether the policeman had telephoned through or not, but that I must circumvent this obstacle.

I spotted a path leading off to the right and winding up behind the village street. Unfortunately, it led to the back gardens and all the dogs started to bark. This took me very much by surprise at the time, as most dogs in Germany had been exterminated, but I learned later that a German police dogs' kennels was situated there. I felt very nervous and elected to scramble up the rocky slope rather than go back to the main road. It was a very stiff climb, but eventually I got far enough up to be beyond the range of the dogs' interest and to a point where the trees thinned out into a little rocky dell where I decided to settle down for the night under a star-studded roof. I set to work to make a litter of bracken and to turn my suit about to sleep in,

as I had done so successfully the night before. I had barely got on to
my bed before I was fast asleep.

The shrill whistle of a train in the valley below woke me up very
early next morning. It was not yet daybreak but the dawn was
coming up fast, for already I could make out the lie of the land much
more clearly than I had managed to do the night before. Once again
I put my suit on right side out and looked about for an observation
point commanding a view of the valley because the presence of a
railway line at this point was baffling to me. By going still further up
the mountainside, I eventually found the solution to the mystery,
and that it was to my advantage. It was not at the nearby and ill-
omened Bad Griesbach that the train was standing but in the
adjacent valley at Bad Peterstal. The sound had clearly carried to
my ears in the still of the night, and I realised from my vantage point,
that I could make my way direct to this spa across the mountain
slope without needing to return to face the dogs of Bad Griesbach.

I came to the edge of a big crag from which I had an excellent view
of the object of my earlier curiosity. Standing in a small terminal
station, all lit up for its departure, was a little locomotive with steam
well up at the head of a train of antediluvian carriages. On impulse I
felt I must investigate its destination, thinking it might well put me
on my way and confident that there was little risk involved at this
hour of the morning.

I came down from my perch into the valley at top speed, afraid
that at any moment I should see the train start up, but it was still
standing there when I reached the station. Three or four travellers
were queueing at the booking office and I took the opportunity of the
delay to take a look at the list of stops displayed near the barrier. I
spotted the name Oberkirch and remembered it was the place where
I had originally planned to take to the woods, the better to negotiate
the Siegfried Line. I promptly asked for a ticket to that town which
was only three stations away.

The little train rushed down the slopes at break-neck speed and in
less than twenty minutes we had arrived at Oberkirch, where, to my
surprise, there was something of a stir afoot. As I came out on to the
station square, I had the nasty shock of finding myself among a
throng of brown-shirted Nazis. The swastikas were swarming like
bees in a hive! No doubt it was a party meeting but feeling in no
mood for political speeches, I set about making myself scarce.

'*Heil Hitler!*, excuse me please,' I repeated in German over and
over again as I forged my way with difficulty through this repulsive

mob. Once through, I took a road leading to the edge of the forest, but on my way I had to have recourse to the Hitler salute repeatedly as I encountered the stragglers.

At last I plunged right into the darkness of the forest, thick with undergrowth and ruggedly uneven under foot. Although it was some comfort to be alone, nevertheless I had a haunting fear of getting lost. What a pity I had to leave without our compass! I could improvise one if only I had a watch... then, thinking along these lines, I suddenly had an idea. I felt in my pocket and found a pencil and my pipe. Using these two articles as the hands, I roughed out a clock face on the ground. Supposing the pencil to be the hour-hand and pointing it in the direction of the sun, I considered it to be eight o'clock on my imaginary dial, which was my rough estimate of the real time, and then placed my pipe as the minute hand, towards the figure twelve. Then I had only to bisect the angle between pencil and pipe to determine the direction of the true south. This I did from time to time during the day, greatly assisted on odd occasions by the striking of a distant clock.

That evening the sun disappeared prematurely behind a bank of clouds, and unable any longer to use my 'compass', I stretched out under a bush and went to sleep. Whether from cold or hunger, I woke very early but until dawn it was useless for me to move. I seemed to have been lying wakeful for hours when suddenly I heard voices. I held my breath while two people passed within ten yards of me, without my being able to distinguish them. I could follow their progress, however, by the beam from the torch that one of them was carrying. I had a strong feeling that they were soldiers.

Dawn came at last, but for my purpose I had to wait for full sunlight. I had just started off when I came upon a sign-post saying: 'Beware! Military Zone. Keep out.'

This gave me a nasty shock and I wondered whether to try to circumvent this area, which would probably have resulted in losing my bearings, so I decided to go straight ahead with great caution. I expected to be halted at every step, but the day wore on without incident until by a stroke of good fortune I heard a clock strike three and crouched down at once to take my compass bearing. It was lucky that I had done so, for almost at once I heard footsteps. By just turning my head, I was able to watch two German soldiers fully armed, as they strolled past. This was my last alarm, for within a few hundred yards I came out of this vast and oppressive forest into the dazzling sunlight of the world beyond.

I felt I could breathe more easily now that I could look out over the undulating plains ahead. About half a mile away, I could see a cross-roads where I thought there might well be a sign-post. I made my way down an easy slope along the hedgerow to the crossing where I was pleased to learn that Bodesbach, the village where I expected to meet Roland, was only three miles away.

CHAPTER TWELVE

The White Cross

Once free from the depressing atmosphere of the forest, and aware that my goal was within sight, I regained my resilience, but I felt a certain trepidation as I came upon the first houses of the village of Bodesbach, for according to Dary's instructions, it was imperative for me to locate the school without making myself conspicuous among the villagers. My fears were allayed, however, as soon as I caught sight of the school among the nearest buildings.

It consisted of one large room, and through the open window, I could see that it had been turned into a dormitory but there was no one in at the time. I tried the door only to find it locked, and realising that it would not do for me to wait about outside, I climbed in through the window taking good care that no one saw me doing so. The sight of all these beds made me realise how tired I was and I could not resist the temptation to lie down on one of them and go straight off to sleep.

The noise of someone coming into the room woke me and I got up with a start. It turned out to be a small dark lad quite astonished to see me there.

'I'm looking for someone called Roland,' I explained.

'I'm Roland. What can I do for you?'

'Dary has spoken to me about you,' I announced, hoping this name would mean something to him.

'Dary! Oh, yes. How is he? I take it he didn't manage to get through, then?'

I told him what I knew about Dary's misadventures and gave him a rough outline of my own escape. He set me at my ease immediately and promised to do all he could to help me. He guessed I was hungry and suggested that we should go off together to the canteen. Reading my anxiety in my expression, he reassured me that it would be full of French workers from the forced labour corps, who would pay no attention to a newcomer.

The canteen proved to be situated two or three minutes' walk away in a different school and I could appreciate how lucky I had been to pick the right building first time. Roland introduced me to his friends as his cousin from Paris, saying that I was with the forced labour corps at Cologne and was on a visit. He told me privately that it was essential to be cautious because of stool pigeons.

I had a very good meal on my new friend's ration tickets, and spent the evening listening to the conversation. At about nine o'clock we all went back to the sleeping quarters where Roland invited me to use his bed, explaining that they were all on the night-shift at the marshalling yards and would not be back until morning. Before he left, he told me that if there was a train that might be 'interesting', he would have me called. So at last I was able to settle down peacefully, free from present anxieties, and confident that my fate was in good hands.

Daylight came next morning, bringing with it the return of the night-shift, and no one had given me a call.

'There was nothing that would have been of any interest to you,' explained Roland when he came in.

It was not until about 11 pm on the third night that I was roused out of a deep sleep by someone shaking me and saying: 'Roland says you're to get up and come with me.'

I was on my feet straight away and it only took me a few moments to get dressed. It was a very dark night with total black-out except for an amber glow at the end of the road we took.

'That's the marshalling yard,' volunteered the man who was escorting me. We stopped before getting there and he made me wait for the next step, flat on my stomach, hidden in the long grass of a piece of waste land adjoining the goods yard. I did not have to wait long, but was beckoned to crawl under barbed wire and numerous railway trucks. Several times we had to crouch in the shadows to let German railway workers go by, but suddenly we came upon Roland himself, standing by a truck. Its sliding door was ajar. He signed to me to climb in hastily and whispered:

'This is bound for Italy via Switzerland where you must jump off.'

He shook my hand and shut the sliding door behind me. I heard him seal it up and then make a stealthy departure. I could discern nothing at all in the blackness of the truck, but could feel parcels and packing cases all round me. I did not move at all for fear of making a noise while the train was stationary. A strong pharmaceutical smell was wafted up to me from the consignment of goods. I listened to every footstep passing on the gravel and strained my ears to catch the guttural words of Rhineland jargon exchanged between the various railway men.

At last, the train began to move and rapidly gained speed. I began to feel my way around and soon discovered that the truck carried three distinct types of goods. There were parcels of every dimension, crates which I could hardly move and a collection of very large casks. Having taken stock of my surroundings, I sat down to think over the situation. I calculated that most escapees would aim at hiding in the furthest corners of the trucks and that, consequently, the Germans would make it their habit to examine these first. I judged it would be prudent to hide myself where they would least expect to find someone, that is near the door, providing I managed to conceal myself completely. This involved shifting a good deal of the truck's cargo, so as to bring the lighter parcels which would afford me moveable cover, near the door.

In the darkness and the confined space, this work proved so exhausting that I had to strip to the waist, but eventually I contrived to build myself a little hide-out, which measured up to my necessarily rigorous standards, right against the door.

Suddenly Dary's words came to my mind, about all trucks being weighed on the frontier. I clambered up on a pile of crates until I was within reach of the ventilator. With considerable difficulty, I managed to open it. Then, I felt around until I had got hold of a couple of parcels which, I judged, together weighed roughly 9 stone, the weight to which I had dropped from my normal 12 stone 4 under POW conditions. I hoisted them up level with the open ventilator, tore off the corners and let a shower of granules pour out on to the track at suitable intervals. I then jettisoned the empty packets and reclosed the ventilator before climbing into my kennel to await events.

The train was travelling so fast that I could feel a current of air through the floorboards with much relief as it helped to disperse the feeling of nausea which the smell of the chemicals was giving me. I realised that this smell was not altogether to my disadvantage as it would cover my undoubtedly strong scent from guards and dogs alike.

After what seemed to be a brief interval, due, no doubt, to my having dozed off, there came a grinding of brakes and the train slowed down to a stop. I was wondering if this could possibly be the frontier when I heard footsteps on the gravel and guttural exchanges outside. There was a sound of shunting and of soldiers marching past on a hard road. A dog barked; an order rang out. After a short silence, heavy footsteps approached the truck. The heavy door slid back noisily and, crouched under my parcels, I felt the impact of the fresh air. Nothing happened for at least ten seconds which seemed interminable to me as I froze there, literally holding my breath. Then, through the parcels, I felt the full weight of two men right on my head. I heard them disperse, one to each end of the truck and could distinguish by ear that they were moving the parcels about, searching behind the crates and thrusting an iron rod between the casks. In due course, I felt them tread over me again and jump down on to the track. There was another silent pause during which I could hear my heart pounding and then the door thundered to with a crash. With a rising wave of silent exultation, I listened to the re-sealing of the lock.

I stayed quite still in my hiding place, for this was no time to provoke the attention of some prowling police dog. After about half an hour the train proceeded in a series of thirty or forty ten-yard jerks which I guessed represented the weighing of the individual trucks, before finally going on its way.

I struggled up out of my nest of parcels and climbed up to the ventilator which I opened in feverish haste. Dazzling though the daylight was, it still did not stop me from discerning the white cross of Switzerland sprawled in paint across a red gasometer. Now I only had to choose the moment to slide out through the ventilator and drop on to free soil.

Thus did the adventure which had started at the gasometer at Stuttgart, come to its conclusion at the much more friendly gasometer of Basle. At last I had escaped from Germany, the accursed country where people of the highest principles rub shoulders with the vilest murderers.

CHAPTER THIRTEEN

Basle

The train that had brought me to freedom slowed down and I knew that this was my chance. I swung my feet out first through the ventilator and lowered myself till I hung against the outside of the truck. Then with a swift, forward thrust of the hips, I threw myself clear. I did not make the classic pancake landing on to Swiss soil, but finished up somewhat ignominiously on my behind.

Two Swiss railwaymen, whom I just missed as I glided in, rushed up to make a grab for me, but I picked myself up uninjured, dived across a mass of tracks, taking good care to dodge the live wires and plunged headlong into a wood which providentially I found on the other side.

The railwaymen were soon shaken off and I was once again alone and in a position to take stock of the situation. I could have let them collar me but I wanted to avoid internment if I could, as I had a little bit of information which I was determined to reveal when I had the opportunity, to someone in a position to communicate it to the Allies. The right place, I felt, for this was the British Embassy or consulate.

I came out on the far side of the wood to find myself a few yards away from a busy main road with a tram route. Within ten minutes, I had ascertained by observation that the next rattletrap was heading for the Basle town hall. I calculated that this town was important enough to have a British Consulate and decided to follow the tram-lines to the town centre but it was further off than I had bargained for and night was already descending when I eventually reached it.

The blaze of light in the centre of the town was dazzling to eyes like mine, accustomed only to the gloomy prospect of the prison camp. The shop windows were crammed with all manner of goods just as in pre-war days, even, to my astonishment, with quantities of chocolate and cigarettes. I wandered from one shop window to another, all ablaze with light since nightfall, gazing at the various displays which so overwhelmed me with nostalgia that I almost lost

sight of my objective. It was essential that I should find the British
Consulate, but I could not bring myself to turn away from the old
familiar bustle of the traffic, the cars, the buses, trams, pedestrians,
the cinemas, the neon lights, the . . .

All at once, there was nothing. The lights had all suddenly been
extinguished at one stroke, and were followed by black, impenetrable
darkness. I could not see to put one foot in front of the other and
wondered if this was a general failure or a deliberate power cut. I
realised it must be deliberate as after some considerable time, the
lights still did not come on again. There was now no hope of finding
the Consulate, all I could hope for was some place to spend the night.

Two or three hundred yards away, I spotted a blue light which I
fortunately, approached cautiously, for, to my dismay, it was a
police station. The next blue light that came into sight turned out to
be the railway station, an even more dangerous locality, according to
the reports of my former recaptured fellow-prisoners, many of whom
had met disaster at this particular spot. It was a railway terminus
under German-Swiss control and consequently patrolled by the
forces of both nations.

A third light caught my eye, which proved to be a smart hotel. I
wondered whether I had the nerve to go and ask for a room, and if my
one and only twenty-mark note would be current exchange here.
Even more important, should I have to produce an identity card? I
walked up the steps to get a peep inside and straightway caught sight
of the pretty receptionist. I could not hope to exert any charm upon
her in my dirty dishevelled condition, but she looked a kindly sort of
girl and my instinct was to try my luck. I felt it would be best to come
straight to the point and tell her the truth, while keeping a close eye
on her reaction so as to preserve the option of losing myself in the
darkness at the slightest sign of trouble.

'Good evening, Madam; do you happen to have a small single
room?'

'Yes, sir. Have you your traveller's card?'

Now I was in trouble. I ought to have realised that I should need a
permit to travel about in war-time even in a neutral country like this,
so by way of a reply I held out my twenty mark note saying:

'I should like to pay in advance because I want to leave very
early.'

'Is that your only currency?' she asked, looking contemptuously
at my note.

'Yes, Madam, it is! I have been a POW in Germany and have just managed to escape. I want to get to the British Consulate with a view to joining up again with the Allied Forces. Will you please help me, without notifying the Swiss police because I don't want to find myself interned. If German money is unacceptable, I will endeavour to get hold of some from the Consulate tomorrow morning and you have my word of honour that I will come back and settle the bill.'

I saw her decide to help me. She asked me my name and entered it on her register. A porter had appeared meanwhile, who signalled me to follow him upstairs.

'After 8 pm there is no more electricity and the lift is not working,' he explained apologetically, as if I were an important client to whom an explanation was due!

It was a large and luxurious room and I was quite taken aback by the sight of so much comfort. He turned back the bed and I was dazzled by the whiteness of the linen, in contrast to the litters I had known in Rawa and the lice-ridden straw of Silesia.

In order to do honour to my royal couch, I took good care to have a thorough strip-wash and then abandoned myself to the newly regained sensual pleasure of sliding naked between the cool smooth sheets.

Next morning, I left the hotel at about 9.30 am without being able to thank my benefactress who was not on duty. The streets were all deserted and the shops closed. In a telephone box, I was able to locate the exact address of the British Consulate and with the help of a nearby town plan I had no difficulty in finding my way there.

The Consulate turned out to be part of a large mansion, the other half of which was occupied by a mining company. I went up and rang the bell but had to wait for some time before getting any reply. Then the door was opened a couple of inches by a man who seemed to be the caretaker and who asked me my business.

'Is this the British Consulate, please?'

'Yes, but it's closed on public holidays.'

'Is today a holiday, then?'

'Of course it is! Where do you come from?'

'Germany. I have just escaped and must see the Consul.'

'Come in.'

The heavy door swung to behind me and the caretaker ushered me up the steps to the vestibule. As the inner door was opened, I experienced one of the biggest thrills of my life-time for there, in front of me was a portrait, larger than life, of Mr Winston Churchill smoking an enormous cigar. Beneath its massive frame was the following inscription: BRITISH AND PROUD OF IT!

The caretaker escorted me through narrow passages to his own quarters and seated me at his own kitchen table, saying:

'The order of the day is to start with a good breakfast.'

He was a very pleasant character and so was his wife, though somewhat more reserved. They gave me eggs and bacon and a good cup of tea – sheer luxury to a POW – and while I was enjoying it, I could hear the caretaker talking about me on the telephone. He came back to tell me that someone would come and see me in about twenty minutes. In the meantime, he pressed me to have more eggs and bacon and another cup of tea.

Very soon, an Englishman of about forty came in and enquired in perfect French if I had had a good breakfast and expressed the hope that I was not too exhausted as a result of my escape. In the course of conversation, he switched from French to English and sometimes even into German before taking me off to his office on the storey above.

'Why did you choose the British Consulate rather than the French?' he asked me.

'Because I want to join up again with the Allies and I don't know whether or not the French Consul is pro-Vichy.'

'You were right to be careful. He represents Pétain.'

Fumbling in the lining of my jacket, I produced a piece of paper which I spread out before him.

'And this is another reason why I have come to you. Here is a sketch-plan of Stuttgart showing its canal. You see this loop in front of the aircraft factory? I have shaded it in because the Germans have concealed it with camouflage, naturally enough, but what I can't accept is the fact that they have reproduced this loop artificially in front of a POW camp, with the result that in the last air-raid, though the factory escaped, not so my fellow POWs who were locked up in the flimsy protection of wooden huts!'

'Were there many casualties?'

'Well, it wasn't my camp, so it's difficult for me to give an accurate picture, but it is said that there were 600 killed including some Russians. I have drawn this plan, making it as accurate as possible, in the hope that you can put a stop to this inhuman slaughter, which is used as propaganda against the Allies. While I was about it, I put in a few details which I thought might be interesting, such as the gas works, the central power station, a huge open-air park for military transport and the HQ of the SS.'

My interviewer took a look at the plan before announcing; 'I'm sure that our intelligence chaps will be very interested to see this document. Can you give them any more information?'

'No, except that I could probably give some details of the layout of the Henschel Aircraft Factory at Schoenfeld where I worked for six months. I could produce a rough sketch of the position of the factory buildings, showing what processes go on in each, all except one, that is, which was top secret and I could never get into.'

'Yes, we should be very interested in that and I am going to suggest that you sit down at this desk and write out a report of everything you can remember about this factory.'

I was very pleased to do this because it showed I was being taken seriously and I felt I was really beginning to hit back at the Germans for some of the hardships I had experienced at their hands. I settled down to work in earnest on my report, taking care to leave out nothing that could possibly be of interest. It was nearly mid-day before I ran out of ideas.

'You've made a good job of it,' said the Englishman, appreciatively, 'and now I'll take you home to lunch.'

We walked to his home which was close by on the Bahrfusser Platz. On the way, he looked round several times and I heard him swear in English under his breath. Seeing that I was curious, he explained his annoyance, saying, 'They even watch us on public holidays.'

I assumed he referred to the Germans but did not care to pursue the matter any further and was still working things out for myself when we arrived at the house.

There I was introduced to his wife, a cultured Englishwoman, who greeted me graciously. She set me at ease at once and her husband took me to a bedroom where he opened a wardrobe and said:

'Here are several suits. Fortunately, we are about the same size, and with luck, you'll find one that will do for you. You can have it to keep. There are shirts in the drawers and ties behind the mirror. Take two or three if you like. I'll leave you to come along when you are ready.'

I could not help feeling that they were being too kind and was somewhat uncomfortable to feel that I was an object of pity. Nevertheless, I got into one of the impeccable suits.

Five of us sat down to the table, another couple being presented as close friends who were anxious to hear a first-hand account of my experiences as a POW. After an excellent meal, I learned that the visitor was a director of the International Bank and that, to my surprise, I was to go next morning to his bank so that he could take me to buy a ready-made overcoat.

'But who's going to pay for it?' I asked, and added, 'It'll soon be summer. I can manage without that for the time being.'

But my protests were ignored. 'Don't worry about that, and by the way, I have sent someone to settle your account at the hotel, so you needn't worry about that either.'

'You are most kind and I much appreciate all you have done for me. Thanks to you, I feel as if I am dreaming, but I can't see why you go to so much trouble on behalf of someone whom you hardly know, and who is after all, only a bird of passage.'

'You are very welcome,' he promptly replied, 'but since what we are doing seems to embarrass you, let me reassure you that it is not entirely disinterested. For instance, I should like you to repeat everything you told me in my office this morning, to our Military Attaché in Berne.'

'Of course I will, with pleasure.'

'Good, I want you to get a train tomorrow morning, after you've been with our friend to the clothiers. Tonight you will sleep here with us. Afterwards, we shall have to see. Perhaps these friends of ours will put you up for a while. In the meantime, as today is a public holiday, I suggest we go to the pictures to see Bette Davis' latest film. Then we will have dinner at an inn where I will teach you the new skittle game, bowling.'

I thought this sounded as if it would be a very interesting programme and I thanked him very much in advance. And so passed my first day of liberty, but my thoughts went often to my unfortunate comrades still in prison camps and particularly to Gino Campi who, had it not been for some unexplained stroke of bad luck, would have been sharing my pleasure.

Next morning, as instructed, I went to the International Bank and located the friend who was to take me to buy the overcoat. We went into a nearby shop and I became the owner of a dark grey raglan. I should have preferred something lighter but for a reason that I could not understand, Jack (that was this friend's name) insisted on my having a less conspicuous one. We parted at the shop door, Jack returning to the bank while I went to the Consulate to meet my host who now told me to call him Frank. He was very satisfied with the purchase.

'That's fine. It fits you well and the colour is just right.'

'Just right for what?'

'Oh, nothing. I'll explain later. Let's talk about you first. Yesterday you gave me some details about your young days when you were in England and we have made a routine check, so far, to our satisfaction. I must admit that first of all I took you for a German spy. We have already had the case of the so-called escaped POW. However, for the moment, we are satisfied that you are genuine. By the way, you lived several years in Brixton, didn't you? What was the name of the Hosiers opposite the Lambeth Town Hall'

'Isaac Walton.'

Frank smiled. He had just laid a trap capable of catching out any spy who did not know that part of London first hand.

'Now let's have a word about your trip to Berne. Your train is at 12.32 pm but when you leave the Consulate, we shall have to take certain precautions for unfortunately, our every movement is watched and my interest in you will not have escaped the attention of the German secret service. When you leave here, you will, undoubtedly, be discreetly followed. Don't take any notice and, above all, don't look round. Last night I introduced you to Mr Hanz (the fourth player at the skittle game) and he has an antique shop. This is his card. Go straight there on foot. It's not far. Just go back past my house and take the first turning on the left. You will see his shop at the end of the street on the opposite side. Go in and he will tell you what to do next. Here is your return ticket and 200 Swiss Francs so that you won't be short of money.'

Just before mid-day, I went casually out of the Consulate and walked towards the Bahrfusser Platz without looking back in spite of a burning desire to see if I was being followed. This little expedition into the world of espionage or counter espionage gave me great satisfaction and an inflated idea of my own importance! I found the antique shop quite easily and noticing that there were no customers inside, I went in and began to take an interest in the various articles on display. Mr Hanz appeared and showed me into a room at the back of the shop. Without a word he opened a door leading into a long corridor at the end of which I could see daylight shining through the glass panel of another door. This led out into a back street where a car was waiting to take me to the Central Station.

The Berne Express was well named, judging by the way it dashed across the lovely countryside. This journey was going too quickly but I was already planning to make up for it by a little sight-seeing in the capital. However, my hopes were dashed as I walked out of the station, for a young man came up to me, asking

'Mr Roland Rieul?'

'Yes, that's my name, but to whom am I speaking?'

'I come from the Attaché's Office and I am to take you back there by taxi.'

Almost at once we were leaving the busy centre of the town and driving through a residential district. We stopped in front of a very nondescript house. I was shown straight in to the Attaché's office. He turned out to be a colonel in uniform. He was very polite but wasted no words after the manner of senior officers. He questioned me at great length and made copious notes. He took me into another room, saw to it that I was fully equipped with a draughtsman's kit and told me to draw the Schoenfeld plan again.

At the end of the afternoon, having completed my little job, the colonel sent for me again for further questioning. The conversation ended pleasantly with him thanking me for my contribution and wishing me a pleasant journey back to Basle. A taxi was waiting at the door to take me to the station.

The return journey was as swift and pleasant as the outward one and I was soon back at Frank's home with my mission completed. During the course of the evening, while I was enjoying an excellent cigar, I was able to tell them a good deal about the Germans, their way of life under the strain of war, their morale under incessant Allied bombing, of their attitude to their leaders, of their perpetual fear of the Gestapo and the total ignorance of the general public of the atrocities being carried out in their name by the ignoble SS troops.

After listening to my impressions, Frank made the comment that I was in such bad shape physically that I must have two months' holiday. He suggested that I should spend this at an inn run by one of his friends. He also said that another friend would take me there next day and that I would have nothing to pay.

'All you need to do is to eat and sleep, and all at the expense of your fairy godmother.'

'I should like to meet that fairy godmother.'

'All in good time. All that matters at present is for you to get fit if you want to get back into the forces again.'

I did not press the point but could not help thinking that this was the first time to my knowledge, that such concern had been shown over a straightforward enlistment.

CHAPTER FOURTEEN

At Porrentruy

Next morning before we set off to the Consulate, Frank made me a present of an almost new suitcase. 'You can put your old suit in that. It only wants cleaning.'

And for good measure, he threw in two or three shirts, socks, ties and a very good pullover. He also gave me a thousand Swiss francs for out of pocket expenses. I felt myself flushing with embarrassment, but cutting short my thanks he added:

'Don't thank me. I know I can count on you when I need you. In your poor state of health there can be no question of sending you to North Africa as you wish. Incidentally, at Porrentruy, which is where you are going, I want you to go to a Dr Duval for a complete medical check-up. He will be advised that you are coming.'

Having said good-bye to Mrs Frank, we went off together to the Consulate to await the friend who was to take me on holiday. While I sat in the waiting-room, I was able to look through a pile of magazines from neutral countries and this brought home to me how damaging was the propaganda dispensed by Goebbels' service. It made such interesting reading that I did not even hear the door open.

'Mr Roland?' enquired a voice which I realised must belong to Frank's friend. 'My name is René Lesage.'

He shook me vigorously by the hand, accompanying this gesture with a little nod of the head which I recognized as typically Swiss. I liked his frank manner and felt there was an immediate bond of sympathy between us.

'You can call me René,' he said.

'Then call me Roland, please.'

As we went off towards the station, I tried somewhat clumsily to pump him on the subject of Frank's activities. I expressed my surprise at his generosity and speculated as to the source of the money which would cover the cost of my stay in Porrentruy. But I elicited nothing but an ironic smile and an evasive reply.

'I know nothing about his arrangements. As far as I am

concerned, I simply do him a few little favours as requested and I don't know anything else.'

My next attempt, a little later, also drew a blank. On this subject, René was silent as the grave! I could not understand what it was all about, but that did not matter for the time being, for everything was going very well. All I could do was let things take their course and content myself with having a good look round and enjoy the easy living of a country not at war. Besides, the countryside was magnificent. The train wound its way through majestic gorges and I could look down on the turbulent torrent which flowed far below me. Every little station was fringed with a border of flowers and the trim dresses of the young girls were all embroidered with tiny florets. The resonant sound of cow bells and the tinkling of station signals, were the only noises to disturb the sleepy tranquillity of the scene.

Porrentruy was a small residential town very near the French border, closely resembling its counterparts in France. Whereas in Basle, Swiss-German is spoken, here one could only hear French coloured by bits of dialect.

René took me across the station square and introduced me to the *patron* of a hotel called Bienvenue des Voyageurs. A young porter took me to my room. It was very pleasant and had a window looking over the square.

I rejoined René in the bar where he stood me a glass of white wine and I said how pleased I felt at the prospect of spending a couple of months in such an attractive spot. My expressions of appreciation were interrupted by the arrival of two Swiss soldiers to whom René also offered a drink. I did not take in their names as I was so intrigued with the contrast of their appearance. They looked like Don Quixote and Sancho Panza, the only difference being that their roles were reversed, for it was the little fat one who wore the stripes. His name turned out to be Sergeant Cartier and it was his duty to be responsible for me throughout my stay at Porrentruy. Any requests or complaints were to be put through him. It was through him, too, that I should have to communicate if I wanted to get in touch with Frank, as all telephone calls direct to the Consulate were forbidden to me, but the sergeant undertook to make contact with me every day.

The time came for René to return to Basle and for the soldiers to take to their powerful motor-cycles. I went into the dining-room where there were only a few people left and had an excellent meal. Then I went out to get a breath of evening air in the deserted streets of this drowsy provincial town. I called in at a *guinguette* decorated with colourful bunting, to have a drink. There I sat and watched the dancers whirling round to the jaunty strains of an accordionist who sat perched high in one corner of the room. In the intervals we were entertained by various Tyrolean turns.

Thus ended the first day of my holiday at the expense of this mysterious 'fairy godmother'.

A few days spent with nothing to do but to eat and sleep soon began to fill out my face again. At mid-day the sergeant always called in for a drink to make sure that all was well and a week had passed before he brought me news of Frank, to the effect that he wished to see me on the following day. I was to take the 9.15 am train and go straight to his house for lunch.

I reached the Bahrfusser Platz almost at the same time that he did. He congratulated me on looking so well and offered me a whisky and water as an apéritif. We then had a very fine lunch and set off for the Consulate, Frank still not having explained why he had sent for me. However, as soon as I was settled in his office, he told me the reason.

'We have now completed our enquiries and I am pleased to tell you that we consider you above suspicion.'

'Thank you very much,' I retorted with some bitterness.

'Don't be offended. We are being subjected all the time to insidious manoeuvres on the part of the enemy and we have to take every possible precaution. So much for that. Now there is something I want to ask you to do for me.'

'Yes, with pleasure, what is it?'

'For reasons which I cannot explain, it's not possible for us to send you back to join up with the Allied Forces in North Africa. Moreover, even if this should become possible some day, in that position you would only be one of a number, whereas if you comply with our request, you could be a hundred times more useful to the Allied cause.'

'What do you mean?'

Frank paused for a long time before replying.

'Would you like to see Paris again?'

'Of course. Nothing would please me more, but how could I?'

'If you will agree to work as a British secret agent, I will send you to Paris. I don't want you to give me your answer now. Go back to Porrentruy and think it over carefully. Then come back and see me in two or three days' time. It's a very serious decision for you to make. You must bear in mind two things; first, this is a very dangerous game where your life will be continually in jeopardy, and secondly, if you accept, you will be rendering an inestimable service to the cause of the Allies who are struggling to free oppressed countries, France among them.'

Two days later I was back again sitting in the self-same chair.

'I accept your proposition on one condition; that I shall be freed from all commitments on the day when the last Boche is driven out of France.'

'I agree to that, I give you my word. I congratulate you on your decision. I think we can do a good job, together. I am going to send you to Paris, where, I'm sorry to say, our previous organisation has been completely wrecked by our opponents. There were too many contacts with the Resistance, which is fatal. Don't forget this when you are there, rule number one is have no contact with resistance groups.'

Frank went on to give me some preliminary tips and then announced that I must report to him every Tuesday and Friday to take a special course with an instructor. He also lent me a thick dossier containing copious information on German methods and organisation.

'Study this very carefully,' he said, 'and make a point of learning the military code system by heart, so that later on, once you have grasped it you will be able to identify at a glance the nature and strength of any enemy unit you may encounter.'

He warned me never to lose sight of the dossier, not to leave it in my hotel room but to take it with me wherever I went, even to the lavatory. I felt a bit dazed by all this and wondered if I hadn't plunged into the deep end a bit too hastily. I began to wonder whether I was up to this job. To learn a code by heart, when I had always had difficulty in memorising anything, was a lot to ask of me at the outset. However, having taken the plunge, I must sink or swim.

I went back to Porrentruy clutching the dossier tightly under my arm for fear someone should attempt to snatch it. It was not until I was safely locked into my hotel room that I dared open it. Then I began studying it page by page and to take in the good advice handed out to Intelligence Service apprentices.

From then on, I spent every morning in my room studying the dossier before parcelling it up and taking it to the dining-room at lunch time. One day, as I sat down to the meal, I took a quick look round the guests and caught sight of a very attractive blonde sitting at a table near the window. Throughout lunch I took an occasional look in her direction and finally managed to catch her eye. Fancying I saw a gleam of encouragement, I could not resist taking my coffee over to her table and saying, 'May I sit down?'

She made no protest, so I took a seat opposite her and embarked on small talk, but I had not been going for more than a couple of minutes, when the waitress passed me a saucer bearing an envelope addressed to 'Mr Roland Fournier'. I looked at it for a moment, thinking it was a mistake. Fournier was not my name, yet the Christian name was right. My hesitation did not escape my new acquaintance.

'Aren't you going to open it?'

Thus pressed, I became aware of a need for caution, so I opened it taking care that she could not read the contents which were printed by hand in minute characters and consisted of three words: 'BEWARE OF ELIANE'.

Just as I was restoring the note to its envelope, my companion commented that I looked worried.

'It's nothing serious, I hope,' she said, in an enquiring tone.

'Yes and no. Just a reminder from the *patron* about my hotel bill.' I was pleased to have found such a prompt and plausible reply, but she had noticed the name on the envelope.

'So your name is Roland.'

'Yes, what's yours?'

'Eliane,' replied my peroxide panther!

That was enough for me. I knew where I stood. Gathering up the packet containing the famous dossier from between my feet, I made a pretext of an imaginary rendezvous at the bar and made a discreet withdrawal from the situation.

I stopped for a moment in the hall to catch the waitress as she went through, to enquire who had given her the letter which she brought me.

'A customer.'

'Which one?' I asked.

'He's gone.'

At the bar where I ordered another coffee, I asked the barmaid if she knew Eliane and could tell me what she did.

'She's the tart of one of the watch-makers.'

I was no further forward in the matter, but at least, I knew now that I had embarked on my new career.

The next day was Tuesday, so I booked the first train to Basle to begin my course on espionage. Frank received me at his office and after asking me if I was enjoying myself at Porrentruy, he said:

'You must avoid that woman, Eliane. She is a very dangerous enemy spy. She tries to discover the destination to which our agents are bound in enemy territory. Then, by means of a photograph taken clandestinely by her or one of her acolytes, she gets them picked up by the Gestapo on arrival at their territory.'

With this advice, Frank took me into another room and presented me to my tutor, an Englishman with a military look. He was tall and thin, and very fair with a tooth-brush moustache. He was very pleasant to talk to and his course was instructive and interesting. I learnt what information was most vital and what was worthless and a waste of time to transmit.

After my interesting lesson, I spent the afternoon in a cinema before going back to Porrentruy. Days and weeks passed uneventfully. I had learnt my dossier by heart and thanks to my training course, I felt I knew what was expected of a secret agent. Only one incident upset the normal routine. One day wishing to stretch my legs, I left the hotel with my dossier under my arm as usual. I went round the block and was passing the rear of the hotel when I realised that I had left my cigarettes in my room. Using the service entrance, I ran up the four flights of stairs, let myself into the room and searched for the missing packet in the pockets of my coat and other suit. Suddenly, there was a knock at the door and as I happened to be standing just inside, I grabbed the handle and flung it open to find myself faced by a hotel porter, obviously taken aback to find the room occupied. He pulled himself together as much as he could and to explain his presence, he blurted out:

'Excuse me, have you got a light?'

This already seemed a very strange request on the part of a hotel employee. He was to become even more confused for as it so happened, I had just picked up my matches. I struck one, only to find that he was now without a cigarette and had to run off and collect one from his room before being able to take advantage of his premature request!

This marked my second contact with the enemy and this time, I had smelt him out myself. It was mostly due to luck and I had no real justification for being conceited about it, but could not help feeling very pleased to be able to make this incident the subject of my first report.

A few days later, in conversation with Frank, I learnt that my suspicions had been justified, that the porter was indeed an enemy agent but that by that time he was already safely in prison.

'When we came to make enquiries, following your report,' Frank told me, 'we discovered that he was an old lag, wanted by the police, so he won't be troubling us again for a long time!'

Although I was very pleased to hear this, I was never quite sure whether he was really after my dossier or only after my money. Having lived like a lord for five weeks, all the time at the expense of my mysterious Fairy Godmother, I was not at all surprised when the Swiss Sergeant Cartier arrived one day with the instruction that I was to take the dossier back to Basle. There, at the Consulate, Frank informed me that I was to undergo an oral examination that afternoon.

'This will be conducted by a high-ranking colleague of mine from Intelligence Service,' he explained, adding by way of encouragement, 'and if you give a satisfactory account of yourself, you will be registered in London as an official agent.'

My fears were quickly allayed when I saw my examiner. He was English and a young man with a disarming smile and no military pomp. His questions were not so much technical as framed to assess my personality and intelligence. I felt I came through all right, even on questions referring to the technicalities of German methods and administration, but was relieved to hear from Frank a few minutes later that I had been accepted and that application would be made to London straightaway for confirmation of my registration there.

After a few more days of vacation, I was recalled to Basle and told that my departure for Paris was imminent. I listened to a good deal of advice from Frank, warning me, especially, against the danger of getting in touch with 'resistance' groups and to beware of so called 'hidden Allied airmen'. On the other hand, my positive duties were once more impressed on me:

Firstly, I was to form an organisation for the purpose of supplying information at short notice on the strength and movements of German troops in the Paris region.

Secondly, on the day following an air raid, I was to transmit details of 'impact', the damage created and the effect that I estimated they would have on the enemy.

Thirdly, I was to ferret out any information which my espionage training made me deem useful.

Fourthly, I was to carry out promptly such special missions as might subsequently be demanded of me.

'Here is an address in France which I should like you to learn by heart. That is where you will send your reports, in a sealed envelope, of course. Make sure that you memorise it accurately because you must never, in any circumstances, carry it on your person in writing. You must not even address a letter when you are taking it to the post. Put your report in a blank envelope and wait till you reach the post-box before writing the address, having made quite certain that no one is watching you. I think it would be politic for us to meet once a fortnight to take stock of the position. Our Swiss friends will make available guides to see you across the frontier. You will be hearing from them very shortly. The only other thing I have to do is to hand over this money, 200,000 French francs – do you think that will be enough to carry on with? – and to wish you good luck and a safe journey.'

I went back to Porrentruy a very anxious man, weighed down with the feeling that I had bitten off considerably more than I could chew!

CHAPTER FIFTEEN

Open House at the Allemanns

The day after my visit to Basle, the weather was so beautiful that I decided to take advantage of it and set out for a long walk through the green countryside. My route led me up into the hills from the top of which I could look down on the River Alaine meandering across the plain. I was plunged in thought and considerably worried, not so much at the prospect of unknown dangers to come, but as to whether I was capable of playing the part allotted to me. I was as nervous as a young actor on the first night.

That evening, contrary to his usual custom, Sergeant Cartier came back to see me again at the bar. Taking me on one side, he announced:

'You are leaving tomorrow at ten o'clock. I will call on you in your room half an hour earlier to give you my final instructions.'

In this way, my vacation came to an end. The next day would bring the onset of a new phase of my life, a nerve-racking phase, perhaps, but certainly not a purposeless one, and my words in the Bois de Thuilley the day I was captured, came back to me, the English saying 'Live to fight another day', and I realised that, now, that day had come.

I spent a sleepless night thinking about Paris and what I should find there, but my overriding anxiety was how to set about the task in hand. I also wondered what to do about living quarters. I knew that hotels were bound to be under German surveillance and that to go back to my own flat, empty though it was, would be folly.

At 9.30 am, exactly, there was a knock on the door but I was already up, shaved and dressed. It was the Swiss sergeant with a travelling case in hand.

He greeted me as usual and then said:

'Strip off and put all your possessions on the bed, your socks as well. I want to see you as naked as a new-born babe.' He fumbled in the case and proceeded to make me a present of a pair of socks. 'Get into those and into this.'

By the time he had finished I was dressed from head to foot in clothes which had come out of the suitcase. When I automatically felt in my pockets, I brought out a number of articles every one of which might have come from Paris, used Metro tickets, the halves of a couple of cinema tickets, a losing voucher from the Paris tote, a packet of Gauloise cigarettes, nearly empty, and a box of German matches. My two hundred thousand French francs I put into the inner pocket of my jacket but the sergeant made me surrender my other personal belongings including my Swiss money.

Before getting on my new shoes, I noticed that they were marked 'Chez André, Paris' but when he came to help me on with my dark grey overcoat from Basle, I thought I had found a flaw in his preparations.

'You've forgotten something, haven't you?' I protested, thinking I had caught out the expert. 'This coat comes from Switzerland.'

'Take a good look at the label,' he replied with a smile.

I did so and realised that the name on it was 'Henri Esder, Paris', and yet I remembered that I had seen another label on it when I chose it at the shop in Basle. Then I understood why there had been a slight delay 'to carry out a little alteration' as the salesman had explained.

'Let's go and have some breakfast before we set off,' suggested the sergeant. 'We'll take the 10.40 am bus to Bure. Don't say goodbye to any one. The *patron* knows you are off and that's all that's necessary.'

And thus it was that we got away as discreetly as we wished and mingled with the other travellers as we boarded the bus bound for the frontier. As we came into Bure, the bus stopped in front of a little café. We went in and were shown straight through to the room at the back, where the proprietor produced a large parcel for me.

'These are the cigarettes and tobacco,' the sergeant told me, handing me a rucksack. 'Shove them in there and put the sack on your back – they're part of your disguise. You're a smuggler if you are unlucky enough to come up against the Germans. If that happens, you can expect to get three months inside, or even to be sent off to a forced labour camp – from which, of course, you would escape, knowing the ropes so well!'

'You talk as if it were child's play! Are you pulling my leg?'

'No, not unless you'd rather be riddled with bullets. It's best to choose the lesser of two evils.'

We left by a door leading straight into a little garden which abutted on to a pine wood and found ourselves following, through dense undergrowth, a path which came out along a hedge and across fields. It was slightly uphill all the way, somewhat to the distress of my friend the portly Swiss sergeant. We stopped for him to get his breath at the lower corner of a meadow whih sloped up away from us, and he warned me that our meeting place was up at the top of it.

'Keep your voice down now. We shall find the people who are waiting for us in a hollow.'

As we went silently up the last three or four hundred yards, I was gripped by a paralysing fear, the same which I had had to master before each of my escapes, and after living at ease for a couple of months in an unoccupied country, the prospect of rubbing shoulders again with the Germans had nothing to recommend it!

All at once, we came upon the hollow to which the sergeant had referred and I was very surprised to find four persons already there; two civilians and two Swiss soldiers, one of whom, a lieutenant, shook me by the hand and introduced me to the two civilians in a whisper.

'Good morning, Monsieur Fournier, here are your two guides, Jacques and Paul.'

Jacques was a strapping young man under thirty but Paul was just the reverse, well over fifty, I reckoned, and of puny stature. It was Jacques who straightway took the lead. With a finger on his lips, he whispered:

'The Boche is fifty yards away down over the brow of the hill. Follow me at a distance of ten paces. Stop whenever I do and if you see me crouch, get down yourself immediately. It's quite easy. You only have to follow exactly what I do and keep ten paces behind me. Oh, and take care not to snap any dead twigs or dislodge any stones.'

'Right,' I answered.

'Good luck, Monsieur Fournier,' said the lieutenant, giving me a salute before he shook hands with me.

Just at this moment, I was feeling far from confident. I felt as if I were about to enter the lions' den. Jacques had just disappeared over the edge and I was due to follow.

We found ourselves at the top of a long slope down through rocky woods. I observed that my guide was making the maximum use of natural cover and I did my best to imitate him. Suddenly, he flattened on the ground behind a bush and I did likewise behind a tree. We froze for a couple of minutes which only gave me time to wonder what I had let myself in for. Jacques rose, took a few steps and then flattened himself again. This time I found myself behind a boundary stone and read its carved inscription which informed me that where I then was, I was still in Switzerland, but that on the other side of the stone, I should be in France. In different circumstances, I should have felt great pleasure to have realised that I was home again, but at that moment, I had no thought for anything but the actions of the man ahead.

This time there seemed to be an interminable delay for no apparent reason. The forest was quite still and no unwonted sound disturbed its peace. However, eventually Jacques got up very carefully and crept forward as stealthily as a cat for a few paces, only to kneel down again behind a large boulder. He watched me as I negotiated this bit of the operation before venturing to set foot round the boulder, but suddenly darted again into the shelter of the rock. He signed to me to be absolutely silent and I wondered what he had spotted. All I could hear was my own heart beat. However, the sound which I still missed had not escaped my guide's supersensitive ear. A few seconds later, the danger which had been threatening us became apparent. A German soldier, with a tommy-gun at the ready, sauntered by within three or four yards of him.

The soldier was making his way along a path which ran right alongside Jacques' boulder. Every now and again I could catch sight of him clearly through the bushes. He was a real square-headed Boche, true to type. Fortunately, he did not spot anything but went on his way with a heavy step. He had hardly gone out of sight when Jacques beckoned to me to come close, and whispered in my ear:

'That's the sentry's beat, we shall have to cross it very quickly and silently, having first made sure that no one is in sight in either direction, and whatever you do – no noise.'

He got up, crept round the rock to make sure the coast was clear, and then crossed the path swiftly, to disappear in the undergrowth opposite. It was my turn next. I did just what he had told me, sonewhat hastily, I admit, because I felt to some extent my nerves had got the better of me. However, nothing happened and I soon rejoined Jacques on the other side of the path. He set off again at once in the lead, this time on the upward slope. We went forward as quickly as possible, taking good care not to step on dead wood or to dislodge any stones.

The further we found ourselves from the sentry's beat, the more confident I grew. However, we were not yet out of danger to judge by the precautions taken by the man ahead, his long pauses and his conscientious listening for the slightest sound. The little chap who brought up the rear had certainly not come for the good of his health.

Using an improvised besom, he took good care to obliterate our tracks as we went.

Our progress had slowed up again. It must have taken a good quarter of an hour to cover three or four hundred yards as we came up towards the summit. I hoped that once we were over it, the danger would diminish, but this was not so. From the cover of a boulder, Jacques signalled to us to come up to him.

'From now on, keep at a distance of thirty paces instead of ten. For the next couple of kilometres we need to look out for ambushes and patrols but fortunately, they are not very frequent.'

We started off through the forest which was sometimes very dense and sometimes sparse. Occasionally, we skirted a clearing but for the most part, the path ran through the wood. We met no hindrance and step by step, I felt myself relaxing. I could not help admiring the skill and composure of these guides. Theirs was no easy contribution to the 'cause' and I could not help wondering whether I should be good enough at my job to justify such men risking their lives for me.

At last, at a gateway into a field, Jacques stopped and waited to speak to me.

'You are out of danger here. See that building over there across the field? That's a cattle shed. Wait there till someone comes and fetches you. We are a bit ahead of schedule, so you will probably have to wait for half an hour. We're off now the other way. Goodbye and good luck to you.'

'Thank you for bringing me this far safely. Do you often do this job?'

'Every day, nearly. So long, then.'

When my guides had gone, I felt horribly alone, abandoned even. The shed was dark, muddy and stinking. My feet were deep in dung and I waited impatiently for someone to come and rescue me, my mind straying to foolish fancies that no one would turn up and I should be left here for ever to take root in this fertile seed-bed. The waiting was preying on my mind but my fears were without foundation. A sturdy form appeared outlined in the doorway, blotting out what little daylight there had been.

'Monsieur Fournier?'

'Yes,' I replied, used as I now was to this pseudonym.

'I am Philippe Allemann,' announced the newcomer, shaking hands with me. He was a very friendly lad, unlike the two guides who were very efficient but dour, and he had an attractive and reassuring appearance.

'Have you had a good journey, without any mishaps, that's the main thing?'

We went out of the shed and across the field. We took a twisting path down to a tarred road where a car was waiting for us. A youth at the wheel started up as soon as we jumped in. I told Philippe all about my stay in Switzerland and tried to get some grasp of the set-up. I learnt that I was on my way to his parents' house but as I was talking, I had no idea of the direction we had taken. The few place names I caught sight of conveyed nothing to me with the exception of our destination, Sochaux, with its pre-war reputation for professional football. It was an industrial region with a concentration of Peugeot factories. We were soon passing between imposing buildings and taking the road to Montbéliard, where we found ourselves going across a district that had been razed to the ground by recent bombing. For a distance of several hundred yards, the only buildings we saw standing were a battered cinema and three workmen's cottages, in front of one of which we stopped.

We went through the tiny front garden, round the back and in through the kitchen. A white-haired old lady was busy at the big coal cooker watching her pots from which issued a subtly appetising odour, particularly promising after the strain and effort of my journey.

Philippe introduced me to his mother, whom I found extremely kind. It was easy to see whence came his engaging smile. She was a wonderful mother and her cooking was not her least accomplishment. She provided an excellent meal during the course of which her son revealed to me something of the contribution that this remarkable family was making towards the cause of victory. The house was in effect a marshalling yard for numerous separate intelligence groups, a place where they could stay in safety between missions. It was also used by Allied airmen who had come down in occupied territory and those members of the escape lines who were conveying them to safety. There was always coming and going. Madame Allemann spent nearly all her time bending over the stove to produce food to satisfy ravenous young people snatching a brief respite between one dangerous escapade and another. Whereas some dropped in simply for a meal, others were needing rest as well, and then the lady of the house found room for them in a bed, or if need be, spread a mattress for them in some corner of a landing or passage, for here all were welcome. No one was ever turned away from this house, no matter how many there were and the inmates were one great family, single-

ght) Madame Allemann, Philippe's
her, on the right and, on the left, a
*nch*man who was a very active
ret agent known as The Penguin,
s Alfred Shorpp. He is seen here
*gu*ised as an old woman. He
ually pushed a dilapidated pram
l was often accompanied by a
ng girl of about twelve. He
ster-minded the blowing-up of
Peugeot Factory and one of the
n in his group was M. Peugeot
self. The reason was to avoid a
etition of an earlier disaster in
ch 1,800 civilians had been killed,
only one bomb had hit the factory
sing little damage. Madame
mann received the *Croix de
erre avec palme* and a citation
n General De Lattre de Tassigny
her two years' of sheltering agents,
groups run by Shorpp and
ther agent, helping them to
omplish their mission.

low) This is what remained of the
al café after the bombardment of
haux. Philippe's father can be
n near the centre of the
otograph leaning against a lorry
ch had been blown into the
ablishment.

With Philippe (on the left) and Liliane at the Swiss Frontier Stone.

minded in their aim to rid France of the invading vermin.

Next morning Philippe suggested getting some false papers made for me in a borrowed name, but since my wife and children were safely in England, out of the reach of the Gestapo, I could see no necessity for this. Moreover, a borrowed name would necessitate a cover story which I might not manage to sustain in the event of interrogation. If I were caught, I should prefer to masquerade as an escaped prisoner doing a bit of smuggling. I felt that this would involve me at worst in a comparatively short prison sentence and a deportation to Germany, a far preferable alternative to being tortured and shot. I stood out on this point and finally got Philippe to agree to getting false identity and ration cards made for me in my real name. He explained that they would serve a temporary purpose until I could get more authentic ones in Paris.

Then we discussed the next stage of my journey towards the capital and decided that I should take the night train from Montbéliard so as to arrive in Paris next morning, if all went according to plan.

'You can even go and see the revue,' added Philippe.

'The revue? Which revue?'

'The 14th July revue! Tomorrow is the National Fête day.'

For a few moments I failed to appreciate the irony of his words, only to realise that in the Champs Elysées I should see more swastikas than tricolours.

CHAPTER SIXTEEN

Birth of an Intelligence Group

It must have been in the early hours when the door of my compartment was thrown open.

'*Heil Hitler!* Your papers, *bitte!*'

Two civilians, accompanied by a military policeman wearing the chain of office of the Feldgendarmerie, were standing in the corridor. I offered them my false identity card and awaited their verdict with resignation. They held a consultation and thumbed the pages of a big black book[1]. Then one of the men turned to me.

'*Arbeit?* Where you work?' he demanded while we waited for the result of his colleagues' deliberations.

'In Paris.'

'Why travelling?'

'Family reasons.'

'I see. Right. Let's move on.'

The door slammed even more noisily than it had been thrown open. It was to be the only incident in the whole journey but it effectively dispelled all thoughts of sleep. I pondered for a long while on my movements on reaching Paris. For want of a better solution, I decided to visit my uncle and aunt at Passy.

They were, naturally, very pleased to see me again and all over lunch I recounted the story of my escape, taking good care to omit any reference to secret service work so as not to involve my aunt. I intended to get my uncle on his own before laying my cards on the table. I had selected him as my first confident, being well aware of his anti-German feelings. I did not expect much direct help from him but felt that his experience as an ex-officer might give me some ideas.

From the outset of our tête-à-tête, my uncle showed interest. He was with me from the first and promised to give me all the help he could. He told me that one of his best friends, a fellow POW from the 1914-18 war, used to belong to the French Deuxième Bureau, and

---

[1] Evidently my name did not figure in this book of 'wanted persons'. This was a further confirmation that there had been a mix-up in the German records.

offered to take me and introduce me to him. He assured me that he, more than anyone else, would be in a position to give me advice.

After thinking it over, I accepted the offer, realising that I must make a start somewhere and that this man might prove useful. I had also realised that it would be impossible to accomplish my task without certain risks. I therefore authorised my uncle to arrange for me to meet him, and then tackled the tricky subject of accommodation. He agreed to put me up for a few days until I could make other arrangements, but this could only be temporary on account of the fact that they were expecting their son to return very shortly.

The rest of the day I spent very pleasantly at their home and early next day, my uncle and I set off to meet his friend, the ex-member of the Deuxième Bureau.

I found that he lived in a large house on the Left Bank. He was a well known ENT specialist and, consequently, we did not find ourselves alone in his luxuriously furnished waiting room. When, eventually, we were shown into his consulting room I was surprised to find that his personal appearance was not in keeping with his impressive surroundings.

After an exchange of greetings, I embarked, straightway, on the matter in hand.

'My uncle has led me to understand that you used to belong to the French Deuxième Bureau?'

'Yes, I did once, but I have lost my contacts, which is a great pity.'

'Why?'

'Because I could supply some important information if only I could get in touch.'

This was the moment for me to reveal my purpose and endeavour to enlist this medico as a sub-agent.

'If you are prepared to pass on your information to me, I can guarantee that it will be transmitted to London.'

I was expecting an objection or an excuse but his reaction was just the reverse. The mysterious doctor fumbled in the bottom of a drawer only to produce a typewritten sheet which he handed over to me.

'Could this be of any use?' he enquired. 'It's the guestlist from the Ritz Hotel. It is compiled daily and a copy is slipped every day to me by a secretary who works at the office under German supervision.'

I glanced through the list of names and noticed that they were all high-ranking German officers, none below a colonel. Against each name was a number.

'What are these numbers?' I asked, trying to estimate the value of the lists.

'They are unimportant to us but they are the room numbers on account of which the lists have to be compiled. The Ritz Hotel is requisitioned entirely for the use of high-ranking Boche officers who are not stationed permanently. It is the only one of its kind.'

I grasped the significance of the information that was being proffered. All these generals, because they held commands or staff appointments, would be personally identifiable by our Intelligence and their presence in Paris ought to be a useful indication of the proximity of their troops.

'I find these lists very interesting. Do I understand that you can get hold of them every day?'

'Yes.'

'How long can you continue to do so?'

'So long as there is no hitch – and let's hope there will never be one.'

I felt it would be wise in the interest of my own security, in accordance with my instructions, to establish a 'safety valve' between this sub-agent and me. I had to take a decision on the spot, so I quickly worked out a plan to avoid picking up these lists myself.

'Would you enclose them daily in an envelope and address them to Monsieur Pierre Benoist at the Café Cyrano, Place d'Alésia, Paris 14?'

'Certainly, I shall be pleased to do so.'

Our business was finished but when I was ready to leave, I learnt something which disturbed me. This one-time intelligence agent had already had trouble with the Gestapo. The house had been surrounded and searched but, fortunately, with no consequences. Nevertheless, it might well be still under observation and in order to allay suspicion and the chance of being shadowed as I went out, I had to go into an adjoining room for the nurse to clap a big dressing on my left ear.

I left my uncle at the Metro station Notre Dame des Champs for he had to go off to his office in the centre of the city and I was on my way to Place d'Alésia so that I could arrange the letter-box for Monsieur Pierre Benoist with my pre-war friend Noel, the proprietor of the Brasserie Cyrano.

His establishment had lost some of its sparkle since the days when I used to visit it regularly, but I had not come here to steep myself in past memories and, in any case, there was no attraction now that the clientèle was so much changed. It was a delicate proposition that I had to put to my friend but Noel was an intelligent lad. He agreed at once to help me, without explanations or even asking why I was using a pseudonym. He seemed quite unperturbed when I added that the mail would be 'hot' and that he must never hand it to me in front of customers. I told him to leave the letters in full view on the cash desk so that I could see the address from a distance. Then, when the café was closed I would come along to the side door which was under cover, to collect them. I realised that I had easy access to this door as two friends of mine occupied a flat in this building.

Incidentally, I thought these friends might solve my second problem of where to stay, which would be ideal as I should then be on the spot to pick up my mail every day. I had the utmost confidence in these people. The husband, Roger, had been my closest friend before the war. We had played football together all over France and his wife, Suzanne, was often present with us.

She it was who opened the door and she was so delighted to see me that she burst into tears. Roger had not yet returned home from work but I was immediately invited to dine with them to celebrate my return.

Naturally, in the course of the meal, I had to tell them about life as a POW and the story of my three escapes. Eventually I came to the most delicate part of the business. Suzanne was most excited to learn that my war was not yet over, but Roger, although ready to stand by me like a brother, seemed more aware of the dangers involved. However, he had no hesitation in offering me his spare room for as long as I wanted.

Now that, thanks to them, I had found an ideal solution to my awkward housing problem, I was free to concentrate on extending the group which I had to build up. Before doing this, however, I went over in my mind the steps I had taken up to the present and wondered what would be the outcome if the secretary who supplied the lists from the Ritz Hotel were caught? I could just picture the very special methods of persuasion which would be employed and the consequences to the doctor and even to Monsieur Pierre Benoist! I realised that my 'safety valve' was not fool-proof and that I must be absolutely certain before picking up my mail that it had not been previously examined. I gave a lot of thought to this matter and evolved a means of control.

It seemed to me that there were two particular dangers both of which would result in the Gestapo taking an interest in my mail; the first that they might suspect me on account of my activities in general and the second that they might capture the secretary and, consequently, the doctor whom they might then force to write to me through the 'letter box' so as to pick me up at the time of delivery. This was the eventuality which I had to forestall.

On the next day, I paid another visit to the ENT consultant, for I needed his cooperation to put into effect my new security plan.

'Experienced as you are in intelligence work, you will understand, doctor, only too well that it is imperative to introduce all possible security checks. In order that I may be alerted in future in advance of any disaster here, this is what I would like you to do. Before you stick down any envelope addressed to Monsieur Pierre Benoist, I should like you to insert this narrow strip across the envelope's glue, which you can withdraw once it is sealed. Thus a check can be made on the unsealed patch in the glue before I pick up the letter. If you were ever forced to write to me under duress you would seal the envelope completely, thus immediately conveying that it was hot.'

When I had arranged this to my satisfaction with the doctor, I went off to see Noel at the Café Cyrano, to put him in the picture.

'I have got to take some additional precautions,' I explained to him as soon as I got him alone. 'My correspondent will never stick down the flaps of the envelopes completely. They will be unglued at one spot and so will the ones I intend to write to myself at the same address every day. You will know my handwriting and you'll soon recognise my agent's. Every day when you receive my mail, I want you to check up and make quite sure that the flap is incompletely sealed before displaying them on your cash-desk for me to see. If any envelope is completely sealed, I want you to warn me before you close up the café.'

I felt I had, by now, covered every loophole in the system and it only remained for me to find further sources of information.

Walking about in the centre of Paris gave me plenty of opportunity of taking note of German military vehicles and identifying them against the code but this I regarded as only 'small beer' and wondered how I could get on to something of greater significance.

After having established that the German HQ for the Paris Region was at the Place de l'Opéra, that the naval HQ for the Atlantic Fleet was at the Château de la Muette and the HQ of the Western Theatre of Operations was at the Château de St Germain, I was really no further forward as this was, obviously, common knowledge in Intelligence circles but, my fortnight being up, it was now time for me to make my way to Basle to present my first on-the-spot report.

I realised that my absence would constitute a particular problem; I should not be able personally to ensure the continuity of Monsieur Benoist's mail! I decided that Suzanne could provide the solution to this difficulty. From the beginning she had been itching to play a part in the group I was trying to form. I explained to her at length the details of my postal system, made her learn the forwarding address by heart and, above all, impressed on her the imperative necessity of taking precautions.

Thus having settled to my satisfaction the continuity of the Ritz Hotel lists, I set out one evening from the Gare de l'Est towards Montbéliard. During the course of the train journey, my identity card was subjected to another check, again successfully, and the rest of the trip to Franche–Conté was uneventful.

For two reasons, I decided to walk from the station to the Allemanns' residence; because I did not know if it was on a bus route or, if so, what stop to ask for. On the way, I passed a factory just as the workmen were going in. At the gate, there were some youths distributing pamphlets and I noticed that some of the workers read them and slipped them into their pockets. Others, who were unwise enough to throw away this Vichy propaganda, were immediately set upon by a band of ruffians, detailed to beat them up.

The house, when I came to it, was just as it had been a fortnight before. Early as it was, Madame Allemann was already installed over her saucepans and two young girls were seated at the big round table, the main piece of furniture in the little kitchen. They were dipping bread in their steaming bowls of coffee.

I introduced myself to these two comrades and learnt that one was called Liliane but I did not catch the other one's name as she was a very quiet type of girl and very softly spoken. Liliane, on the other hand, was most exuberant. From her accent, she could only be a Belgian.

Our conversation was trivial to begin with but we soon got round to the one topic which was of common interest to all those who foregathered in this stronghold of the special service. I soon learnt that Liliane, a pleasant looking girl, was a member of the Swiss Intelligence and that it was an open secret that this department was unreservedly pro the Allies. As I guessed, she worked the territory beyond the Quiévrain River which separates France from Belgium, whereas her reticient companion carried on her activities somewhere in Northern France.

As I looked at these two girls, I thought what little resemblance they bore to my ideas of a female spy which was based, no doubt, on the influence of the cinema; but Liliane had the effect of bringing me rudely back to reality by producing a revolver from her handbag, dismantling it and then cleaning it with the dexterity of a gunsmith.

Meanwhile, Philippe Allemann had come in saying he had had a good trip which I took to signify that he had been into Switzerland. He sat down by us and announced:

'All three of you will be crossing tomorrow at midday with my father.'

I had not realised that his father was a frontier guide and I was to learn that even his young brother of sixteen was working in France as a courier for the Intelligence Service. I was certain that, though this family was supported financially by various foreign agencies, their work was inspired essentially by their devotion to the Allied cause.

I liked the father very much when I met him next morning at breakfast. He was Philippe over again but an older and larger edition. His smile and mannerisms were those of his son but without something of his son's authority. At any rate, it was undoubtedly Philippe who organised the frontier crossings. It was he who issued revolvers and ammunition to all of us except Liliane who was already equipped.

'You will have to carry arms today,' he said, 'since the Germans may well repeat their ambush of yesterday.'

'Oh, so there was an ambush yesterday?' asked Liliane's young friend, suddenly finding her tongue.

'Yes, and we shed some feathers,' replied Philippe.

'Was anyone killed?' I asked.

'There were two dead or wounded. We're not sure yet.'

This was not reassuring for a tenderfoot like me, nor, apparently, to the quieter of the two girls. Liliane, on the other hand, was quite unperturbed and her comment was:

'All the better; it's a long time since I had an excuse for a pot-shot!'

At nine o'clock a car was waiting for us at the door. Philippe was getting agitated because the girls were dawdling in the kitchen quarters. 'Hurry up! You must be at the frontier by midday to have a hope of getting across without trouble.'

I was intrigued at this statement and tried during the course of the journey to find out from Old Man Allemann what Philippe had meant.

'Simply that the Fosse crossing, which you took a fortnight back, is better on the stroke of noon than at any other time.'

'Why noon exactly?'

'Because we have to slip between two sentries attached to different groups of guards. The change-over takes place at midday and the men right at the end of each line of guards have a natural tendency to walk towards their replacements one minute before time, thus leaving open a gap of about a hundred yards or so.'

The car did not deposit us at the exact spot where it had picked Philippe and me up a fortnight earlier, so I did not recognise the lie of the land. We took a forest path which sloped steeply upwards until we came to a fork in it where there was a sign-post bearing the following notice in German –

'BEWARE! Frontier zone. All entry forbidden on pain of death.'

I realised that we must be very close and was not surprised when Old Man Allemann announced that we must walk in silence in Indian File ten paces apart. I brought up the rear with Liliane ahead of me. I recognised the route and realised we were not far off the summit from which we would have to wend our way stealthily down towards the line of guards. Suddenly our column halted for what seemed nearly half an hour. I wondered all the time what was going on. From my own hiding place under the drooping boughs of a huge pine tree, I could see Liliane sitting in the long grass and she might well have been any girl out for a walk on a Sunday in the forest at St Germain. I admired her composure but felt she might have taken a bit more trouble to hide herself properly. As I watched her, I could not help remembering what Frank had said about women in face of danger: 'They're either scared of a mouse or else they are so fearless that they are b . . . foolish.'

In the end we were going forward by leaps of five or six yards at a time. Liliane turned towards me frequently to shake her head in disapproval of the crawling pace. Fifty yards out from the pine tree under which I had been lying, I saw what might have accounted for our delay; the remains of a smouldering fire round which were scattered fresh stubs of cigarettes and an empty German tin, proved that we were not the only ones in the neighbourhood.

Just afterwards, we came to the beginning of the long slope down towards the crucial point of our expedition and this part of the slope being less densely wooded, I could watch my three companions ahead as they moved cautiously forward from tree to tree. From the height, I had a view of stretches of the line of guards though none was actually visible. The colour of their field-grey uniforms certainly blended in very effectively with the bushes and boulders around them. I could see that Old Man Allemann was already right up close to the path, motionless behind a huge rock. He seemed to be listening but then I wondered if he was just waiting for zero hour. Looking at my watch I saw that it was just four minutes off noon.

Suddenly a German appeared on the path round the corner of the boulder behind which our guide was concealed. I knew now why he had frozen like a pointer. The German went on his way down the path and presently we could hear raucous voices in the ravine below. Allemann slipped round the rock and disappeared.

I watched the first girl follow suit, imitated in turn by Liliane. Then I came down to the rock myself. It was not a pleasant sensation to be bringing up the rear in this kind of enterprise but my ordeal was soon over; I was across the path without mishap and on my way up the steep rocky slope towards the frontier boundary.

As soon as we were on neutral soil, our guide took us to the nearest frontier post. He explained to us on the way, that this was to comply with an agreement with the Swiss Customs Department which stipulated that all special service agents should notify their crossing in this way. When we had fulfilled this formality, we took the bus to Porrentruy, all except Mr Allemann who, no doubt, was due to go back, to use a Swiss phrase, 'up to France'.

We found Sergeant Cartier having a drink at the bar of the Hôtel des Voyageurs. He had been notified of our crossing by radio and was waiting for us. He had even warned Basle of my arrival and made an appointment for me with Frank for the following morning.

I enjoyed the train journey much more than on the other occasions because the weather was so good. The countryside was no different but to breathe the free air of Switzerland gave me a greater sense of exultation after my sojourn in the depressing atmosphere of occupied France.

I was received with great enthusiasm at Basle, my lists of German officers being very much appreciated and it gave me a sense of considerable satisfaction to learn that they were considered by London as of top priority, which implied that they were transmitted daily in code before less important information.

'The radio link is only used for matters of top priority,' added Frank, to emphasise my initial success. We then talked about all the things I had seen in Paris. I answered his questions to the best of my ability and let him realise that I was at a loss to know what steps to take next. I had had a bit of luck over the lists but you could not expect that kind of strike every day. He reassured me and gave me a tip:

'One of our Paris agents told me, before the group was destroyed, that the underworld could provide a good source of information. I must warn you, however, that there are dangers in this. In the underworld, more than in any other section of the community, there is a large proportion of people working for the Germans and, those who do not, are not much good either. If you could worm your way in you might well be able to winkle something out but don't forget to get the measure of the men you are dealing with.'

I could not quite see how I could become a member of the underworld without having a criminal record, nor that anyone would take me for a gangster or a burglar. Neither, on the other hand, could I pass for a pimp or a ponce. However, I took notice of his advice and promised to investigate the possibilities.

Mr and Mrs Frank took me along to a brasserie that evening with some friends to celebrate my return and we had a game of bowls in the basement but, next day, I was on the move again. I went back to Porrentruy to await my marching orders. There, I managed to snatch a couple of days' holiday in the country before the portly form of the sergeant came on the scene.

'You will be leaving tonight at ten o'clock,' he announced over an apéritif.

'I thought the coast was only clear at noon?' I queried.

'You won't be crossing by the Fosse this time. Your route will be through Paradise,' he replied.

'Paradise?'

'Yes, Paradise is a farm just near the border at Boncourt.'

'Oh, I was beginning to wonder!'

Ignoring my cynicism, the sergeant went on giving the orders.

'You are to take the bus to Buix. Liliane will make the crossing with you, so there will be nothing for you to worry about. She knows the farm very well.'

I located her at dinner time and told her that I was very pleased to be crossing again in her company, not out of gallantry but because I had considerable admiration for the quality of cool courage which this girl had exhibited.

Our trip in an ill-lit bus was somewhat depressing. I could not help thinking that in France, in similar circumstances, the bus-load of passengers would have been animated to the point of rowdiness. A few tales would have been told in the darkness. There might have been some altercation to help pass the time away, but there, in Switzerland, all the passengers were silent and the night seemed steeped in gloom.

Fortunately, we did not have far to go and Liliane led me to a house just outside the village. There, we were welcomed by a family of four or five people who offered us coffee and liqueurs, during the course of which someone produced two packets which turned out to be the tobacco parcels, all ready for our rucksacks.

The approach to the farm was long and tortuous and I wondered how I could have managed to find it had I been on my own. When we reached the brow of the hill, Liliane stopped to point out a distant light.

'It's down there,' she said.

Ten minutes later we were making our way into the living-room of this ancient farm-house where we found several young people already installed round the table, partaking of packets of food. In one corner, sitting round a long table over a bottle of wine, several older people were having a quiet discussion. The floor was strewn with rucksacks and parcels as if it were a railway station waiting-room on market day. Obviously, we were going to attempt the crossing in considerable numbers that night and I wondered whether this were not imprudent. I calculated that unless it were an entirely different type of crossing from the Fosse, the whole enterprise would be sheer madness.

One lady who, judging by her grey hair and general appearance, was well over fifty, was continually darting about. She went from one to the other of the younger people there talking in an undertone. She did not leave us out, but came across to ask us how we were getting along. Liliane introduced me as one of her friends and carried on a friendly conversation with her.

'Do you know her?' I enquired as the old lady departed.

'Yes, she is the one who collects parties of Allied airmen who have evaded capture and have been escorted down through occupied territory by Resistance groups. Her job is to see that they negotiate safely the final stage, that of crossing the frontier into Switzerland.'

We spent a long time listening to snatches of conversation which held little interest for us and I was just going to ask Liliane why there was this delay, when the farmer stood up and addressed the assembled company which amounted to some fifteen people.

'If you ladies and gentlemen would like to get ready, we are going to put the lights out in five minutes' time.'

At this, there was a general reshuffle, everyone making sure of getting hold of his or her personal belongings. Then the farmer switched off the lights leaving us all standing in the dark. I wanted to know what was going on and asked Liliane in a low voice, 'Why have they put the lights out?'

'The farm is right on the frontier and in full view of the Germans. The farmer switches off downstairs and puts the lights in the bedrooms to make it look as if they are going to bed.'

We waited in the dark for what seemed to be an eternity, though from the luminous dial of my watch, I could see that it was only a quarter of an hour. Someone asked for absolute silence. Then the back door was opened and a draught of fresh night air soon dispersed the fumes of stale wine and tobacco from the atmosphere within. From the cover of the darkness, I could see the large form of the farmer outlined in the doorway. He stood stock–still for two or three minutes and then disappeared into the black night, followed by a long line of shadowy forms.

Our course lay across the farmyard and round the farm buildings. Then we went through an orchard, climbed over a gate and took a path along a hedge until we came to some barbed wire which, I realised, the farmer was holding back for us in the darkness.

'From now on you are in France. Good luck and a good journey to you!'

I had to hurry to keep in sight of the girl in front of me. We went down a slight slope across a field to some more barbed wire and on till we came to the edge of a wood. There, the front of the line was halted strategically to enable those of us in the rear to close up before penetrating into the even deeper darkness of the forest where visibility was, in fact, practically nil.

The old lady who had spoken to Liliane back at the farm, took advantage of this pause to pop back and have a word with us.

'Are you all right?' she asked, in a whisper. 'Don't be afraid, if we do come across any Boches, we'll soon finish them off.'

Then we went on walking without any mishap for two and a quarter hours, finishing up in another farmyard. There the farmer's wife, still half asleep, handed out bowls of steaming soup to all of us before we went off to spend the rest of the night in the cowshed. It seemed that there was a long passage strewn with straw to serve us as a communal bed. As all was in total darkness, no one could have accused me of engineering this, but I found myself installed between

Liliane and another girl. Nevertheless, it was not the choice position one might imagine, as I came to realise later on finding that a cow had her head wedged between two bars so that she kept dribbling on my face all night!

In spite of the stifling stench of a billy-goat tethered in one corner and the natural warmth of the herd of cows, the night was so fresh that we had to huddle together which would have been more to my taste in less anxious circumstances.

At day-break, we were very glad of the hot *café-au-lait* and bread and butter which the farmer's wife provided. Then we broke and dispersed, some of the party making for the nearest station and others, like Liliane and me, going off to the nearest bus stop.

Later that day, in front of the railway station at Belfort, my companion was saying goodbye to me when, taking me quite by surprise, she flung her arms round my neck and kissed me fervently. Although I was never one to resist such an invitation, this time my illusions were short-lived for my apparently amorous partner whispered in my ear, 'This is all for the benefit of the two Gestapo thugs who are watching us. Keep waving to me as you leave.'

We parted. She went towards the trains and I went diagonally across the station square towards the autobus station. I turned several times, as she had asked, to wave to her and, to my horror, the last time I realised she had been accosted by the two sinister-looking civilians.

I avoided the Sochaux bus, which I had intended to take, and plunged into the back streets, getting as far away from the station as possible. As I had plenty of time and taking the bus seemed risky, I walked the twelve kilometres to Sochaux without any incident and arrived at the Allemann house in time to partake of a good lunch.

I told Philippe what had happened at the station and my fears for Liliane's safety but he gave me some reassurance by saying:

'Don't worry about Liliane. She can take care of herself. She's no novice. I would go so far as to call her the smartest of all our agents.'

I hoped for her sake that it was as he said but the realisation that I might easily have been behind bars made me shudder.

CHAPTER SEVENTEEN

The Munition Factory

We finished what had been an excellent meal with coffee and kirsch and then discussed my return to Paris. On my first trip, I had had to take the night train, due in the early morning, to ensure having a day ahead of me in which to find somewhere to live, but this time I was able, on Philippe's advice, to take the 5 pm train due in before midnight.

'I must give you another tip, too,' he added. 'Never come straight here without first calling at the baker's.'

'Why at the baker's?'

'Come along with me and I'll show you.'

At the end of the street we went into a shabby little shop of a country-style master baker. He was a dark, portly little chap, wearing a floury beret and vest of wide mesh.

'Roger, this is Roland,' said Philippe as we shook hands.

'Roger is our radio operator,' he explained. 'He keeps his set stowed away behind his baker's oven.'

'Is he in contact with London?' I asked, in surprise.

'No, only Switzerland. He just announces the crossings so 'they' know who to expect. You must always call here first before coming to our house. If there is someone in the shop, ask for a cut *baguette*. Then Roger will cut the loaf up for you, either in two pieces or into three. If he cuts it in two, you will know that all is well at the house and you are safe to go there. But if he cuts it into three, it will mean that it's in your own interest to get the hell out of it!'

After this little interlude, when it was time again for me to depart, I gladly accepted Philippe's offer to come with me as far as the station at Montbéliard. On the way, he memorised my Paris address so that he could get in touch with me in case of an emergency.

In accordance with the usual routine, there was a Gestapo check on the course of the journey to Paris, with no ill effects so far as I was concerned, in spite of the traditional big black book. My arrival at the Gare de l'Est was heralded by an air-raid warning but fortunately, it did not last long. The Metro soon disgorged its complement of sheltering *souris grises*[1] and *Feldgrauen*[2] and resumed normal services.

Before going up to my friend's flat, I called at the brasserie where I learnt, to my satisfaction, that Monsieur Pierre Benoist (alias Suzanne) had received his mail regularly during my absence.

Next morning, I woke up early and lay thinking about various aspects of the problems inherent in my assignment. The previous night's air-raid had reminded me that in cases of aerial bombardment in my region, I was expected to make a report on all incidents. To enable me to do this, I had to have a bicycle and decided to buy one that very day. I then pondered over what my chief had said about the underworld being a fruitful source of information, and realised that I had yet to find a means to penetrate it. I thought it would be a sound idea to probe around the Montmartre area and determined to start visiting the bars and night-clubs on the night of the following day.

During the day, I paid a visit to some first cousins of mine to thank them for the efforts they had made early in my captivity to obtain my release, unfortunately without success. I learnt, incidentally, that the husband was now employed by a very large engineering firm well known before the war for its electric motors, cookers, refrigerators etc.

'Now, I suppose you must be working for the Germans?'

'Yes, but on very different products.'

'No more cookers now, then?'

'No . . . shells,' he answered.

A hound on a fresh scent could not have been more on the alert than I was, but I contrived to hide my interest.

'You are working in the provinces, then?' I queried, hoping to draw him out.

'No, I'm not actually at the factory. I'm with the Head Office in Paris.'

'What's your job?'

'I'm in charge of the welfare services,' he replied.

This all seemed most interesting. I felt I had to know more about this famous shell factory. My first idea was to find some way of getting into the company's head office in Paris. I had no particular plan in mind but, following intuition, I asked him for the address and

[1] Grey Mice as the German girls in the services were popularly called.

[2] Feldgrau was the name by which the German soldiers were known – because of their grey uniforms.

The Crow and his brother Pierre passing frontier stone 455 in the Combe Semone Ravine at Charmesol.

The Crow, Liliane and myself.

Three cheers! The Crow, Liliane and I reach safety after a perilous passage. We never carried revolvers unless we were forewarned to expect trouble.

if I might call and see him at his office when I had the opportunity.

He agreed, but conventionally, I should have waited a week or two before taking up this invitation. However, scenting a particularly good trail, I strained the leash of etiquette and called at the office in a couple of days' time.

As an executive, my cousin had his own private office, which suited my purpose as I had decided, if necessary, I would take him into my confidence. I soon learnt the locality and even the exact position of the factory which was nearly a hundred miles south of Paris but there was one serious obstacle from my point of view.

'The factory is completely hidden by the trees of the surrounding forest so that it is quite invisible from the air,' explained my cousin, as if he could read my thoughts. Whether this was an artless or a deliberate revelation on his part, I felt that the die was cast and that now, there was no turning back.

'I'm pretty sure I'm right in judging that you deplore the important contribution that your factory is making or having to make towards the success of France's hereditary enemy,' I parried.

'I certainly do deplore it.'

'Then would you be prepared to help me to turn the tables on this state of affairs?'

'Yes, I would.'

'I shall need a detailed plan of that factory.'

I was well aware that I had waded right in and my cousin was looking most embarrassed, frowning and biting his lips. It would not have surprised me at all had he refused to pursue the conversation further, but my fears were groundless, as his next words showed:

'There's only one really detailed plan and that's in the managing director's office safe. I have access to it but I can't possibly take it on the quiet as I have to sign a receipt for it. I could let you have a look at it but would have to return it almost immediately.'

'That's fair enough but I think we could do even better,' I commented. 'I will come and see you again in a few days' time – I'll let you know the exact date – and I should like you to have that plan available on your desk.'

We agreed to this arrangement and we parted after exchanging a few words on the political situation. The reason why I had fixed the visit for a few days ahead, was because I intended to photograph the plan and, for this, I needed Frank's assistance. He had once shown me a minute camera designed to photograph documents on micro-film which could then be readily concealed and had told me that if I ever needed it, he would lend it to me. I decided forthwith to ask him for it and so as not to waste time, I straight away went to the nearest post office. There, I wrote him my request briefly on a leaf torn from my note book, without giving any explanation. I slipped it into a ready stamped envelope and, carrying out my instructions, refrained from adding the secret address until I was about to pop it into the letter box.

Three days had gone by without any progress from my various peregrinations when, on returning to my friends' flat, I found Suzanne waiting for me on the landing.

'Someone's waiting for you in the salon,' she whispered.

'What's he like?'

'Very young, fair and quite good-looking but, my goodness, you can't call him chatty! He has been sitting there for two solid hours without uttering a word in spite of all my efforts to get friendly.'

My first reaction was one of suspicion, but then I remembered my request for the camera and realised that this must be the courier who was bringing it to me. Nevertheless, I had to be cautious. The courier could have been intercepted and the final stage arranged by the Gestapo. I asked Suzanne to make some pretext to go into the salon and to leave the door ajar so that I could get a good look at our visitor without being seen. My precautions were superfluous for it was Philippe's young brother. There could be no mistaking the remarkable likeness.

'Hello, I'm Roland Fournier.'

'And I'm Marcel Allemann. I have a little package for you.'

The micro-film camera was a little gem, so tiny that I could palm it like a conjurer.

Having warned him in advance by telephone, I went to my cousin's office next day. I found him more at ease than previously and he went straight off to the manager's office to get hold of the plan of the factory.

'Here it is,' he announced on his return.

'Well done!' I complimented him. 'Now, all you need do is to leave me alone for a few minutes. You go off to the toilets and leave me to get on with my photography.'

As soon as I was alone, I spread the document out on his desk and took photographs of different sections of it. There was a risk of someone walking in while I was carrying out this operation but, nothing venture, nothing gain. All went well and when my cousin returned from his little excursion, all he had to do was to restore the plan where it belonged. I, on the other hand, went off towards the Champs Elysées to mingle with the motley crowd dotted with green and grey uniforms.

As I was almost due to make another trip to Switzerland, I decided to take back the micro-film camera myself and have the pleasure of seeing the effect that the document created. In the meantime, my efforts to penetrate into the underworld had had little success. So far, I had only managed to meet the small fry in the night-clubs round the Moulin Rouge and Pigalle. They were only small beer and no use to me at all. I had to get after the big noises but they make a point of keeping quiet. No doubt the police were aware of their hide-outs but I had no idea and despaired of making any progress in this direction in spite of all Frank's suggestions.

One evening, when I was near Place Clichy, I remembered that I was not far from the home of Lucien Tarsitano's parents. He had been a very good friend to me during our captivity and I decided to look them up to give them news of their son and thank his mother for the very much appreciated parcels which she had sent so regularly.

I found them in very humble circumstances, reduced by his mother's ill health. The father, who was of Italian origin, was like all his self-respecting compatriots, in the building trade. Unfortunately for him at this juncture, there was more demolition than building going on and plasterers' jobs were particularly scarce; all the more so when any of them, as he did, refused categorically to work for the Germans. This was why Victor Tarsitano had to content himself with whatever small commissions were offered to him by a bookmaker operating clandestinely in opposition to the official Tote. His work was in the *pesage* which is the French equivalent to Tattersals, and consisted of both collecting bets from his personal customers and of laying off money on the Tote, as and when his boss demanded. He suggested that I should come and see him at work one day and he offered me a 'cert' by way of encouragement.

This Victor Tarsitano was very like his son Lucien, so nothing could have been more natural than that I should have felt friendly towards him. I accepted his invitation gladly, all the more so because I felt like a break from my special work for a few hours, and also of steeping myself in an illusion of pre-war atmosphere. But, even at Maisons Laffitte, the leprous *Feldgrau* infected the normal colourful tableau of bustling racegoers. I could not help wondering what proportion of that pleasure-going crowd were working either directly or indirectly for the enemy, while our brother allies were fighting on all fronts and the rubble of what had been the French Army was left to rot in the prisons of their oppressors.

Victor introduced me to some of his racing friends and also to his employer, the bookmaker, who, in turn, introduced me to his girl-friend with whom I spent quite a lot of time that afternoon. She was a pretty little tart with a provocative figure, as light in her conversation as in her morals, judging by the ease with which she led the conversation into suggestive channels.

'Shall we be dining together this evening, then?' she persisted.

'I should be pleased but I wouldn't know where to take you.'

'Never mind about that. I'll show you a little place in Montmartre that's absolutely first-rate, where all the big noises go.'

'The big noises?' I murmured with the scent of game in my nostrils.

'Yeah, the big noises, you know, the barons of the underworld, the gang leaders.'

Now I had taken the point and realised that this was no time for hesitation.

'All right, I'll see you at eight o'clock at the Balto, near the Gaumont Palace.'

A little later on, I managed to get Victor on one side between two of his trips to the Tote, to tell him about my date and ask him what he thought about the girl.

'She's a little bag,' he told me, 'and very greedy but, if you are out for a bit, you couldn't do better. Corsicans are hot stuff, you know. She used to go with one of the big boys, a fellow named Lulu Lippe because of his scarred mouth.'

I really felt that I had killed two birds with one stone, (and what a bird!) so I was doubly afraid of being stood up as I was waiting for her at the appointed time at the Balto Café. However, she did not keep me waiting long. She jumped out of a 'cyclo-taxi' only a quarter of an hour late and we had a drink before going off to her restaurant.

We were very quickly on Christian-name terms. She told me her name was Renée and that she was the mistress of Louis the bookmaker.

We made our way to the restaurant through the back streets. It was a drab looking place but its gastronomic qualities were remarkable, particularly in view of current shortages and rationing. Renée introduced me to the proprietor.

'Here is the *patron*, Louis le Mexican, a good friend of mine. Meet Roland!'

'Roland who?' he asked.

'Roland Potier,' I said, spontaneously appropriating the name of my pre-war partner.

'Don't know him,' he disclaimed, as if he might have expected to know everyone.

To draw her out about this tough and obviously suspicious Mexican, I took advantage of his preoccupation with some new customers to comment to Renée on his strange form of address.

'Don't know him!' I repeated. 'Indeed, why should he expect to know me?'

'Because everyone knows everybody else, in the underworld, and he knows you aren't one of them.'

This was only too true but little did Renée know how eager I was to graduate! At least I felt I was now on the right road, so long as I played a careful game and ensured that this little friend of mine did not suspect me of other than amorous intentions.

'Why "the Mexican",' I asked between the bites. 'Is he from Central America?'

'No, he's no more Mexican than you are. He got his nickname because at one time, in Mexico, he was commissioned to lay on a banquet for six hundred guests in honour of the French Ambassador. He ordered the lot, food, wines, cigars, decorations, garlands, flags, head-waiters etc. It was a fine do. All the guests went off pleased as Punch while he went off with the caterers' dibs!'

'Jolly smart,' I said with a laugh. 'He's a bright boy all right. Some of these chaps take some beating.'

I was deliberately playing up to her obvious approval of these sharp practices, which I could detect in the saucy flashing of her dark eyes. Psychologically, I must have been on the right track, for she responded at once by saying, 'I'll take you into the Bar des Sports for coffee. The Mexican's small fry against the chaps that go there, Jacques Grandes Dents, for instance.'

'Why "Big Teeth"?'

'Because when he had to be fitted for false teeth, his horse must have opened its mouth!' she explained. 'Then there's "Counterfeit Joe".'

'Why "counterfeit"?'

'Because he makes better five-pound notes than the Bank of England. And there's Joe Polish.'

'A Pole, or just shoe-polish?'

'Shoe-polish. He planned to pinch a lorry-load of ball-bearings worth a fortune, but finished up with a load of a hundred thousand boxes of boot-polish.'

I could not help laughing at this anecdote but there was more to come.

'You'll think they're all called Joe in the Underworld but it is a coincidence. Up to yesterday, there was Joe the American too, but he got bumped off as he stepped out of the bar.'

'By the Germans?' I asked.

'Oh no, he used to work for them. I should think someone was paying off an old score.'

By this time I felt quite certain I was on the right track. This lucky introduction on the race-course would probably enable me to achieve what had appeared impossible, an entry into the underworld circles; but I was well aware that there was all the difference in the world between getting to know them and being really accepted by the "big noises" and their henchmen.

After an excellent meal, true to her word, Renée took me along to her Bar des Sports, which turned out to be no ordinary café. The furnishings and fittings were flashy in the extreme and so was the female clientèle, but the men were commonplace enough. The uneasy hush which greeted my entrance left me in no doubt that I was regarded as an intruder. Renée must have noticed it too for no sooner had she perched herself on one of the high stools at the bar, than she introduced me to the man on her right.

'Here, Pierrot, this is my friend Roland.'

'Hello,' came the surly acknowledgement.

'And this is Louis.'

'Pleased to meet you,' said Louis, giving me a warm handshake.

Pierrot seemed less anxious to know me but this man, Louis, was more affable, more sociable and probably more dangerous!

I asked Renée, on the quiet, if these were really some of the big noises.

'Oh yes, of course, Pierrot is "Pierrot the Cop". He is nicknamed "Cop" because he once dressed up in police uniform and went right into the nick to pinch a piece of incriminating evidence. Louis's quite different. He's a lone wolf. An artist in his work. They call him Louis Scales because he limps so badly that he bobs up and down like a pair of old fashioned scales.'

We stayed for a long time in this interesting establishment, which enabled me to recognise various other personalities, among them one Pierrot Pastis and a Momo the Mohican who surely must have been the last of something or other.

When we left the bar, I was careful to notice the address with a view to returning there regularly. Renée, little though she knew it, had sown the seed for me but, if it was to bear fruit, it was up to me to cultivate the soil.

The very next day, I started dropping in regularly, in spite of Victor Tarsitano's frequent warnings that one day I should end up with a 'second belly button'.

He was right enough that, dealing with a crowd like this, I had to watch my step very carefully, but he could not appreciate my motives. Up till this time, my luck had held and I trusted that it would continue to do so as I took the train one bright morning at the Gare de l'Est.

CHAPTER EIGHTEEN

The Smuggler

There were no Gestapo hitches on this journey to the Franches Contés but sabotage on the railway line near Romilly caused considerable delay. It was late that evening when the train pulled into Belfort Station. As soon as I had given up my ticket, I found myself passing between two individuals who could only be the Gestapo.

I walked across the station square to a café and, not daring to look round, went inside. There were no customers, so I was able to order straight away a coffee and liqueur and then took a peep over the curtains in the direction from which I had come. The two suspicious characters had followed me and were only about fifteen yards off. Without a moment's hesitation, I made straight for the toilet, but, coming upon another door marked 'private'. I took a chance, opened it and found myself in the big kitchen. Two women were peeling vegetables at a table in the middle but I scarcely noticed them, so intent was I to find a possible exit. This presented itself in the form of an outside door with a transom above it. Though I did not stop to study the two women, I could feel their astounded eyes following me as I darted round the table and, in less time than it takes to tell it, was out in the cobbled yard. Providentially, there was an archway leading into a side street and I was able to make myself scarce in the back streets and alleyways. I never found out whether the two blackguards had a long wait outside the toilet or whether they settled my bill!

My first precaution on arrival at Sochaux was to go to the baker's, as arranged. There were no customers in the shop at that late hour, so there was no need to ask to have my loaf cut up. I found out all was clear at the house and that Philippe was at home. Before I left, Roger, the baker, asked me when I proposed to cross the frontier.

'Tomorrow at noon, I expect.'

'All right, I'll notify them, then. You'll probably be going with Philippe. Goodnight.'

'Goodnight to you.'

When I reached the well remembered kitchen, the scene was just as usual, except that there were many more inmates and Madame Allemann was busier than ever, if that could be. However, she found time to greet me with a gracious smile. Philippe too, gave me a very friendly welcome and was not at all surprised that I had had trouble in Belfort. He advised me to give that 'sticky joint' a miss.

This comment made me think of Liliane and her trouble at the same spot. I asked Philippe what had become of her. He confirmed my worst fears that she had been arrested and could tell me that she had been stripped of all her clothes and interrogated at the Gestapo headquarters. She had then been transferred to the Feldgendarmerie to be locked up pending further interrogation but the officer in charge, not wishing to lose such an opportunity, announced to her unequivocally:

'You'll spend tonight with me.'

Naturally, Liliane did not agree but she had to choose between this alternative and one even less attractive.

'If Mademoiselle does not like sleeping with an officer, I could arrange to turn her over to my men. I'm sure they would enjoy taking turns to have a French bitch!'

She had to make a choice but the wily Liliane already had a plan. She played up to the officer, how far no one will ever know, but, at the first opportunity, she slipped away into the streets of Belfort in her homespun nightdress, covered a couple of dozen kilometres barefoot and crossed the frontier near Delle.

'The Swiss guard who arrested her had to carry her on his back to the nearest police station, so exhausted was she. Liliane is now in Porrentruy Hospital,' Philippe informed me.

We all spent the rest of the evening discussing happier topics and not only in French, for there were five American airmen present, all crew of the same Flying Fortress which had been brought down in flames. Only one of the five showed any traces of his parachute jump – he had lost most of his teeth. He took all the leg-pulling of his companions with stoicism, very thankful to have got off so lightly. So far as I could understand, his parachute had split open in two and failed altogether to break his fall. Another of them had landed in a tree in the middle of the night and had waited till dawn, clinging in desperation to a branch. When, at last, it was light enough to see, he realised that he had spent the night six feet above the ground!

Next morning there was such a queue waiting to shave in the wash-house that it might have been the ablution room of a barracks.

We let the Americans take first turn as they had to leave early to make their way to Le Russey where they were due to join another guide. The house was very soon cleared of most of its temporary occupants who had already crossed the frontier from Switzerland and were on their way to their various assignments in France or Belgium.

Philippe came and asked if I was ready.

'We're leaving a bit earlier because I want to go via Pont de Roide so that I can point out to you the house of a guide commonly known as "The Crow".'

We travelled on a bus which was very overcrowded on account of some neighbouring market day.

'All the better,' said Philippe, reassuringly. 'When it's as crowded as this, the Gestapo won't bother with controls.'

We got off at Pont de Roide, a pleasant town on the banks of the Doubs, crossed an ancient bridge and found ourselves on a council house estate. The Crow's house was one of a kind with all the rest and Philippe instructed me to make a point of memorising its position so that I could return there alone if ever the need arose.

The Crow was not at home and his brother, another guide, was away with him in Switzerland.

'I'm not at all surprised,' commented Philippe. 'They go across every day with the mail. They're the ones who have the job of conveying the messages from all different intelligence groups to Switzerland. They have a most hazardous occupation. It would he hard to find one more so because they are continually at it, but then, they're professionals in their field. They used to be smugglers.'

We made our way up wooded slopes towards the green hills of Villars. At the highest point we passed close to the disused fort of Lomont and I soon recognised that we were on the familiar track towards the Fosse. A glance at my watch showed me that we had only a quarter of an hour in which to reach the German sentry-beat.

We made the approach correctly, ten paces apart, and got across our obstacle without any hitch. Barely a hundred yards after the frontier stone, we found ourselves confronted by a Swiss guard who, covering with his rifle, escorted us triumphantly to the nearest frontier post, but he was somewhat disconcerted when his commanding officer greeted us with the words:

'Good morning, Philippe. Good morning, Monsieur Fournier, how are things in Paris?'

I made no comment in front of the officer but on the way to

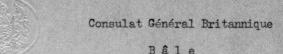

Consulat Général Britannique

B â l e

le 21 février 1946.

Je, soussigné, Leonard A. FRENKEN, Vice-Consul à Bâle,

certifie que Roland RIEUL, 4 rue du Commerce, Paris, a

participé efficacement à la victoire des Alliées à qui

il a rendu de fidèles et appréciables services au risque

constant de sa vie.

Vice-Consul.

My testimonial from Frank

Porrentruy I protested to Philippe that I was most astonished to realise that my location was known to a customs official, even though an officer. I felt there had been indiscretion and insisted that Philippe should thrash the matter out with the appropriate authorities.

That afternoon I went to the hospital in Porrentruy to visit Liliane. I found her still suffering from shock and not yet completely recovered from her strenuous ordeal. The sister advised me to keep my visit brief so as not to overtire her but I was there long enough to get general confirmation of the account which Philippe had given me.

At Basle my microfilm of the munition factory was much appreciated. Moreover, I learnt that there had been a further aerial attack on Stuttgart and that this, apparently due to the plans I had submitted, had three parts destroyed the aircraft factory.

This news I found particularly acceptable as I felt I had made an important contribution to the war effort. At last I was giving back knock for knock, instead of always being on the receiving end.

Furthermore, Frank made no secret of how pleased he was about my work in Paris. He did not know and I took good care not to enlighten him, that in all three cases, the officers' hotel lists, the microfilm and my contact with the *Milieu* (French underworld) were all achieved by chance. But luck or no luck, up till now I had given satisfaction and I was beginning to feel more self confident than at the start.

At the outset of my interview with Frank we discussed at some length my effort to get into touch with the ringleaders of the *Milieu*. We arranged that I should take back with me an assortment of gold watches and try to establish myself with them as a watch smuggler.

And so it came about that when I left Porrentruy two days later, I had in my possession a small but very valuable parcel. It was a relief to me that this time there were to be only two of us, Philippe and myself. I was not so pleased to hear that we would be travelling by way of Paradise Farm but my friend reassured me that we should be making the crossing alone.

We arrived at the farm rather early, so whiled away the time by eating scrambled eggs and Swiss cheese. When it was quite dark, we hitched on our haversacks, made our farewells to the assembled company and went through the orchards at the back of the house.

Philippe knew the track well and we made very good progress. Against the starlit sky, I could make out the edge of the forest which the long line of agents had followed on the last occasion. When Philippe paused for a moment, I went on ahead into the impenetrable darkness of the surrounding forest.

Suddenly, there was a blinding flash and an ear-splitting report as a shot was fired at me literally at point-blank range and I felt a sharp pain in my left eye. Instinctively, I flung myself down and an answering shot rang out from Philippe in the background who was firing over me. Following suit and aiming at random towards the spot where I had seen the flash, I emptied my revolver into the darkness.

Immediately ahead there was no sound or movement but while my last shot was still echoing, the whole frontier came to life. Dogs started to bark all over the place and lights were flashing but Philippe was already tugging me away by the wrist towards the left of our course.

Crouching down and taking long strides, we made ourselves scarce, skirting the forest laterally for about a hundred yards. Then, all at once, Philippe dragged me straight into the undergrowth.

We made the best speed possible, barging into tree trunks, tearing ourselves through the brambles and tripping over unseen obstacles but gradually getting further and further away from the danger spot. Eventually, we stumbled on to a path carpeted with pine needles which enabled us to proceed much more quickly and silently. We could still hear shouts in the distance but they grew fainter as we went on.

When we had been travelling for about half an hour, my companion halted and told me to stay exactly where I was and to wait for him. He was gone for what seemed an eternity for I was now aware that my left eye was closed and I was in considerable pain. I did not know what had hit me but it certainly was not the bullet. My clothes smelt strongly of gunpowder which showed what a near miss it had been.

Philippe returned as we set off again. When I asked where he had been, he said: 'You'll see.'

'Whatever it is I shall only see half of it because I've only got one eye!'

Till then, Philippe had been unaware of my injury and he was most concerned about it and tried then and there to examine it in spite of the darkness.

'I can't see anything,' he said.

'Nor can I, as far as that goes!'

However, we went on our way and soon passed in front of a sentry box.

'Don't worry,' said Philippe as he saw me hesitate. 'That's why I left you just now, to make sure it was empty.'

Finally, we made our way down a rough rocky path to a small village where my guide took me to some friends of his. They were all in bed at this late hour and we had to bang on their windows to get them to open up.

Our host, still half asleep, gave Philippe a welcoming smile and shook hands with me enthusiastically. He heated up coffee for us and gave us a cognac each to put new life into us while his wife attended to my eye and put a dressing on it.[1]

We did not spend long there, however, as we were still a long way from Sochaux, but in due course, we reached our goal, weary but with a sense of satisfaction that we had got the better of a difficult situation.

We were not the only members of the company at Sochaux to have had a brush with the Germans that day. We learnt that Father Allemann was in bed with a bullet wound in his hand from a frontier incident. We paid him a visit to get a first-hand account of his story.

'I ran into a patrol. I didn't see it till too late and they began to chase me. I could have outdistanced them except for their dogs. As I passed the Devils Well, a small pool concealed by a dense thicket, I took a header into it and guessing that they would spray the pool with bullets, I hauled myself up into the cover of the overhanging roots. The dogs, urged on by their masters, nevertheless refused to go down into the black waters, so the Germans changed their tactics and fired their tommy-guns at random into the thicket. They moved off leaving me for dead but they were unlucky except for this one ricochet and the fact that they had smothered my mug with mud.'

In our turn, we explained why I appeared with my eye in a bandage and we all agreed that it might have been worse.

Once back in Paris, I enjoyed a good night's sleep at Place d'Alésia before resuming my secret duties. My first action was to pay a visit to the Bar des Sports where I ran into Louis 'Scales'. In an effort to appear one of themselves, I made a point of using their

---

[1] I learnt later that this man was the Post Office worker who extracted the secret letters sent in by all agents from the general mail. Just before the Liberation the Germans found out that this village was being used as a clearing house but could not identify the culprit. Pressed as they were for time by the rapid advance of General Delattre de Tassigny, they shot every male in the village.

jargon whenever possible, I explained away my 'pied peeper' attributing the damage to customs officers. When I came to the point of offering Louis and the *patron* a drink, I felt the time had come to produce surreptitiously from its cache a little gold watch.

'What about one of these for your bird?' I suggested. 'Dirt cheap at two thousand francs.'

Louis cast a cautious eye round the customers present and then examined it minutely, opening the back to have a look at the works. Then, with the assurance of a connoisseur, he announced:

'Not at all bad! Eighteen carat and jewel mounted. If I find a buyer for you, is there a cut for me?'

'If you like,' I replied, only too pleased to do business with him, even at the expense of losing ten quid.

'Right,' he said, 'I'll keep it. When shall I see you?'

'Tomorrow, I expect.'

A game of rummy was being organised and Louis was to be one of the players. They still needed a fifth and I agreed to participate, fully aware that I should need four pairs of eyes if I wasn't to lose my shirt. I calculated that I must expect to pay the price to gain the confidence of the clients of this exclusive establishment.

Nevertheless, the game did not prove too expensive, in spite of the persistence with which my neighbour on the left, known as the 'Chemist', kept popping Jolly Jokers into his pocket and pulling them out again. I nonchalantly passed round my American cigarettes, with the effect I had anticipated.

'American cigarettes! How d'you get hold of these?'

I put on a knowing air and said nothing but Louis 'Scales', quick to take up the connection between watches and the cigarettes, gave the explanation for me.

'It's his line.'

This tab reminded me that I had read somewhere that in the Paris underworld, every one was known by his particular racket and I felt confident now, that Louis would lose no time in circulating mine. News travels fast in such circles as these and in one week, with three or four games of rummy and some twenty pounds on my expenses account, I had become known as 'Roland Contraband' – a very interesting fellow to those appreciating Virginia tobacco and the darling of the girls whose morals were so light that only the weight of their shoes kept them on the ground.

Right from the start of my association with the *Milieu*, I overheard a few interesting bits of gossip about working with the Gestapo.

Once the information was so precise that I managed to warn a police station in a Parisian suburb that it was due for a raid. This was to be carried out in order that the Gestapo might seize a clandestine arms store and effect arrests. I learnt later that my telephone call triggered off prompt action and that the raid was a failure.

Of all these new acquaintants, it was with Louis 'Scales' that I most often had a drink. Although I thought that he was probably more crooked than the others, his Mediterranean wit and dialect kept me amused and he was much too discreet to embarrass me with questions. Moreover, we had a common interest – opera and *bel canto* – and so it came about that Louis introduced me to one of his lady friends (or acquaintances) who had popped in for a 'quick one' at the Bar des Sports.

She was a woman of ripe age who, throughout the course of her career as a musical comedy star, had skilfully contrived to keep youthfulness of complexion and attractiveness. At this stage, Madame Denay had to content herself with the modest earnings of a singing teacher.

During the course of our conversation, which was naturally focussed on our common interest, I learnt that one of her pupils had a voice of quite exceptional quality and I accepted an invitation to be present at her lesson next day, to hear for myself.

She turned out to be a pretty girl of twenty-three who certainly had a beautiful voice with quite exceptional top notes. Her name was Pierrette Giraut. Was it really her voice or was it perhaps her physical attraction which made me hope that I should be able to follow the professional development of this outstanding pupil?

My wishes were soon fulfilled for Madame Denay recommended a little restaurant to me and I made a point of lunching there as often as possible and usually in the company of this lady and her protégée. Sometimes, Madame Denay could not manage to be present and this gave me a chance to get to know her pupil better and to realise that we had a great deal in common, the hate of the Germans to say the least, the outcome of which being that she became the latest recruit in my group.

I had felt the need of a courier for some time and for this kind of work, Pierrette had the advantage of having no family ties and thus being foot-loose. I also felt that, as a woman, she would be better able to conceal secret documents.

I was soon able to put my new recruit to work to good effect for, thanks to a man named Paulo with whom I had got into conversation at the Bar des Sports, I hit on another source of information. I learnt that Paulo's mistress was an ex-prostitute. He told me so himself, for it was quite the thing in these circles to be 'hitched up' with a whore. Louis the Mexican himself, respectable hotelier as he now was, made no secret of the fact that he had married a woman from the Panier Fleuri, an establishment whose commercial slogan at that time was 'Five Francs including the towel'. I was not interested in Paulo's mistress' past profession but rather in what she was accomplishing at present for the Germans. She was employed at the German Central Military Bakery. I thought how interesting it would be to know the production statistics as a guide to estimating the strength of the enemy. The arrival or departure of a division would surely make itself felt in the new provisions.

Possibly, probably even, this woman would be unable to be of any help but I had a hunch that it would be worthwhile pursuing the idea. Meanwhile, before embarking on it, I needed time to think it over and contented myself with sounding out Paulo's political views. I made a point of criticising the actions of the British on all counts but my listener's reponse was a look of disapproval. He even found ingenious excuses which led me to feel that, although I should have to proceed warily, this shady customer was, nevertheless, of a different kidney from most of his fraternity. This was my first impression, but I could not depend on this alone. Before stepping on such dangerous ground, I had to be absolutely certain that I had not hit a nark.

Leaning towards him, I said in an undertone, 'I'm on a job but I need a partner.'

'It all depends what it is.'

'I know a Jew-boy who is well loaded and who would think nothing of parting with a packet to get safe custody into Free France.'

'That's very interesting but what do you expect me to do about it? I don't know any escape routes but what about you with your smuggling?'

'My way would be out of the question. You have to swim for it and he's an old man. But I thought perhaps you, with all your friends . . .'

'You mean with the Jerries, don't you?'

'Well, yes,' I admitted, tentatively.

'Well, in the first place, they're no friends of mine. I'll be b . . . if they ever will be.'

By talking in this vein to me, I felt that he had plunged in head first. For all he knew, I might have been an informer. Had he been in the pay of the Germans, I reasoned, he would have accepted my proposition and invented an escape route to ensure that I would produce my Jew. He would then only have to pocket the cash and get me and my client arrested.

By refusing the tempting offer, he convinced me that he was genuinely pro the Allies, unless of course he was a particularly subtle German spy but this I could not believe; his speech, mannerisms and appearance, all seemed to suggest the successful petty crook and ponce. However, there was far too much at stake for me to be guided only by an impression. I felt that I must find out more about this man before I got involved with him.

I had a scheme in mind which necessitated my knowing Paulo's surname. Of course, I could not ask him directly or he would have taken me for a 'rozzer'. On the other hand, none of his circle was likely to know it because in the underworld, nicknames are found to be both convenient and colourful. I decided I must have time to think and not pursue the subject more deeply for the time being.

'All right, mate, I'm sorry I mentioned it. I just thought you might know the right guys for getting dud papers.'

'What made you think that?'

'Well, you told me your "wife" worked for the Jerries, so I thought perhaps . . .'

'You've got plenty of imagination, mate, but you're quite on the wrong track.'

I did not press the matter further but soon left the bar and made my way back to Place d'Alésia. That night I thought out my best way to establish Paulo's identity. I decided, first of all, to shadow him and find out where he lived so as to try my luck with his concierge.

Next day, at noon, I had no difficulty in tracking him home to rue Berzélius, then, five minutes later, I called on the concierge and asked her a name at random.

'Monsieur Boudoin, please?'

'Ain't got no one of that name.'

'Oh yes, you know who I mean, he's known as Paulo.'

'Ah, Monsieur Lesage. The fifth floor on the right.'

'Thank you, Madame.'

I then made my way very slowly up and down four flights of stairs so as not to arouse the good lady's suspicions and went out satisfied that I had attained my objective.

That afternoon I called at the Préfecture de Police where I had a good friend from pre-war days in a position of importance. This enabled me to kill two birds with one stone. I equipped myself with the much needed authentic papers in place of the now obsolete ones which Philippe had supplied and I was able to establish that Paulo had a record, and a lengthy one at that, complete with photographs full face and profile. I felt that this was a satisfactory indication that he was not a German spy and most unlikely to be even one of the narks and I decided that I could now put my cards on the table.

In fact, at our next meeting I had no hesitation in bringing the subject up.

'Am I right in thinking that you have no love for the Boche?'

'They're a lot of b . . .'

'You're all for the Allies, then?'

'Well yes, why not?'

'Because you can do them a good turn.'

I had burnt my boats and wondered how he would respond. I could not read his expression. His face remained enigmatic so I had to embark on an explanation of what I hoped his 'wife' would do. I asked him if he thought she would be prepared, for a consideration, to keep me supplied with the appropriate production figures.

'What's it worth?' he asked.

'Ten thousand francs a week for as long as it lasts.'

Paulo tried to push the price up by pointing out the risk his good lady would be incurring but I stuck to my figure. I was well aware that she would be taking a risk but realised only too well that I should be sharing it by dealing with such people. Even if the scheme worked out well, there was always a chance that she would be caught and betray me.

Next day, I received word that his 'wife' was agreeable to my proposition but could not see a means of carrying it out as she was only employed at the canteen of the establishment and had no access to the information I required. I suggested to her through Paulo that she might, nevertheless, be useful as there were other means of estimating production than by actually counting the loaves. It would be sufficient, for instance, if she could even tell me how many sacks of flour were used each day. To my satisfaction, this shot in the dark proved rewarding. The number of sacks supplied by the store turned out to be chalked up daily on a blackboard visible from the corridor through a glass partition. From then on, Paulo's mistress kept me informed daily of the number of sacks and I only had to notify appreciable changes as they occurred. Admittedly, at first I was somewhat dubious as to whether or not she invented the figures simply to collect her ten thousand francs a week but, as time went on, I was able to confirm their reliability by comparing them with information about troop movements received from another source.

I then put Pierrette in touch with Paulo and arranged for her to give Suzanne the figures every day by telephone as I was now due to make another trip to Switzerland.

CHAPTER NINETEEN

A Sudden Move

This time Philippe Allemann decided that I should go to Pont de Roide to make the crossing into Switzerland under the expert guidance of the Crow. We followed the same route that I had taken with Philippe on a previous occasion. All went well and we reached the disused fort Lomont where we stopped to have a drink with the fort-keeper and to pick up a French girl agent and two British airmen.

We left in the usual formation, with me bringing up the rear. When we reached the long wooded slope leading down to the German sentry beat, someone ahead slipped and dislodged a stone. We all, instinctively, took cover and listened with bated breath to the stone crashing on down the slope to alert the sentry waiting at the bottom. It was a hair-raising moment. Suddenly, something quite unexpected happened. The forest resounded with the raucous cawing of a startled crow gradually growing fainter as it took to flight. It was certainly the most realistic imitation of that bird that one could possibly imagine and I realised how apt was my guide's nickname. The German, doubtless deceived by this subterfuge, took no further notice and went off, as usual, at one minute to noon to meet the up-coming sentry.

At Porrentruy, life was much the same, except that there were some new faces and fewer of the original ones. Eliane was still in evidence in the *salle-à-manger* and the *truite au bleu* was more appetising than ever.

I spent one day in Basle and was quite ready to return to the fray. This time Sergeant Cartier insisted that I should take yet another route across the frontier, over Franches Montagnes and the Doubs River under the guidance of a very young man.

The journey started, as did the others, by a trip in an ill-lit bus. The route was longer than the others and very hilly. We alighted at a cross-road and struck off across wild and desolate country, walking for at least an hour under a star-lit sky before reaching the cover of a wooded region. Our route seemed to be dropping all the time and I asked the guide if it was much further.

'The River Doubs flows in the bottom of the gorge and, across it, you are in France but we must stop talking from now on and make no more noise. In a few minutes, we shall be passing near to a house where we must try to avoid waking the dog. If he barks, it'll put the Germans on the far bank on the alert.'

We crept stealthily past some kind of saw mill and made our way down towards the cascading river. The nearer we came to it, the louder grew the thunder of the cataract so that we were soon able to talk again out loud without the least fear of being overheard.

We crossed the sentry beat of the Swiss frontier guards and, a few yards further on, came to the water's edge. The moaning of the wind in the leaves, the rush of the torrent and the eeriness of the murky gloom conspired to bring back the old sensation of unease.

On the opposite bank, a little to the right towards the waterfall, I could see a yellow light flickering in the darkness.

'What's that light over there?' I asked with some concern.

'That's nothing. It's only the German police post.'

I was so surprised by this nonchalant reply that I was glad to keep quiet and, in any case, this was no time for argument. My guide had started to strip and signalled me to do likewise. We took off our shoes, socks, trousers and pants and put them all into a bag which he had unrolled.

'Draughty, isn't it!' he remarked as he gathered up the bundle and put it on his head. I dealt with my parcel of tobacco and watches in the same way and followed my guide into the cold water. He turned to me and explained that, at every step, I must put my foot alongside his before putting my weight on it, as we were about to make the crossing on submerged stepping stones.

We went forward very cautiously for the slightest false step would have hurled us into the swollen torrent and the force of the current, with the water swirling round our thighs, made it very hard for us to keep our balance; but the guide was very experienced and able to overcome these difficulties and we eventually reached the other bank some thirty yards away.

We crouched in the cover of a natural inlet in the sandy bank to dress again. I was just going to say something when the guide checked me by putting his finger to his lips. We must have been very close to the German sentries' beat and the waterfall would not have been loud enough to have drowned my voice if one of the guards had happened to be passing. In a few moments we were ready to go. The guide peeped over the top of the bank, paused for a moment and then climbed up and crawled through the long grass. Needless to say, I followed like his shadow and, ten yards further on, we passed under some barbed wire. Then, bent double, we made our way swiftly across a path only to drop down into the long grass again and crawled another twenty yards till we reached a rocky path.

At this point, the guide stood upright and I did likewise and followed him into the cover of the woods. This path rose sharply up till I noticed that the roar of the cataract was gradually diminishing. We went on climbing for, at least, half an hour and, finally, the serene silence of the night was disturbed only by our heavy breathing.

'So far, so good.' This was the guide's first utterance since we had set foot in France. I noticed a building on our left which I took to be a barn and just then we went through a little gate and along a path through a vegetable garden till we found ourselves on the threshold of an old thatched farmhouse. My friend gave a special knock on the shutter of one of the windows and soon someone came to open the door.

By the light of the flickering oil lamp, I could just about make out that our host was a man, in spite of his misleading night attire. His first and most welcome attention was to give us both a bowl of hot coffee from a pot still simmering on the hearth. As he poured it, he asked if we had a good trip.

'There wasn't anyone down below?' he asked in raspy tones.

'No, it was all quiet but there was more water than usual.'

'You've been lucky. The Germans had orders to double the guard tonight and we didn't find out in time to let you know.'

'Well, Dad, here we are all the same and we'll get our heads down till daybreak.'

My friend had no sooner said this than we stretched out, fully dressed, on a high country bed with sagging springs. Hanging on with one hand to avoid slipping into the crater, I managed to get enough sleep to be fit for the next day.

After breakfasting on country bread dipped in ersatz coffee, we continued our journey along a path that ran through the woods and the undergrowth. An hour later, we came to a cross-road where we took an old gas bus heading for Maiche.

Our destination in this town turned out to be the house of the coach terminus superintendent. This cannot have been the company responsible for the derelict bus we had just left, for the vehicles in the garage were modern and the building itself was of very recent construction. The superintendent, to whom I was introduced, was one of us. He was a likeable man and his wife was very pleasant too. They seemed to have a whole brood of young children round them, together with numerous employees of the coach company, not to mention a bustling throng of passengers. In fact, the whole atmosphere struck me as incompatible with any kind of clandestine activity. However, perhaps it had something to recommend it after all as no one would be likely to be suspicious of a house like this, open, as it were, to the four winds.

My guide put me on the coach for Besançon and then went off. I reached this town on the stroke of noon, after a picturesque journey. This city of watchmakers had had a reputation of beauty but I was very disappointed in what I saw of it. It is true that strong forces of German soldiers did not contribute to its gaiety. I sat down at a little restaurant in a square planted with plane trees and endeavoured to satisfy the insatiable appetite which I found I had acquired. After lunch, I took the Paris Express.

On my arrival in the capital, I made haste to get in touch with Paulo at the Bar des Sports to find out what news there was from the bakery. All was well there, which served to allay my remaining doubts. I decided, moreover, that as Paulo was in the habit of spending most of his time gossiping with the arch-traitors of the underworld who were in the pay of the Nazis, I would ask him to pass on to me any information he could glean in return for a supply of cigarettes.

I did not often get any useful information from this source but one day he put me wise to a tip that came straight from the Todt Organisation[1] to the effect that certain existing fortifications were being redoubled and reinforced and this I was able to transmit direct to Basle.

At just about the same time, Paulo was tipped off that a very important meeting of the German General Staff was to take place in Rheims. I decided to investigate this personally so, consequently, I took the train to the capital of the Champagne district. There, I was quite easily able to locate the hotel where the meeting was actually in session. Naturally, I could not get into the building and was entirely ignorant about what was under discussion but I managed to tack

[1] The Todt Organisation was the name given by the Germans to the department responsible for the construction of fortifications such as the Western Wall or Wall of the Atlantic.

myself on the the front of a small crowd already waiting at the main exit for the delegates to emerge.

When they came, to my astonishment, the central figure was Reichsmarschall Goering himself and I realised what an important conference this must be to draw so big a fish. One thing was clear, however, this conference was essentially concerned with aviation, judging by the importance of the representation of that service. This was not exactly what Paulo had led me to believe but I had to admit myself that the tip had been pretty good all the same.

Acting on intuition, I elected to follow two smaller fry, junior officers of some sort, and snatches of their conversation which floated back to me, indicated that the conference had been planning a renewal of the intensive bombing of England. Losing no time, I transmitted that message to Basle that night.

One evening when I went into Noel's brasserie for a drink. he said, while serving me, 'Your wife's looking for you.'

This was a pre-arranged signal to warn me that my letters were being tampered with and that some suspicious personage was in the company of those present. I took a casual look round as I sipped my drink. One workman was leaning on the bar and two strangers were seated at a small table in the window. I knew that Noel was too intelligent to use this signal irresponsibly and that, consequently, it was up to me to get clear as quickly and as far as possible. I paid up and strolled out nonchalantly.

I took every precaution to make sure that I was not followed and when I was well in another district, I decided to telephone Noel, watching my words very carefully in case the line were tapped.

'Your wife is looking for you,' he repeated and added that Suzanne had been searching for me all the afternoon, before cutting off rather abruptly.

I pondered on this reason for mentioning Suzanne and decided that he meant me to get in touch with her, which I did immediately by telephone. Her very first words were – 'Don't come here. They're downstairs,' and she went on with unconcealed anxiety in her voice, 'Noel wanted me to warn you. The mail is all stuck down and since 4 pm there has been a continuous string of strangers visiting the bar.'

'Right, and thanks. I shan't be home tonight but will 'phone you tomorrow.'

My first concern was for the doctor and I telephoned him at once. He had not heard or seen anything, so it looked as if the revelation had not originated at that end of the circuit but he and the secretary were still in great danger, for it would not take the Gestapo long to work back to the source. I therefore had to instruct the doctor to warn the girl to suspend operations until further notice.

My next problem was to find somewhere to sleep. I thought of returning to my uncle but even there, it would be risky. The Gestapo were quite capable of acting swiftly, of making the secretary talk by means of persuasion of which they had the secret, then of arresting the doctor and of investigating and contacting his closest friends.

For want of a better idea, I went off towards the Bar des Sports. There, at least, I could stay up all night but, on the way, I remembered some other good friends of mine living in the vicinity, my ex-partner Roger Potier and his wife. I decided, despite the lateness of the hour, to knock them up. They were obviously very pleased to see me again and we spent most of the night talking. To my great relief, they agreed spontaneously to put me up for as long as I wished. I was afraid lest when I disclosed the nature of my business, they might withdraw their offer in view of the enormous risk they would be incurring. But I need not have worried. They were, on the contrary, whole-heartedly in favour of out and out resistance and accepted their embarrassing guest with stoical unselfishness.

Next day, I telephoned Suzanne and learnt that Noel had put up a very good show when the Germans, on my failure to turn up, had shown their hand and run him in for questioning. He disclaimed all knowledge of course, stating that the letters were collected by customers of unknown addresses. This was quite a usual custom in France where men, for reasons one can easily imagine, found it convenient to have separate letter-boxes. When charged with having warned me, Noel denied this most vehemently and the incident seemed closed, at any rate, for the time being. However, from my point of view, one thing was certain – I had lost my letter-box.

I had to wait only a couple of days for further news of the Germans' efforts to put a stop to my activities. The doctor warned me by telephone that all the personnel of the Ritz Hotel had been screened and given a thorough search. The secretary, who had typed the lists herself, was subjected to a particularly gruelling inter-rogation. She must certainly have made great play of the point that though she typed the lists, plenty of other people had access to them and, for the time being she was not arrested.

In the course of setting up a new letter-box in another restaurant in the Clichy neighbourhood, I told the doctor to warn the secretary not to re-start her activities for the time being, although all seemed tranquil. I shall always congratulate myself on having taken this precaution because, before that week was out, the Gestapo pounced a second time on the personnel of that hotel and searched even more thoroughly than before.

CHAPTER TWENTY

Special Mission

The night before I had planned to make my next trip to Switzerland, one of the suburbs of South Paris was shaken by a violent bombing and my first task the next morning was to cycle over to get first-hand information for my report.

As I went along Rue Cambronne in the fifteenth district, I came upon a cordon of German troops sealing off the access to Rue Lecourbe, where I used to live before the war. There was quite a crowd of onlookers at the cross-road and, from force of habit, I stopped and made enquiries as to what was going on. I learnt that all streets in the vicinity were similarly blocked so that no one could go in or out of them. I could not discover anything further, even by asking one of the sentries, so went on my way to the blitzed area, where I was able to make a satisfactory survey of the damage done.

A few days later, on my return from Switzerland, I had reason to call on my ex-landlord in Rue Lecourbe.

'You're a week too late!' he announced, by way of greeting.

'Why do you say that?'

'Someone was very anxious to get in touch with you.'

'Who was that then?'

'The Germans.'

By checking up on the date and time, I was able to establish beyond all doubt, that I had been intended to play the lead in a scene, staged by the Gestapo, which I had in fact watched, blissfully unaware, from the wings!

I saw the funny side of this and was still able to laugh, even when I was told that they had confiscated a trunk of books belonging to me, containing, among other things, my prized stamp collection. However, I found myself laughing on the other side of my face when the full significance of their attention dawned on me. One thing was evident, that they were looking for me under my own name, which made it essential for me to leave my ex-partner's home immediately.

The question was where to go next? It was Paulo who found the solution. He took me to a little hotel at the Porte Clichy where the *patron* was a friend of his. He introduced me as a pal who needed to lie low. He did not have to reveal my true activities because the fact of being wanted by the police constituted the very best reference in Paulo's circle of friends. A room was found for me on the fifth floor, together with an assurance that my name would not be submitted to the local police station as regulations demanded. A sudden impulse made me ask for a second room under the pretext that I wanted to install a lady friend there unbeknown to my regular girl. The landlord accepted this as a matter of course, so long as I paid him well for it. My idea was that this second room on the first floor, might effectively cover the existence of the one on the fifth floor if I found myself arrested and knew that I had incriminating possessions. I was thinking, in particular, of my stock of contraband tobacco and watches.

I was satisfied now that I had guarded myself against discovery through my pre-war contacts and I was free to pursue an idea which had come to me through meeting someone at Potier's appartment. This was a man about forty who had been introduced to me as an engineer attached to the railways. In the course of the conversation, I had learnt that he was head of the traffic control at the Gare St Lazare and had pricked up my ears because in the course of my initial training, his kind of job had been designated as 'of special interest'. From the turn in his conversation, I formed an impression of his political standpoint which led me to think that he might make me a very useful agent. However, before pursuing the matter further with him, I wanted a chance to discuss him with the Potiers.

It turned out that he was well known to them for his pro-Allied convictions. We agreed to arrange another meeting with him, at which I had no hesitation in putting the cards on the table and, from then on, he made a particularly useful contribution to the group by keeping me informed in advance of all proposed German troop movements by rail, immediately he received the notification.

Now I was in a position to affirm that the Germans would have the utmost difficulty in moving units into or out of the sector without my prior knowledge, from the hotel lists (when again available), from the bread rations or directly from the railway.

My days became full of activity now that I had to keep in touch with so many different sub-agents and to haunt the various services in the hope of getting on the track of new lines of enquiry. At the Hôtel Ritz all was quiet once more, so I was able to put the finishing touches to a new letter-box by checking its efficacy with a few blank communications. I then advised the doctor of the new arrangements and the daily delivery of the lists soon made its reappearance.

Meanwhile, I was due for another visit to Switzerland and to ensure that all went well in my absence, I had to brief Suzanne about the new letter-box. This unfortunately, necessitated that she should go right across Paris every day by metro to collect the mail, a trickier business than at the Brasserie Cyrano because it had to be done during working hours. She also had to telephone the railway traffic control superintendent and be home at the right time to get Pierrette's figures from the bakery.

This time when I reached Sochaux on my way to Switzerland, the house was full of people, most of them coming back into France. The rest of the outward-bound folk left that night on a nocturnal route but, for me, there were different orders. I had to join the Crow next day at Pont de Roide.

My coach journey there was disturbing to say the least of it. At Audincourt, the Militia had decided to be particularly zealous. A whole platoon of this nauseous force barred our way and made us all alight. Everyone had to show his papers and submit to an inspection, presumably for firearms. Fortunately, I had foreseen such a possibility and as soon as we had left Sochaux, I had felt about for somewhere to hide my revolver, if need be. As I fumbled the underside of the seat, I noticed that it was covered in coarse hessian. Unobserved by my neighbour, I managed to rip it open with my pocket knife and this proved to be a timely bit of foresight. Only a few minutes later I found myself in the urgent necessity of slipping my revolver into this prepared hiding-place. Even then, it was in agony of anxiety that I watched the Militia climb into the coach to carry out a search. But my fears were groundless. The foraging vultures found nothing and the passengers were allowed to get back into the coach.

As soon as we were under way, I tried to recover my weapon but without success. No doubt, egged on by the vibration, it had slipped down out of reach and, without tearing off the whole cover, I could see no hope of retrieving it. I had to consider it lost, unless, by chance, the coach belonged to the company of our friend at Maiche. On the off-chance, I made a mental note of the registration number of the coach in the hope that I might trace it.

This delay at Audincourt took the best part of an hour and I was quite that much late on arrival at Pont de Roide. I found the house easily enough but the Crow and his brother had been gone for twenty minutes. I wondered what to do, whether to return to Sochaux or try to catch them up. I decided on the latter course and started off straightaway.

At the beginning of my climb towards Fort Lomont I made good progress but at every step the sky grew darker. I had still not overtaken the others when a violent storm broke with torrential rain. There was no cover nearby and I was drenched to the skin almost at once. As the deluge showed no signs of abating, I realised that I could not proceed as the path would be impassable and, in any case, my clothes would be in such a state by the time I reached Switzerland, that I could hardly hope to be otherwise than highly conspicuous. I felt that my best plan was to return to the Crow's house to dry off.

The crossing from which I had turned back was that known as the Fosse which was only practicable at noon, so there was no question of going back again for twenty-four hours. To enable me to save time and cross that night, I thought of the waterfall route over the Doubs. As soon as my clothes were dry, I took the bus to Maiche and went to the traffic superintendent's house. When I arrived there, I found my luck was still out. I had missed my guide and had little chance of overtaking him as there was no bus for three-quarters of an hour. These successive setbacks unnerved me to some extent and led me to make a rash decision; I would go alone.

Although I was doubtful about making my way again to the thatched farm, I did fairly well and got there in the end. The farmer and his wife were surprised to see me arriving alone, especially as the guide was only a quarter of an hour ahead of me. I was not at all sure of my way from then on but the farmer's son very kindly put me on the right track.

It was very dark but I could easily find my way down the hill and heard the torrent roaring far below at the bottom of the gorge. I had to screw my courage to the sticking point to overcome my sinking sense of fear at the thought of crossing both the German sentry beat and the submerged stepping stones of the ford.

Realising that I was now within a hundred yards of the perilous path, I crept forward cautiously with stealthy steps until I was almost upon it. Then, I heard a sound and was just in time to crouch and let a German patrol pass not more than ten yards away. I was surprised that I had not spotted them before, as they were sweeping the dark water with beams from their torches.

Giving the patrol time to get well away, I crawled under the barbed wire and made my way on my hands and knees towards the cover of the bank. I took off my clothes, shoes, socks and trousers, which had been soaked once already, but not my underpants so eager was I to put some distance between me and the inhospitable bank. Sounding the stones with a stick, I made slow but sure progress, except for a minor set-back near the Swiss bank, when I Iran out of stones and had to retrace my steps a little. Eventually, succeeded in negotiating this hazard and was once more on Swiss soil.

I made a wearisome but uneventful climb to the heights of Franches Montagnes where I caught the little dawn train along a branch line to St Ursanne, on the main line to Porrentruy. I finally arrived there, tired out but gratified to have made the crossing for the first time without a guide.

After a bountiful breakfast, I went up to my room for a rest. I began to feel ill with rising temperature and a rapidly worsening sore throat. I managed to send word to Sergeant Cartier that I had arrived but was laid up and he came to see me immediately.

'So you are here after all!' he said, as he came in. 'We thought it was all up with you. Yesterday morning, we got a radio message to expect you via Pont de Roide and the Fosse but the Crow and his brother ran into an ambush.'

'Surely, they can't have done,' I cut in, aware that had it not been for my enforced delay, I should have been included.

'Yes, they did, right into the middle of it. Fortunately, the Crow was fifty yards ahead of his brother but, all at once, a German soldier jumped out of the hedge and thrust a tommy gun under his nose.'

'"*Halt!*" he shouted. "Hands up," and frisked him for firearms. Then, pointing to the Crow's half empty rucksack, he signed to him to take it off his back. At the very moment that the Crow was pulling it off, he took aim at the German with it. With all his colossal strength he brought it down on the Jerry's head and then was off into the undergrowth in a single bound but not before he had received a salvo from all sides from numerous concealed Germans. However, knowing the frontier well, he got through to Switzerland. He is now in Porrentruy Hospital where the doctors have already extracted six bullets.'

'How is he now?' I asked.

'Swathed in bandages like a mummy, with one leg up to the ceiling, otherwise in good spirits.'

'And what happened to his brother?'

'Oh, he fired just one shot at the Germans and then his revolver jammed and he dashed back into France at full tilt. We've already heard that he got back safely. At first, we were terribly worried about you, because we thought you were with them. By the way, how *did* you get across?'

'All by myself, like a big boy, via Maiche and Franches Montagnes,' I replied.

'Well, I must say you've got a nerve. And what's the matter with you now?'

'I've got a temperature and a very bad sore throat.'

'You stay where you are and I'll get a doctor.'

A few hours later, I was told that I had severe tonsilitis and would be laid up for at least a fortnight.

Towards the end of this dreary period, the Swiss doctor allowed me to have visitors, one of whom was particularly interesting. He was an Englishman whom I had often seen in the hotel bar. He was a British Intelligence Service agent, like myself. I had already suspected this and he confirmed it as soon as we were alone. To be exact, he had been one before an incident took place which had resulted in his enforced retirement. His story was as follows:

'My mission was to go to a small house near Belfort to meet another agent and collect from him a document. As I pushed the door open, I found myself peering down the barrel of a service revolver, held by a huge German military policeman. He made me face the wall with my hands against it above my head and searched me to make sure I was not armed. Then, taking a chair at the table in the centre of the small room, he told me to sit opposite him. Taking care to keep me covered all the time, he told me that the game was up, my contact had been arrested and was, at that moment, being escorted to the police post by his mate who would be back shortly. Not satisfied with dismaying me with such disastrous news, he kept on needling me by mournful allusions to my compatriots or by anything else that came into his head.

'I noticed a bottle half full of red wine and two glasses on the floor in a corner. To create a diversion, I assured him that I bore him no grudge for having arrested me but fully realised that he was only doing his duty as I was doing mine; we should drop the antagonism now and if he would care to have a drink on it, I wouldn't say no. To my surprise, he agreed and told me to do the honours, but took good care to follow every move with his revolver. "Cheers", I said and drank. I then suggested another one which he also accepted but, I had hardly finished pouring when I flung the contents of my glass in his face and grabbed the pistol at the same time.

'A violent struggle followed. Table and chairs were hurled over, while bottle and glasses went crashing to the floor. We also crashed down, interlocked in a desperate effort to gain possession of the gun. Suddenly, I saw my chance to grab hold of the bottle and bring it down with a crack on his skull. The blow knocked him out completely and I looked for the revolver but could not see it. He must have rolled over on to it but in my haste, I did not realise this. I remembered his mate who should be shortly returning and instinctively rushed out of the door towards the woods. But I could not have hit him hard enough for he was very soon on to me again. He was the bigger and very soon overcame my strength.

'Feeling I was lost, I made one last desperate effort and forced my fingers into his eyes. He was screaming with pain as I ran away. I managed to get back to Switzerland but the experience had so undermined me that I had to go into hospital and now my nerves are so bad that the IS feel I'm no longer suitable for this kind of job and that is why I am waiting here to be sent back to England.'

I was not surprised that such a violent incident had made this fellow lose his nerve, especially when later I learnt that the fight in question had been much worse than the Englishman had admitted. He had actually killed the German and when his body was found one of its eyes was hanging out.

Soon after hearing this story, I was fit again and on my way to Basle to meet Frank at the Consulate. On arrival, I found that Suzanne was still sending the daily communication regularly in spite of my long and unforeseen absence. Frank expressed himself as being very pleased with the work going on and, by way of recognition, entrusted me with my first special mission. I was to make a trip to St Nazaire and back to do some checking up on battery disposals in the submarine base.

Back at Porrentruy, Sergeant Cartier was anxious to persuade me to go by way of Paradise Farm but I was not in favour of this; the first time I had used that route, there had been such a crowd that I felt we were as conspicuous as a hiking party and, on the second occasion, I had been shot at in the face. I preferred to go by La Fosse or by Franches Montagnes.

'You can't use those crossings because there are no guides available for them,' he replied.

'All right, then, I'll go alone!'

'You please yourself but I won't be responsible. How will you go?'

'Tonight, by Franches Montagnes.'

My stubbornness put the Swiss sergeant to a bit of extra trouble as he had to go up to Paradise Farm on his motorcycle that afternoon to collect the contraband tobacco which he had arranged to have waiting for me there.

Having fortified myself with a good Swiss meal, I experienced no difficulty in making my way back across Franches Montagnes to the winding rocky path down the slope.

As I drew near to the saw-mill, I tried to take great care not to wake the dog but one false step snapped a twig with what might easily have been disastrous consequences; the dog barked furiously and the sound was taken up by the German dogs on the other side until the whole gorge re-echoed with their yelping. For a few moments I was unnerved and undecided whether or not to turn back, when a most unexpected and providential event took place. A plane came thundering right through the gorge immediately scaring every dog into silence and my particular aggressor went cringing back into his kennel and silence reigned once more.[1]

For more than an hour, I dared not proceed further for fear of the 'reception committee' on the other bank but when I judged that I had waited long enough, I went on very cautiously, watching every step, until I reached the ford.

I had not bargained on finding so much water and current, particularly in view of the fact that the weather had been relatively dry. I had to hitch my shirt up round my neck to keep it from getting wet. The water was cold and I could not keep from shivering, be it from the chill or the tenseness of the situation.

My progress from stepping-stone to stepping-stone was most perilous and several times I nearly lost my balance and fell in. It seemed a lighter night than last time and I felt that the whiteness of my body must be visible on the opposite bank. I kept thinking with every step that a shot was bound to come but all remained silent and I reached the French bank without opposition.

I dressed quickly, crawled up into the long grass and under the barbed wire. A few seconds later I was making my way up the path to the thatched farm.

The farmer and his wife made me welcome and gave me coffee made from roasted barley but added a tot of cognac which soon

[1] I learnt, subsequently, that the RAF had made a parachute drop to the local Maquis.

pulled me together again and I made an untroubled journey on to Paris.

My first thought on arrival at Porte Clichy was to seek out Pierrette to make sure that all was well at the central bakery. I always had a feeling that this was the most vulnerable part of my set-up. However, all was well and I now telephoned Suzanne to set her mind at rest about my long absence. I could hear her exclamation of joy at the sound of my voice. She had given me up for lost but had, nevertheless, continued to carry on faithfully with the task I had given her.

'You'll have to carry on by yourself a bit longer, old girl, because I'm off to the coast and then back to where I have just come from. I expect to be away for at least a week.'

'Where are you off to?'

'Nosy!'

Suzanne asked no further questions being well aware of my distrust of the telephone.

I took a train to St Nazaire, on the south coast of Brittany. As I alighted I suddenly noticed that the passengers were being rounded up by the German guards and that military police assisted by Gestapo agents were forming them into small groups to check identities. Before it came to my turn, I realised from the questions they were asking, that they were probably on the hunt for candidates for enforced labour camps in Germany. Those whose occupation seemed indefinite or non-essential, were being set on one side, while the rest were allowed to move through the cordon in little groups with their wives and children.

There was a good deal of shouting and gesticulating, in fact, of general disorder, in which I saw a chance to try my luck. I sauntered over nonchalantly to the tail-end of one little group and walked in their wake straight through the German cordon.

My mission was relatively straightforward. I had to check the position of some light batteries of the port defences. All I had to do was move about, keeping my eyes open, without necessarily having to penetrate into a forbidden zone. Unfortunately, it was nightfall before I had finished the job to my satisfaction and I felt I must stay until next day to round it off.

Contenting myself with a sandwich in a water-side café, I set off in search of a room but all in vain. All accommodation was taken either by German soldiers or by employees of the Todt Organisation on the Atlantic Wall project. I had to resort to going right out of town and had a five-mile walk into the country to a farm before I managed to find some sort of makeshift bed in a granary.

Next day I had to cut short my informative peregrinations because I had a feeling that I was being followed. I deliberately took to the back alleys behind the port so as to throw off my unwelcome shadower. When I was satisfied that I had done so, I went straight to the station and took the next train to Paris.

On arrival, I did not even stop to telephone Suzanne but went across the city to the Gare de l'Est where I was just in time to board the express to Montbéliard, thus saving a day.

The bus to Sochaux was packed to capacity and I could not get on, so had to walk. To call at the baker's first necessitated my walking straight past the Allemanns' house. If two strange bicycles had not been propped against the garden fence, I might have been tempted to disobey instructions and walk straight in but it was a good job that I did not for Roger cut my *baguette* in three!

Needless to say, I made myself scarce immediately – in the opposite direction. I managed to pick up a bus on the main road, bound for Audincourt and from there another direct to Maiche where, at the Traffic Controller's house, I was soon sitting down to a good meal.

I learnt that the guide was in Switzerland and that I had no choice but to go alone. I left early to allow time for a good rest at the thatched farm-house and it was not even dark by the time I reached the forbidden zone.

As I made my way slowly along a winding path through an open stretch of woodland, a faint chink of metal caught my ear. I plunged swiftly and silently into the long grass and listened to the unaccustomed sound as it grew nearer. Almost immediately a German patrol of eight or ten men filed into the clearing where I lay hidden, the leaders walking so silently that I could never have heard them coming had not a little fat chap, bring up the rear, been kind enough, in my view, to sling his mess tin on his belt in such a way that it clicked against his bayonet sheath at every step.

It was a near shave but the rest of my journey to Switzerland went smoothly. Frank seemed duly satisfied with my report and, without delay, entrusted me with a second mission. He even read me the message received from London about it:

'Furnish precise information with view to bombing re fortifications under construction between Soissons and Laon' (or words to that effect).

'How long do you need for that?' he enquired.

'I've no idea.'

'Well, as this is marked "Urgent" I can only give you five days including the journey,' he announced.

I did not reply, my thoughts wandering to the fact that I considered that 'the Firm' was getting a bit too demanding! I had not the slightest idea how to tackle this and Frank had nothing useful to suggest. He stuck to his original schedule and left me to sort it out.

I was a very worried agent as I took the train back to Porrentruy and the news I received there was not likely to boost my morale. It was Sergeant Cartier, leaning against the bar, who put me in the picture.

'What do you think of the Sochaux business?' he asked.

'What Sochaux business?'

'Didn't you know? Philippe's brother was arrested as he got off a coach. It happened like this; you know the Germans had a price on Philippe's head – that's why he only operates in Switzerland now, organising the frontier crossings – well, his young brother whom you know very well, was arrested in mistake for him. Of course, Allemann is an easy name for them to remember. The fact of the matter is that they have kept him in prison. Not only that, they found his address on him, raided the house and arrested his parents. We were fortunate enough to hear about it at once and to prevent other agents from going there. Apart from the Allemanns, no one else has been picked up.'

'Have you any news of them?'

'No, except that the priest from the prison at Belfort, who is one of us, told us that the young lad of sixteen had been tortured.'

Now I could appreciate why that *baguette* had been cut in three!

CHAPTER TWENTY-ONE

The Second Mission

I spent the long trip back to Paris racking my brain in vain for some line of approach to the problem. My first concern on my arrival was to call on the Potiers to explain my long unforeseen absence and set their minds at rest on my account. In the course of conversation, we got talking about one of Roger Potier's fellow POWs and it turned out that he was actually working for the Germans in their Todt Organisation. He was on a building site near Soissons! This was a strange coincidence, with Soissons so much on my mind, and I suggested that I should like to meet him.

No problem arose in arranging this meeting as the fellow was on leave in Paris at the time. Roger thought our best plan was to call at the little draper's shop run by his wife in the Monge district of Paris and this proved to be right.

Roger performed the introductions but I cannot recall the name of this young couple. As prearranged, Roger told him that I should like to get a job with the Todt Organisation.

'He wants to find out about the working conditions,' he explained.

'Yes, that's so,' I added. 'Do I understand from Roger that you are at Soissons?'

'Yes, that's right.'

'What kind of a job are you on?'

'Concreting.'

I began to think I had struck lucky.

'Concreting? What are you making, then?'

'Gun emplacements and blockhouses.'

Now I knew that I had hit the jack-pot. I was certain that this young man could supply me with very useful information if I could risk putting the cards on the table. Now I was not at all sure that I ought to trust him, particularly in the presence of his wife. I preferred to hold my hand for the time being, contenting myself with asking numerous questions about how to join the Todt Organisation, the working conditions there and the kind of work I might be expected to do. During the conversation, I saw, to my satisfaction, that the wife was preparing to depart which would give me the opportunity I was seeking to speak to him alone, though I still felt some reluctance in broaching the matter at all. I realised that my profession was inherently dangerous and I must be prepared to take the plunge in accordance with the dictates of my intuition.

As soon as his young wife had gone, I dropped my hitherto pleasant manner and appreciative acknowledgements of information received and, giving him a very straight and severe look, said, choosing my words very carefully:

'Working for the Germans is an unpardonable crime in the eyes of the Resistance.'

'But I've been forced into it!' he protested.

'Unpardonable,' I reiterated very deliberately, 'except in cases where the coercion is maintained and cannot be avoided. This is not your case. You are quite free to fail to return after this holiday of yours. You could go and join the Maquis, for instance.'

'Are you from the Maquis?'

'I might or I might not be.'

'Well, what do you want with me?' he stammered.

'Information about the fortifications you are building at Soissons.'

'Five miles from Soissons,' he corrected me, from which I concluded that he was acquiescing to my demand.

'All right, five miles from Soissons then, and along which road?'

'The road to Laon.'

So far, this checked. It was the district Frank had mentioned. I carried on interrogating him.

'What kind of fortifications are you building?'

'Gun emplacements.'

'How far apart are they?' I asked, insidiously.

'It's all according to the lie of the land, sometimes far apart and sometimes very close together.'

This reply had an authentic military ring and convinced me much more readily than the answer 'at a distance of three hundred yards' would have done, that this young man was not trying to invent his replies.

I then got him to give me full details of the construction of these subterranean gun posts. I ended up by putting a few questions to him to attempt to establish the quality and resistance of the concrete in the face of bombing.

'What kind of cement do you use?'

'Portland.'

I understood this to indicate first quality. 'What are the proportions of sand, gravel and cement?'

I managed to get detailed information on all these points except that this casual bricklayer was unable to tell me for certain how thick the reinforced concrete was above each emplacement but he was able to inform me that they were covered with approximately one yard of earth. However, I did get a final worthwhile tip from him to the effect that the railway line from Soissons to Laon was closed because the Germans were storing ammunition in the nearby tunnel.

I could think of no more questions to ask him and was turning over in my mind how best to ensure his silence. It seemed to me that to play upon his fear would be the most forceful argument I could use so, once more adopting a most menacing attitude, I invented the following story.

'My superiors would wish me to thank you on their behalf for the help you have given to the Cause. On my account, I must warn you that I did not come here without the knowledge of my friends. In fact, at this very moment, your shop is being watched. If you say anything to anybody, and that includes your wife, you will have *them* to deal with and they are not known as the "Killer Squad" for nothing. If you are discreet it won't be forgotten after the war, so it's up to you to keep you mouth shut.'

I realised that this was something of a theatrical tirade but it was effective. Moreover, in betraying me, he would have also to betray Roger and much depended on the closeness of their friendship. In any case, there was nothing more I could do about it. We all went off for a friendly drink and then Roger and I went back to Place Clichy.

I felt that my time had not been wasted but that, nevertheless, I needed more reliable information than the unsubstantiated word of a casual bricklayer. It needed an on the spot check to verify the facts and I realised that, even if I could manage to penetrate a military site of this kind, it would be tantamount to putting my head in the lion's mouth. The utmost precautions were necessary and I spent a sleepless night thinking over the situation.

By dawn, I had evolved a plan. I called at my uncle's office and asked him for a list of his customers in the Soissons area and a collection of samples of webbing and processed materials. My request caused him some surprise but he was ready, as always, to help me in any way possible. He gave me everything I asked for without hesitation. He also briefed me on the essential points of his merchandise so that, by the time I came away, I had adequate information to call on his clients as his representative.

Next morning, I arrived at Soissons by the first train. In a nearby café, I took stock of the topography of the town and drew up a schedule of my visits for the day. Then I drank up my ersatz coffee and called on my first customer.

I do not know whether it was that, in spite of three years' absence, I still had not lost the knack, or simply because the goods I was offering were in short supply but, whatever the reason, I picked up an order. Nor was this the last one. By three o'clock in the afternoon, I found myself, by design, visiting the last two customers in the vicintiy of the Todt site, on to which I wandered.

No one questioned me and I was soon strolling among piles of planks, heaps of cement and stacks of girders. There were huts of all kinds and a variety of lorries, military and civilian. The work was in full swing. I noticed a team of labourers handling planks and a detachment of soldiers marched past. In the middle of all this bustle, I noted the fact that the electricity was still supplied from the Central Power Station at Soissons, which was worth remembering.

I had soon passed through the busy centre on to a new road which ran along the edge of the wood when, suddenly, I found myself in front of one of the block-houses which appeared quite unoccupied. I took a good look round to make sure that no one was watching me and judged that I should have time to go right inside and inspect it before anybody came along. I needed only a few seconds to calculate by simple arithmetic the thickness of the roof underneath its yard of earth. I counted the number of steps as I went down and found that each step was equivalent in depth to the width of my hand plus two fingers. Standing upright inside, I noticed that my head almost touched the ceiling. This was all I needed to know and was on the point of leaving when I heard a sound and saw, to my horror, a pair of jack boots on the steps.

''*Raus!*' barked a raucous voice which re-echoed ominously round the empty vault. There was no option but to come out and I was forced to approach the man holding me covered with his pistol.

'*Spion, Mensch. Weiter!*'

Which I clearly understood as, 'Come along with me, you dirty spy!'

I knew that I had been caught red-handed and I could feel the gun in the small of my back. An appalling sensation of mingled panic and despair held me almost paralysed. I cursed myself for my folly and lack of prudence, telling myself that I had asked for whatever I got. I was still in this frame of mind when we reached the police post and I was pushed before an officer.

The man who had picked me up explained how he had come to arrest me.

'Pig of a spy!' was his final comment.

They made me empty my pockets while they searched my case of samples. The officer studied my list of customers and then asked me calmly, in fairly good French, if I could explain my presence in a German military fortification.

I told him that I was travelling in webbings and processed materials and that I had got myself lost in the suburbs of Soissons and had accidentally got on the site. I added that I had been in the Maginot Line during the war and, consequently, was very interested in such fortifications purely from an innocent curiosity.

The officer was listening to my explanation apparently without hostility and asking me questions about my work in a friendly voice, then, suddenly, he screamed savagely at me.

'You spy! You filthy spy!'

For two hours at least, I was subjected to this Scotch shower bath treatment, heat alternating with cold at regular intervals. At one stage, a cigarette would be courteously offered and then snatched from my lips, or a glass of water given to me and, as I began to drink, I received a blow on the back of my neck causing it to spill on my lap.

At last, the officer changed his tactics.

'We are going to check your story,' he announced, sending for the local telephone directory.

In consultation with my schedule, he rang up one of my customers and asked if I was known to him and had called on him that day. Somewhat to his disappointment, I thought, the officer learnt that this client had even placed an order with me. The German then asked him for details of the order so that he could check it with my book. Ignoring me completely, he went on telephoning customer after customer and as he got towards the end of the list it became only too plain to him that I was not the fine 'catch' he had hoped. His last and, to me, much too obvious strategy, was to leave me unguarded in the room with the outer door ajar.

And there I was, waiting, when at last the officer and his henchmen returned.

'I am going to have you flung out and if I catch sight of you hereabouts again, I'll see to it myself that you get a bullet between your eyes.'

This threat was followed up immediately by an order and the scoundrel who had arrested me earlier that afternoon, no doubt feeling that he had been thwarted of his prey, shoved me down the steps and took a running kick at the base of my spine. This indignity and the many others that were, subsequently, showered upon me until I reached the edge of the military zone, did nothing to quench the satisfaction I was feeling at having outwitted these fellows just as if they were a pack of choirboys.

I made my way straight to the Central Station and was lucky enough to find a Paris Express on the point of departure. I sat back in my corner with my eyes shut and, soothed by the rhythm of wheels, went over in my mind the startling events of the day, chuckling to myself over a dénouement which was more than I could have hoped for.

CHAPTER 22

A Tight Corner

The day after my escapade at Soissons and just before I was due to leave for Switzerland with the result of my mission, I received a telephone call from my old friend Roger, Suzanne's husband, to let me know that someone had called on him and asked for me, purporting to be one of my acquaintances in the Intelligence Service. He had claimed to have had a meal with me in Switzerland and to have arranged to meet me in Paris. He said he had unfortunately lost my address but remembered that I had mentioned my friend Roger, the Paris director of a well known film company, during conversation. He had, so he said, taken the liberty of following up the clue with a view to obtaining my address.

'Naturally, I gave nothing away,' said Roger. 'But I did promise to try to get in touch with you and agreed to meet him again the day after tomorrow to tell him if I have had any luck.'

'You were right to keep quiet, Roger. It's an obvious trap. In the first place, I have never disclosed my address to anyone and secondly, I've never mentioned you in Switzerland. The best thing for you to do when he comes back is to sling him out, the dirty Boche!'

'All right, you can count on me,' he promised.

'By the way, Roger, where are you ringing from?'

'Oh, don't worry about that. I'm not just hatched. From a public call box, of course.'

When I hung up, I began to think over this disturbing enquiry. It was the Gestapo, I had no doubt. But how could thay have got right on my heels like this? I could only see two possibilities. Either they had not yet exhausted the trail from the Hôtel Ritz or they were on to me from the Swiss end, in which case it really spelt danger. As it is always as well to know which way the wind blows, I decided that I would request a special investigation from my own department.

Roger's description was so accurate that Sergeant Cartier had no difficulty in identifying a suspect in his own mind, which, if correct, indicated one of our own agents and this would be a very serious matter. A minute investigation was imperative, the result of which was not disclosed to me until my next visit to Switzerland.

To make it clear how the Gestapo had got on my trail, I must go back a few months in my story. One day, Roger had approached me to see if I could help a mutual friend of ours from pre-war days. He was a Jew and the nephew of a very well-known film producer. He had been warned in time that the Gestapo were raiding his home. His fiancée, Mireille, had been arrested together with his servant and his concierge. Naturally, he went into hiding straight away with some friends and Roger wanted to know if I could get him to Switzerland.

From my point of view he was, to say the least, a very embarrassing 'consignment' but I let myself be persuaded and our Jewish friend was soon safely over the border. What was more, by a letter of introduction, I was quickly able to get him a post as an accountant with a firm of timber merchants. All he had to do was to stay there and lie low until the end of hostilities but, unfortunately, this proved to be too much to ask. During my periods of absence in France, he had made a habit, having an inquisitive and pushing nature, of trying to attach himself to various secret agents whenever he could manage to get into conversation with them at the bar of the Hôtel des Voyageurs. This had already been a source of annoyance to me because Sergeant Cartier had called my attention to his indiscretion and I had been forced to reprove my friend, with little effect. One day, he had the audacity to write to his fiancée, Mireille, who had since been released by the Germans, probably because she was not a Jewess, and to get an obliging agent to take the letter across and post it in France. As luck would have it, the agent fell into the hands of the Gestapo and the love-letter along with him. The sequel was easy to follow; a Gestapo agent was put on to the case and was soon checking up in Roger's office, with what would have been disastrous results for me had Roger not stalled and so given himself time to warn me by telephone.

Needless to say, Frank did not congratulate me on letting my feelings of friendship obscure my obligations to the job I had undertaken. Having made this reproof, my chief went on to say that it was probably a good thing for it had had the effect of exposing a very dangerous enemy spy.

'What has become of him?' I enquired, tentatively.

'He's found a new job.'

'A new job?' I queried.

'Yes, as a stoker,' he gibed, grimly. I understood that he was referring to the fires of hell.

In the meantime, very serious developments were taking place. London was being subjected to an attack from flying bombs or buzz bombs as the British radio was calling them but they were already known to us as V1s. According to information received, these deadly contraptions were launched from fixed launching ramps, one of which had already been pin-pointed. The heads of the Intelligence Service believed that, taking London as the centre, the ramps must fall on a known arc passing through the one already discovered. It was a matter of urgency that they should be bombed but first, they had to be discovered. Therefore, with that in view, every available agent was detailed off to comb out a small section of the arc. My portion, as luck would have it, was near Soissons where there was, virtually, a price on my head! My first thought was to wonder whether the gun emplacements, into which I had penetrated, might be connected with some such ramp.

During the journey from Montbéliard to Paris, while thinking over my V1 commission, I remembered a snatch of conversation overheard in another train. It was as I travelled back to Paris after being thrown off the Todt site at Soissons. At the time, I had been too excited at my recent adventures to pay much attention to what was said. An old lady was telling her neighbour that the Germans were turning everything topsy-turvy in her village. She also mentioned a tunnel and the fact that she had been on foot to see her daughter at Bucy. Why should this conversation suddenly come to mind? Would the ball be bouncing in front of me? I felt that this might offer a possible line of investigation and, for want of better, decided to follow it up.

Once in Paris, I procured a map of the Soissons region but it was some time before I could find Bucy which turned out to be much further away from the town of Soissons than I had thought and this was some comfort! Having regard to the age of the old lady, only six villages were within walking distance of Bucy. I selected the one nearest to the tunnel shown on the map. This was a fortunate intuition for, even before I reached the village, my mission was accomplished.

As a precaution, I was walking the last couple of miles and while I was still in the open country, all at once, I saw rise from what, to all intents and purposes, appeared to be an ordinary farm, a mysterious short-winged device, trailing fire and smoke in its wake.

Now that I had pin-pointed the site, all I had to do was to return to Paris and send a report of this mission which had been accomplished with such ease, thanks to a conversation heard and recollected in a train. This reminded me of the notices stuck up on the walls of the factory back at Schoenfeld, already so far away: DER FIEND HÖRT (The enemy hears).

How right they were!

*

By the time I was making my twenty-seventh trip to Switzerland, there was universal and open rejoicing there at the good news from the Normandy front, but Frank drew my attention to the fact that my work was not yet over and, to illustrate his point, he sent me off on yet another mission.

Although Hitler's Atlantic Wall had now been breached, he was still noising it abroad that ultimate victory would be his on account of his secret weapons. One of these was a new kind of guided missile called V2, destined, according to him, to be infinitely superior to the V1 of whose failure to obliterate London, thanks to the RAF's precision bombing, we in France were the enthusiastic spectators. Information received from Headquarters in London indicated that it was believed that some of these V2s were being manufactured in the suburbs of Paris. Frank had received direct instructions to delegate the task of locating this factory to me.

Losing no time, I went straight back to France but what a surprise awaited me at Maiche. Pierrette, in a great state of consternation, had decided to come to meet me to bring an urgent report from Suzanne that there was marked German activity on the railway and ominous fluctuations in the bakery figures. These facts pointed to troop movements only to be expected in view of the Normandy push. However, I felt Pierrette had been right to come, particularly as the room list of the Hôtel Ritz which she had also brought showed significant changes in the German High Command.

To take advantage of her initiative, we had to go straight away to the Pont de Roide in an attempt to catch the Crow before he crossed the frontier with the mail. Unfortunately, he had had trouble and was again in hospital but his brother agreed to take our message straightaway while we went off to Montbéliard to take the train to Paris.

But it was not to be as easy as we had thought. At the station, we found out that the Germans had requisitioned all the trains and we watched all civilians being forcibly turned out of the very one we had planned to take. Not that this stopped us getting into it from the opposite side and, thanks no doubt, to Pierrette's charm we managed to get ourselves hidden by the German troops in one of the compartments. She was concealed in a corner, behind a cunningly draped army great-coat and I stood at the ready near the door so that I could disappear into the toilet whenever an officer showed up along the corridor.

As the main line had been sabotaged by the Maquis, the train made a diversion via Dijon but, at the first sizeable station, a little bit of tragi-comedy was very nearly our undoing.

A stolid square-headed Teuton, looking out of the window of our compartment, read out the name of the town Besançon. His typical German pronunciation gave the word an obscene twist which caused Pierrette to laugh loudly, so loudly that she was heard right down the corridor by a sergeant-major. It did not even give me time to disappear into the toilet and I had to stay crouching behind two Germans.

'Mam'sel, mam'sel?' The enquiry came from the corridor. But our compartment managed to preserve an air of convincing innocence and the incident was soon passed over and forgotten in the pandemonium which followed.

The train had come to an unscheduled halt when it was attacked by the Maquis. The Germans seized their rifles and returned the fire through the windows. The exchange was short and sharp and no serious damage appeared to be sustained on either side but it gave us a double and ironic satisfaction to feel that they were unwittingly providing with transport two enemy agents in the very act of carrying out a mission.

Under cover of the night, Pierrette and I took advantage of a halt at a Paris suburb to jump out on to the track on the wrong side of the compartment and soon found a bus to take us to the Porte de Vincennes.

In the Clichy district, near my hotel, I ran into one of the regular clients of the Bar des Sports.

'How are you, Roland?' he said, coming up to me.

'All right, any news?'

'I'm in trouble. Perhaps you could give me some advice?'

'What's the matter?'

'Well, in two or three weeks, it's a dead cert the Yanks will be here and I'm working for the Germans . . .'

'Well, what of it? Isn't everyone in the same boat, more or less? What's your particular worry?'

'I'm working in an armament factory.'

'Making what?' I asked, with a stirring of interest.

'Rockets.'

I could not believe my ears. I had been racking my brains to think of some possible means of getting on this trail and here, with a bit of luck, I had the quarry within my sights!

'V1s I suppose?' I egged him on derisively.

'No, it's new. It's a kind of reactor.' (Now commonly known as 'jet'.)

'And where are you working?'

'At Houilles, in an underground factory.'

'What's your particular job?'

'I'm private secretary to the production manager.'

If there is a patron saint of secret agents, mine was certainly in action just then. Very discreetly, without arousing his suspicion, I gleaned a whole heap of information about this weapon, although my main interest was the location of the factory. In return, I gave this rogue advice, as requested. I suggested that he should join the Communist Party immediately it was reformed!

In accordance with accepted practice, all I now had to do was to carry out an on the spot check to locate the position of the electric sub-stations and transformers, the factory sidings, the bridges to be bombed etc.

Next morning, when I got out of the train at Houilles, I fitted perfectly into that highly industrialised setting. A shabby grey jacket covered my blue bib and brace overalls. A scarf round the neck and a beret added a finishing touch. I spent two hours wandering round the environs of the factory to make a study of any possible targets, taking into account the serious risks to the civilian population in the neighbourhood. In the same connection, it was essential for me to find out when there would be the least possible number of French personnel actually at work in the factory. With this in view, and with the hope of picking up some further item of interest, I walked straight to the entrance where German guards were posted.

'Personnel department, please.'

A messenger showed me to a nearby building. I realised that this did not give me the chance to see much but, at least, the hours of work were posted up. They worked three eight-hour shifts for six days with Sundays free. As far as my own request for work as a miller was concerned, I was taken on subject to passing a test which, fortunately, could only be given next day.

I should dearly have liked to pursue this line of enquiry but not only was I pressed for time, but also I would have made no better a miller than I would have made a Benedictine monk.

That night, back in my room at the hotel, I made a sketch of the factory while it was still fresh in my mind, using a map of the district to help me pin-point the vulnerable targets. This done, I folded the paper carefully in such a way as to reduce it to a very small square, concealable in the palm of the hand. This was a routine I had learnt during the course of my spy-training apprenticeship in Switzerland. The object is to make it easy to slip into the grass or under a bush in the case of an untoward encounter near the frontier. I put the tiny packet on the shelf of my wardrobe before going to bed.

Every morning, while dressing, I was in the habit of being entertained through the open window, by the conversation of two neighbouring tarts whose regular clients were Germans. They exchanged 'pillow-case confidences' when their men had gone. This morning I learnt of the imminent departure of the nearby garrison to a south-westerly destination.

It was nearly time for me to go to the Gare de l'Est to take the train to Montbéliard on my way to Switzerland, when I suddenly remembered that I had promised to take the Potiers a few pounds of potatoes which I had been lucky enough to manage to get hold of. Looking at my watch, I realised that I had just enough time to cycle round with them before leaving. I ran down the five flights of stairs so quickly that before I realised what I was doing, I found myself in the middle of a German raiding party. The foyer of the hotel and the reception office were full of military police and Gestapo agents. I gathered as I walked through that they were there to arrest a woman who, according to what the *patron* was asserting, had checked out a fortnight before. As this was no concern of mine and the hotel was certainly not a healthy spot for me to loiter in, I picked up my bicycle which was standing in the back courtyard and pushed it out on to the pavement. Several cars were pulled up conspicuously in front of the hotel and out of one of these, sprang an officer.

'Your papers, please,' he demanded.

I presented my identity card without any hesitation or misgivings, since it had stood up to all scrutinies so far, but this officer was a tougher proposition. He frowned and his mouth tightened. He examined my card closely for a long time. Then he told me to go back into the hotel.

This unexpected hitch took me aback somewhat but I was not unduly disturbed until I remembered, with a sudden sense of disaster, the little folded document lying on the shelf of my wardrobe upstairs! It was with a hollow feeling in the pit of my stomach that I turned round to face the officer in the foyer, as he put the first question to me in German.

'Do you speak German?'

'Nix,' I replied in pidgin German so as not to divulge my knowledge of his language in case he might be smart enough to deduce from that that I was an escaped POW. He said something else to me which I genuinely failed to understand and then, satisfied that I was to all intents and purposes quite ignorant of Goethe's language, he turned to one of his men and said:

'There's something odd here! This fellow has genuine French papers and yet he looks English.'

These words set me very much on my guard. This German constituted a real danger to me. He had intuitive intelligence, a rare quality in his race. What a fool I had been! I had given up my reserve room on the first floor at the end of the previous month in the belief that it would not be needed any more. I had held all the trumps for months past and now had thrown the game away through a careless slip!

'Search him!' my persecutor ordered. This did not worry me as I had nothing compromising on me.

'What's your room number?'

This was the dreaded question I had been waiting for and, with sinking heart, I gave the right number, not daring to invent one as I was not in sight of the key-board.

'Take your key and go up with these gentlemen!' he commanded and a Gestapo agent stepped forward. He gave a further order in German and a corporal with his tommy-gun at the ready took up his position behind me.

We began to mount the stairs and I realised that in the course of the five flights ahead, I must hit on some plan on which my life would

By this

Certificate of Service

I record my appreciation of the aid rendered by

ROLAND RIEUL.

as a volunteer in the service of the United Nations for the great cause of Freedom.

B. L. Montgomery

Field Marshal
Commander-in-Chief, 21st Army Group

Date_____12.5.48.
Serial No_____EL/HA3

Top: My certificate of service from Field Marshal Montgomery.

Bottom: Letter enclosing the certificate from the British Embassy, Paris.

**BRITISH EMBASSY,
PARIS.**

2/148/48

31st May, 1948.

Sir,

    I have pleasure in sending you the attached Certificate, signed by Field Marshal Montgomery, in recognition of your services to the Allied Cause during the war.

    I am requested by His Majesty's Principal Secretary of State for Foreign Affairs to express to you, on behalf of His Majesty's Government, their high appreciation of your conduct.

    I am, Sir,

        Your obedient Servant,

depend! I racked my brains furiously as each step took me nearer to disaster but, had already reached the fourth floor without any hint of inspiration. Right at the top, I realised that there was only one possible thing to do and that I had only one chance in a thousand of bringing it off but, at worst, it would give me the satisfaction of selling my life dearly; this was to take advantage of the narrow, dark corridor leading to my room, to swing round, grab the tommy-gun and shoot it out!

We were right there and I was just about to make the thought the deed when a sudden inspiration made me change my tactics.

'Bluff them!' I told myself.

I unlocked the door of my room, grabbed the key of the wardrobe which I had left on a small table and, with a dramatic gesture, flung wide the door.

'There you are, gentlemen, search!'

My carefully folded plan was there in full view, right in front of the shelf, but as I intentionally gave them the impression that I was trying to take over and run the search for them, these clever sleuths rose to the bait and, disdaining my offer, concentrated their attentions on the bed and the bed-side table. The Gestapo agent felt systematically, inch by inch, along the piping round the mattress while the corporal seemed certain that the legs of the little bed-side table must be detachable. All the time, I was on the watch for the split second when they would take their eyes off me. Suddenly, I saw my opportunity; with one swift movement my hand shot out, palmed the little packet and thrust it into my trouser pocket.

The bed and the table both having failed to reveal any secret, the searchers turned their belated attention to the wardrobe, then the washbasin and all its gear, the curtains, the carpet and every square inch of the room received their minute inspection, all to no avail. At last, they had to admit failure and go down to report that the search had been fruitless. The officer still seemed unconvinced. He frowned das he had done earlier and was still obviously turning his suspicion over in his mind. I only hoped he would not have me seached again. Suddenly, he clicked his heels, saluted me and said:

'You must accept our apologies. We were only doing our duty.'

At that, he turned on his heel and ordered his riff-raff out of the hotel.

'How white you were!' exclaimed the *patron* as soon as we were alone. I felt like saying, 'and with good reason, too,' but decided to leave well alone. I wheeled my cycle across the wide pavement, got on to it and pushed off but I did not get far. The strain on my nerves had been so great that after about ten yards I lost my sense of balance and capsized on to the ground and my precious potatoes rolled all over the street. It took a brandy in the café at the corner to pull me together.

I failed to catch my train and my friends, the Potiers, failed to get their potatoes but this near-shave was, fortunately, to be the last of the series. The Americans were at Chartres, the Leclerc Division closer still and the Liberation of Paris had begun.

INDEX

Index